The
1900s

The

1900s

Bob Batchelor

American Popular Culture Through History
Ray B. Browne, Series Editor

GREENWOOD PRESS
Westport, Connecticut • London

Library of Congress Cataloging-in-Publication Data

Batchelor, Bob.
    The 1900s / Bob Batchelor.
        p. cm.—(American popular culture through history)
    Includes bibliographical references and index.
    ISBN 0–313–31334–2 (alk. paper)
    1. United States—Civilization—1865–1918. 2. Popular culture—United
States—History—20th century. 3. Nineteen hundreds (Decade) I. Title. II. Series.
E169.1B248 2002
973.91—dc21   2001050132

British Library Cataloguing in Publication Data is available.

Library of Congress Catalog Card Number: 2001050132
ISBN: 0–313–31334–2

First published in 2002

Greenwood Press, 88 Post Road West, Westport, CT 06881
An imprint of Greenwood Publishing Group, Inc.
www.greenwood.com

Printed in the United States of America

∞

The paper used in this book complies with the
Permanent Paper Standard issued by the National
Information Standards Organization (Z39.48–1984).

10 9 8 7 6 5 4 3 2 1

To the two most important women in my life:
my mother, Linda, who has provided love and support,
and my wife, Katherine Elizabeth, my best friend and
inspiration

Contents

Series Foreword

Popular culture is the system of attitudes, behavior, beliefs, customs, and tastes that define the people of any society. It includes the entertainments, diversions, icons, rituals, and actions that shape the everyday world. It is what we do while we are awake and what we dream about while we are asleep. It is the way of life we inherit, practice, change, and then pass on to our descendants.

Popular culture is an extension of folk culture—the culture of the people. With the rise of electronic media and the increase in communication in American culture, folk culture expanded into popular culture—the daily way of life as shaped by the *popular majority* of society. Especially in a democracy like the United States, popular culture has become both the voice of the people and the force that shapes the nation. In 1782 French commentator J. Hector St. John de Crèvecœur asked in his *Letters from an American Farmer*, "What is an American?" He answered that such a person is the creation of America and is in turn the creator of the country's culture. Indeed, notions of the American Dream have long been grounded in the dream of democracy—that is, government by the people, or popular rule. Thus, popular culture is tied fundamentally to America and the dreams of its people.

Historically, culture analysts have tried to fine-tune culture into two categories: the "elite," or the elements of culture (e.g., fine art, literature, classical music, gourmet food) that supposedly define the best of society; and the "popular," or the elements of culture (e.g., comic strips, bestsellers, pop music, fast food) that appeal to society's lowest common denominator. The so-called educated person approved of elite culture and scoffed at popular culture. This schism first began to develop in

Western Europe in the fifteenth century when the privileged classes tried to discover and develop differences in societies based on class, money, privilege, and lifestyles. Like many other aspects of European society, the debate between elite and popular cultures came to the United States. The upper class in America, for example, supported museums and galleries which exhibited the "finer" things in life, which would "elevate" people. As the twenty-first century emerges, however, the distinctions between popular culture and elitist culture have blurred. The blues songs (once denigrated as "race music") of Robert Johnson are now revered by musicologists; architectural students study buildings in Las Vegas as examples of what Robert Venturi called the "kitsch of high capitalism"; sportswriter Gay Talese and heavyweight boxing champ Floyd Patterson were copanelists at a 1992 SUNY New Paltz symposium on literature and sport. The examples go on and on, but the one commonality that emerges is the role of popular culture as a model for the American Dream, the dream to pursue happiness and a better, more interesting life.

To trace the numerous ways in which popular culture has evolved throughout American history, we have divided the volumes in this series into chronological periods—historical eras until the twentieth century, decades between 1900 and 2000. In each volume, the author explores the specific details of popular culture that reflect and inform the general undercurrents of the time. Our purpose, then, is to present historical and analytical panoramas that reach both backward into America's past and forward to its collective future. In viewing these panoramas, we can trace a very fundamental part of American society. The American Popular Culture Through History series presents the multifaceted parts of a popular culture in a nation which is both grown and still growing.

Ray B. Browne
Secretary-Treasurer
Popular Culture Association
American Culture Association

Preface

Never in the history of the world was society in so terrific flux as it is right now. The swift changes in our industrial system are causing equally swift changes in our religious, political, and social structures. An unseen and fearful revolution is taking place in the fiber and structure of society. One can only dimly feel these things, but they are in the air, now, today.

Jack London (1907)

I have always had the suspicion that the 1900s, that is, the decade from 1900 to 1910, is a vastly understudied period. Books including the decade in broad surveys between the Civil War and World War I usually skip lightly over the 1900s, or merely mention the years in passing. After examining the decade more closely, I am convinced that it is a virtual gold mine of unclaimed territory, even through historians have had more than 100 years to examine it. I have tried to imagine why so much is still undiscovered about the 1900s. Perhaps the ghost of Teddy Roosevelt hangs too heavily over the era. Maybe the political and diplomatic events during the Roosevelt administration have soured younger historians from studying the decade's nuances. I am sure some scholars even believe that everything that needs to be said about the period has already been covered in one of the many works examining the Progressive Era.

The Progressive Era derived its name from the political and social advocates who dominated the scene from the 1890s through the 1920s. Progressives worked to make American society a better place by creating stronger governmental institutions and passing legislation that countered the evils they felt were ruining the promise of the nation, including big business and political corruption on all levels. Progressives also fought to reform working conditions in factories, clean up slums and ghettos, and enact environmental legislation that would conserve the nation's natural resources.

The crusading efforts were not just confined to the United States. Progressives thought that America could serve as a beacon for democracy and decency around the globe. During the Progressive Era the nation intervened in the foreign affairs of other countries more than at any other time up to that point. Traditional historians spent so much time examining the Progressive Era through the lenses of political and diplomatic history, that they overshadowed the social history of the period, notably the first decade of the twentieth century. They explored the many political and diplomatic machinations at the expense of what was happening to people on an intimate level.

Today, most people recognize the 1900s as the period in which the United States established itself as the world's preeminent superpower. However, the advances the country made as an economic, military, and diplomatic leader should not overshadow the developments in other endeavors. In many areas, such as art, literature, and music, artists in the United States were just beginning to establish a truly "American" style distinct from Europe. For the first time, authors, composers, and musicians looked to the everyday world around them for inspiration, a critical step in developing a creative scene that either rivaled or could some day surpass that of the Old World. It could be argued that the daily influences on people's lives, such as advertising, technological innovations, or the growing consumer culture, meant much more to them than what was happening on the international stage or the halls of Congress.

In any case, I think the overriding problem for those investigating the decade is that many scholars and writers have labeled the 1900s as the "quiet years" or "the peaceful decade." As a result, the era is interpreted as a kind of bridge between the separate sagas of the Civil War and World War I. I view the period as an indispensable foundation for the rest of the twentieth century—a blueprint played out during the rest of the century. With its concentration on popular culture, this book shows the decade as a foundation across a wider spectrum.

Both primary and secondary sources were used to examine the first decade of the twentieth century, but *The 1900s* is primarily a synthesis. This book, which focuses on the popular culture of the decade, draws on the work of many scholars and historians who have studied the Progressive Era. In contrast to traditional historical studies of the period, however, I treated lightly many areas covered in depth in the past, particularly political and diplomatic history. Given the thrust of the American Popular Culture Through History series, the confluence of history and popular culture is the main subject. I spent more time on areas underserved by others studying the Progressive Era, such as the lives of everyday people, youth culture, architecture, and travel, among others. Special emphasis is placed on how people lived their lives on a day-to-day basis and the issues and ideas that affected them directly.

I have also drawn parallels and links between events that occurred in the 1900s and the present whenever possible. As the foundation of the twentieth century, the 1900s brought to life many ideas that were later expanded on as the century progressed. For example, the rise of the modern corporation in the 1900s, including the merger wave and emergence of the celebrity chief executive, has had a tremendous impact on defining the United States. Yesterday's John D. Rockefeller and J.P. Morgan compare nicely to today's Bill Gates and Warren Buffett. The federal government's intervention in several high-profile monopolies, most notably the breakup of Rockefeller's Standard Oil, is seen repeatedly throughout the rest of the century, including the breakup of AT&T in the early 1980s and the recent legal wrangling with Microsoft.

The United States experienced great changes at the turn of the century, from solidifying its position as the world's reigning economic and military power to acclimating millions of new citizens from all over the world. The transformation might have crippled other countries, but Americans brought a significant trait to the forefront—adaptation—which enabled them to endure the change and adjust to new circumstances.

People who lived in the 1900s would have balked at hearing their decade labeled "quiet," which modern scholars have done. Almost uniformly, the newspapers, magazines, novels, and nonfiction works of the period examined its chaotic nature and blurring pace. It is a testament to President Theodore Roosevelt that he presided over such an era and matched its energy with his own. Although no formal study has been conducted, I would hazard a guess that the nation was split evenly between those who looked at the 1900s with great optimism and those who feared the disarray of the age. Imagine a 60-year-old person looking back on their life in the 1900s. The change must have been breathtaking, perhaps more than at any other 50-year span in history.

America rapidly modernized during the Progressive Era, especially as the nation came to terms with the influx of immigrants, multiculturalism, industrialization, and the rise of an urban society. Culturally, these social movements had a profound influence on the development of arts, recreation, and leisure time. The flood of immigrants into the United States, for instance, altered urban neighborhoods, which became distinct enclaves that helped ease the assimilation into the country. The cultural relationship between immigrants and the United States was not a one-way street. As immigrants adapted to their own New World, they brought influences from their own cultures, which were added to the American melting pot.

African Americans, although still facing despicable racism in an era that averaged a lynching once every three days, had a pervasive influence on popular culture in the 1900s. The syncopated beats of black music helped created the ragtime craze, while black athletes, such as world heavyweight champion Jack Johnson, proved that African Americans were not physically inferior to whites, as had been promulgated by those who wanted blacks to remain subordinate.

Society in the 1900s was not just broken along racial lines; it was also divided by class. The industrial order widened the gap between the owners and workers. Many of the day's leading thinkers, including historian Henry Adams, worried that technology was spinning out of control and crystallizing the wall between the extremely rich and working poor. On one hand were the ultra-rich corporate giants—Carnegie, Rockefeller, and Morgan—while on the other were the semi- and unskilled workers who toiled for them, working 12 or more hours a day, six days a week, and making barely enough money to live on, from $250 to $450 a year.

Despite the massive cultural change that occurred in the 1900s, for many groups the overall impact was dubious. Women were able to gain greater freedoms and more equality during the era, but these gains were primarily for white women. For the most part, immigrant and black women were left behind by their white counterparts. At the same time, advertisers targeted middle-class and wealthy women with images of elegance and domestic bliss as a means of getting them to buy products.

Sweeping change characterized the age, but not in all cases and not across the board. For example, women could see forms of modern feminism appear in the 1900s, but countless little girls worked in highly dangerous factory jobs in the North and the South. This was also an age in which the automobile was born and electric lights illuminated the night sky, but children died in infancy at an alarming rate and urban ghettoes were disease-ridden and overcrowded. The heart of the 1900s resides in these fluctuations.

Acknowledgments

I have incurred innumerable debts over the past two years while researching and writing this book. I wish to thank my family members, who provided encouragement, love, and support throughout the process. They put up with me when I was distracted at family dinners, talking about the latest and greatest item I had learned about the 1900s, and through long hours of writing in near isolation—with our cat, Sprite, lurking nearby—pounding out draft after draft on my computer. First and foremost, my mother Linda and her husband Jon Bowen have given me years of support and encouragement. I'm lucky to have the greatest little brother in the world, Bill Coyle, who humors his bookwormish sibling. Without their love, this book would not have been possible. Special thanks also go to Peggy, Tom, and Megan Wilbert. My grandmother, Annaboll Berghigler has been a source of inspiration since I was a little boy. I would also like to thank my in-laws, Jerry and Nancy Roda, and their sons, David and John. They have been encouraging and kind over the years.

Several outstanding historians taught me to love history: Sidney R. Snyder at Slippery Rock High School, James A. Kehl at the University of Pittsburgh, Richard H. Immerman at Temple University, and most of all, Lawrence S. Kaplan at Kent State University. They have all given me years of encouragement and, in their own works, shown me what it means to be a scholar. Dr. Kaplan has been a constant source of inspiration. His seminars in graduate school helped me develop the critical thinking and writing skills necessary to take on a wide-ranging work like this. Several people have read parts or all of the manuscript, including my good friends Chuck Waldron and Anne Beirne. Chris Burtch, my best friend for more than 20 years, has put things into perspective—getting my mind off the book by talking about basketball, music, and golf. His friendship means the world to me. Fellow historians Tom Heinrich and Jim Fisher have provided many hours of great conversation and debate. Thanks also to my friends Bill Halko; Frank and Regina Natale; Reid Muchler; Bill and Tina Nesbitt and their family; Kevin and Liz Mershimer; Jason and Emily Pettigrew; Maria Thomas; Gene and Tina Roach; Jack and Sue Burtch; Chrissy, Anna, and Lily Burtch; Bob, Marina, and Emerson Osmond; Claudia Carasso; Dennis and Susan Jarecke; Mike Menser; and Christine Cupaiuolo. These people have given more than they know.

In the course of my research, I received valuable support and guidance from librarians and archivists at the Cleveland Public Library, Lakewood Public Library, Cleveland State University Library, and the Oakland Public Library. Indispensable help with the photographs came from Joan Morris at the Florida State Archives (photographic collection), the Cleveland Museum of Art, the Oakland History Room staff at the Oakland Public Library, the staff at the Contra Costa County Historical Society, and the Frank Lloyd Wright Foundation. I would also like to thank my former colleagues at The History Factory, Ernst & Young, and UpStart Communications, as well as Kent State University and Cleveland State University. Debby Adams, the editor of the series at Greenwood provided wonderful and thoughtful edits, as did production editor, Emma Bailey.

Without a doubt, this book could not have been produced without the love and encouragement provided by my wife, Katherine. Over the years, she has been patient and kind, giving me great editing advice and listening to me ask over and over again, "How's this sound?" or beginning yet another story, "Hey, baby, back in the 1900s." She is an outstanding, compassionate teacher and I learn from her on a daily basis. I have loved Katherine since the first second I saw her. She is my best friend and has made me the happiest and luckiest man in the world.

Introduction

Modern life is both complex and intense, and the tremendous changes wrought by the extraordinary industrial development of the last half century are felt in every fiber of our social and political being.

—Theodore Roosevelt, Inaugural Address (1905)

The United States experienced explosive growth in the 1900s. Settlers built new towns, older towns grew into cities, and cities became metropolises. Everywhere a person went, crowds were just round the corner: on electric-powered trolleys, in gargantuan department stores that stretched out over city blocks, at ballgames and community picnics, in saloons—all over the place. Even the country and more rural areas seemed congested with people, especially as socialites began spending the day driving their new toys—the automobile.

Immigration pushed American cities to their breaking point. The most rapid growth happened in cities with more than 100,000 people. From 1860 to 1910, the number of cities with more than 50,000 residents jumped from 16 to 109. Fueling this increase were the nearly 9 million immigrants that arrived in America during the first decade of the twentieth century. Cities were so cramped that engineers and architects came to the realization that the only way to build was up, and skyscrapers soon defined city skylines. Down below, the ghettos and tenements, which filled the cracks between, pulsed with life in ethnic enclaves which made up the great American melting pot.[1]

Rapid growth carries with it wide-ranging consequences, and these consequences were major factors in determining how people lived in the

1900s. For some Americans, explosive growth meant competition for un-skilled jobs from immigrants from Eastern or Southern Europe. For oth-ers, expansion symbolized the opportunity to start a business and hopefully live the Horatio Alger rags-to-riches story. On a practical level, housing had to be built, sewage systems dug, telephone lines strung, buildings erected, and local governments elected.

In the face of the seemingly problematic aspects of life in a rapidly growing United States in the 1900s, people were optimistic about the future and looked to the new century with a fervor that was nearly palpable. When observers predicted what the country would be like in the next hundred years, they pictured a world filled with technical and scientific wonder. People believed in the American Dream, the nation's technological, economic, and military prowess, and had high hopes for the future. Their hope sustained them through difficult times.

Americans believed in justice and humanity, even when they saw pain and squalor all around them. In a vile contradiction, equal opportunity still meant something in a nation that allowed blacks to be lynched and the poor to starve. Through it all, the majority of Americans felt the 1900s were the last of the good old days. For many of them, the decade served as a quiet pause between rural America of the nineteenth century and the horrors of World War I and the modern world. A closer look, with some historical perspective, however, proves the period was much more.

The 1900s were more than a bridge between the nation's rustic past and harried future: the decade was a foundation which set the tone for the rest of the century. Time and time again, in music, art, literature, business, and societal interactions, events that occurred in the 1900s were replayed later in the twentieth century or were the basis of new ideas that others would build into permanent institutions. For those of us growing up in the second half of the century, the 1900s should have been an important learning tool.

For example, black rhythms and beats brought from Africa and influ-enced by life in the South served as the backbone for the ragtime sound that swept the nation. The black artists however did not benefit from the craze—the predominantly white writers and composers of New York's Tin Pan Alley co-opted the black sound and made it acceptable to the masses. White composers aped the sound without shame, and the artists who drew the cover art for the sheet music drew racist and stereotypical images of blacks, Asians, and poor whites.

Later in the century, the same thing happened to black jazz and blues artists who essentially founded the rock-and-roll sound. In this case, white performers, such as Elvis Presley, took the black music and legit-imized the sound for white audiences. In the 1980s and 1990s, the same thing happened with rap music, which came out of the black community but turned mainstream when white rappers such as Vanilla Ice and the

Beastie Boys made it palatable for suburban teens with disposable income to spend on compact disks, concert tickets, and other memorabilia.

The 1900s, as the foundation upon which the rest of the century was built, laid out the blueprint America would follow for the next hundred years. The nation established its international military superiority by winning its first overseas war and acquired an overseas empire by annexing Hawaii (1898) and Wake Island (1899) and by winning the rights to the Philippines, Guam, and Puerto Rico in the Treaty of Paris with Spain. This expansion of the American empire, especially in the Western Hemisphere, increased the prestige of the nation and assured its place in world affairs. The nation's entry into global affairs in the 1900s forced it to throw off its isolationist chains, which dated back to George Washington's farewell address. The first president of the United States cautioned that the country should "steer clear of permanent alliances with any portion of the foreign world." Like Pandora's Box, once diplomacy was let loose, the box could never be shut.

Economically, big business transformed into Corporate America during the era. Men like John D. Rockefeller, J. Pierpont Morgan, and Henry Ford instituted a wave of mergers and acquisitions which formed monopolies in most industries. These powerful business leaders created hegemonies or private fiefdoms that ruled the nation's economy until the federal government felt forced to intervene. The supremacy of corporations remained a constant throughout the century and actually intensified over the years. Government intervention also became a constant. In more recent years this is evident with the breaking up of AT&T in 1984 and the antitrust ruling against Microsoft in 2000.

Culturally, the 1900s wiped away many of the lingering standards of Victorianism, and the nation entered an entirely new era—perhaps the development of Modern America. However, the move toward modernity did not necessarily mean that people became more tolerant. In 1903 the United States witnessed the greatest flood of immigrants in its history, which frightened many Progressive leaders. A chorus of reformers, from local political leaders to artists and writers, reacted strongly, promoting racism and xenophobia, which carried through until after World War I.[2]

Timeline of Popular Culture Events

1900

November 3–10, the Automobile Club of America sponsors the first automobile show in Madison Square Garden.

Sister Carrie is published by Theodore Dreiser.

The International Ladies' Garment Workers Union (ILGWU) is founded.

The first Davis Cup tennis match pits the United States against Great Britain.

Kodak introduces the $1.00 Brownie Box Camera.

The College Entrance Examination Board is established by representatives from 13 colleges and preparatory schools.

"A Bird in a Gilded Cage," written by Arthur J. Lamb and Harry Von Tilzer becomes a hit song.

1901

President Theodore Roosevelt causes a national controversy when he dines with black leader Booker T. Washington at the White House.

General Electric develops the first corporate research laboratory.

United States Steel is formed and is the nation's first billion-dollar corporation.

The United States declares the war in the Philippines is over.

President William McKinley is shot by anarchist Leon Czolgosz and dies nine days later. Vice President Theodore Roosevelt takes oath of office.

1902

Owen Wister publishes *The Virginian*.

Dr. Charles Wardell Stiles discovers hookworm, a parasite affecting countless poor whites in the South.

Michigan defeats Stanford 49–0 in the first Tournament of Roses Association football game.

Congress authorizes the building of a canal across Panama.

1903

May 23–July 26, Dr. Horatio Nelson Jackson and Sewall K. Crocker complete the first cross-country automobile trip.

The Boston Red Sox defeated the Pittsburgh Pirates in the inaugural baseball World Series.

The 23-story, steel-framed Fuller Building is completed in New York City; because of its unique shape, it becomes known as the Flatiron Building.

The Great Train Robbery, directed by Edwin S. Porter, is the nation's first action movie.

1904

The U.S. Supreme Court declared the Northern Securities Company a monopoly and ordered the railroad holding company dissolved.

The first organized automobile race, dubbed the Vanderbilt Cup race, after William K. Vanderbilt, a wealthy auto enthusiast, takes place on Long Island.

The first Olympic Games held in the United States took place as part of the Saint Louis World's Fair.

The first segment of the New York City subway, from the Brooklyn Bridge to 145th Street, opens.

1905

First nickelodeon (nickel theater) opens in Pittsburgh.

The radical labor union the Industrial Workers of the World (IWW) is established in Chicago as a reaction against the conservative policies of the American Federation of Labor (AFL).

May G. Sutton becomes the first U.S. player to win a Wimbledon singles title.

The Rotary Club, the first business-oriented services organization is founded in Chicago.

1906

Upton Sinclair publishes *The Jungle*, a novel that reveals impure food-processing standards in Chicago.

Theodore Roosevelt wins the Nobel Peace Prize for his efforts in negotiating a settlement to the war between Japan and Russia.

A race riot erupts in Atlanta, leaving 21 people dead (18 blacks), and the city is placed under martial law.

Devil's Tower in Wyoming is declared the first national monument by Theodore Roosevelt.

Socialite Harry K. Thaw shoots and kills architect Stanford White for his alleged affair with Thaw's wife, Evelyn Nesbit, a former chorus girl. Thaw is later found not guilty because of insanity.

1907

As a result of the Immigration Act of 1907, Japanese laborers are excluded from immigrating to the continental United States by presidential order.

Ziegfeld's Follies opens on Broadway.

The *Lusitania*, the world's largest steamship, sets a new speed record, crossing the Atlantic from Ireland to New York in five days.

1908

Henry Ford introduces the first Model T, which sells for $850.

New York City passes the Sullivan Ordinance, which bans women from smoking cigarettes in public.

The first airplane fatality occurs when Lieutenant Thomas W. Selfridge dies in the crash of a plane piloted by Orville Wright, who is also seriously injured.

The first blood transfusion is performed in New Jersey by Doctors E. Zeh Hawkes and Edward Wharton Sprague.

The electric razor is introduced.

1909

George Bellows paints *Both Members of the Club*.

The Federal Bureau of Investigation (FBI) is established.

Football is banned from New York City public schools.

Alice Huyler Ramsey is the first woman to drive across the United States—from New York to San Francisco.

Scribner's pays former president Theodore Roosevelt $500,000 for an account of his hunting trip in Africa.

Frederick Cook and Robert E. Peary both claim to have reached the North Pole. The suspense gripped the nation, but experts determine Peary was the winner.

Seventy-year-old Edward P. Weston walks from New York to San Francisco in 107 days, 7 hours.

The Pittsburgh Pirates win the World Series by beating the Detroit Tigers four games to three.

Part One

Life and Youth During the 1900s

1

Everyday America

GOVERNMENT

We must keep ever in mind that a republic such as ours can exist only by virtue of the orderly liberty which comes through the equal domination of the law over all men alike, and through its administration in such resolute and fearless fashion as shall teach all that no man is above it and no man below it.

—Theodore Roosevelt (1903)

America's growing fascination with national fairs fueled the growth of the Pan American Exposition, which was held in Buffalo, New York in 1901. The United States showed off its technological prowess with the spectacular Electric Tower, which rose 375 feet in the air and illuminated the night air. Surrounded by fountains and magnificent gardens, the Electric Tower symbolized the realization of American military, economic, and industrial power. The Buffalo fair, designed to link together North and South America, ultimately showed visitors that the United States dictated matters in the Western Hemisphere. Colonial exhibits, for example, included a Filipino village, which actually represented the nation's conquest of the Philippines and Hawaii.

President William McKinley accepted an invitation to visit the Pan American Exposition and arrived on September 5 with his wife. The president delivered a speech applauding the industrial growth demonstrated at the fair and discussed reciprocal commercial relations between North and South America. The next day, at four in the afternoon, McKinley stood in the Temple of Music greeting and shaking hands with the hundreds of well-wishers filing past. The crowd was anxious to get a glimpse of the president. One young workman, whose hand was band-aged, approached McKinley. The workman, anarchist Leon Czolgosz, had concealed a .32-caliber Iver-Johnson revolver in his bandage and shot the president twice in the stomach at close range.[1]

A Secret Service detective on the scene recalled that Czolgosz was "a boyish-looking fellow, with an innocent face, perfectly calm." Firing through the cloth "set fire to the linen," and immediately a dozen or more men jumped on the assassin, while he tried to fire off more shots.[2] McKinley, the native of Canton, Ohio, seemed to recover over the next week while staying in Buffalo. Late in the second week, however, his condition worsened considerably. Gangrene set in from the gunshot wounds to his stomach, and he died on September 14. His vice president, Theodore Roosevelt, risked life and limb to get to Buffalo from his moun-tainous retreat in the Adirondacks. Roosevelt did not make it to Buffalo in time, but took the oath of office in the house where McKinley lay dead. The outpouring of grief for McKinley took up the next several days. Businesses suspended operations, telegraphs and cable messages took a five-minute pause of silence in his honor, and for 10 minutes, every railway in the nation stood still. The assassin, Czolgosz, was in-dicted and executed in the electric chair in late October, less than two months after the attack.

To some, McKinley's death showed a seedy underbelly existed in the United States that threatened the serene view many people held. Divi-sions ran deep along class, ethnic, and racial lines that would flare up countless times throughout the decade. For every rich millionaire living on Park Avenue in New York or Euclid Avenue in Cleveland, the famous "Millionaire's Row," there were hundreds, if not thousands, of Leon Czolgoszs. These were men on the edge of society who felt beaten down by the system that kept them downtrodden.

Theodore Roosevelt

Theodore Roosevelt embodied the best and the worst of the 1900s. A war hero of the Spanish-American war, an adventurer, and a public in-tellectual, he captured the public's imagination long before he ascended to the presidency after the assassination of McKinley in 1901. On one hand, he was a hero and much more to American citizens—a true guid-ing light. On the other hand, he preached, cajoled, and basically de-manded support on numerous moral crusades from the "bully pulpit" and charged forward with nearly reckless abandon. His foreign policy, which centered on extreme nationalism, had little regard for indigenous populations. Roosevelt's moderate course between labor and corporate America, while in line with his conservative views, actually hurt the working class, who had little artillery in the battle against capital. The

Pencil drawing of Theodore Roosevelt.
Overland Monthly, July 1908. Courtesy of
the Oakland History Room of the Oakland
Public Library, Oakland, California.

degree of righteousness in Roosevelt's public persona seems a bit forced
to today's ear.

Like all political leaders and presidents, Roosevelt had his detractors.
Henry Adams, one of America's finest historians, once said that Roosevelt was "never sober, only he is drunk with himself and not with rum."[3]
Others accused the president of establishing a cult of personality, obviously against the democratic principles of the nation. Some of Roosevelt's
earliest biographers, including Henry F. Pringle and Thomas G. Dyer,
criticized him for his views on race and gender. However, political scientist Max J. Skidmore cautions against judging Roosevelt by today's
standards. Although Roosevelt was a product of the Victorian age and
held what we would consider racist and sexist views, when compared
to his contemporaries, Roosevelt comes across more favorably. "Certainly," Skidmore explained, "Roosevelt was politically incorrect, and
actually wrong, in some of his Victorian views." But, the scholar contin-

ued, "Nevertheless, he bridged the centuries and made it possible for America to develop its modern greatness. . . . When one considers all things about Theodore Roosevelt, he emerges as a true hero not only in war, but in peace as well. His flaws were evident, but so were his virtues." Roosevelt is given credit for paving the way for the New Deal and the Great Society by building a government strong enough to control big business but still hold the will of the people sacred. In the end, Skidmore asserted, "TR—whatever his views—also laid the foundation for a society based on justice and equity in matters of race and gender."[4]

Roosevelt became a folk hero at a time when the people truly believed in the righteousness of the United States. He served as the nation's ultimate cheerleader—he fervently believed in the might of the young country, the sanctity of democratic ideals, and America's deserved place at the forefront among the world's powers. Roosevelt believed in a romantic nationalism that came to define the era. He built a strong alliance with the middle class, embodying their hopes and aspirations, while turning a blind eye on extremists from both ends of the political spectrum. Although he would use both to his advantage when necessary, Roosevelt was no friend to organized labor or to big business conglomerates.

At the beginning of the new century, people were filled with optimism and hope, but they also worried that in striving to advance, the nation might be losing its soul. Roosevelt earned the reputation as a reformer, but his notion of reform was to support a middling activism that never bordered on extremism. When he gained the presidency, only seven months into McKinley's term, Roosevelt recognized the need to define the center, and he convinced the nation that he could steer it in the right direction. According to historian John Whiteclay Chambers II, progressive presidents like Roosevelt and later Woodrow Wilson "often muted the differences among their followers. They sought to maintain their coalitions by avoiding conflict among their members as much as possible and by promoting conciliation and compromise when disagreements threatened to disrupt the alliance."[5]

Roosevelt often spoke with religious overtones. His fire-and-brimstone speeches are filled with such words as "gospel," "faith," "preach," and "crusade." Concepts of morality and efficiency were not just ideals; they were the core beliefs that made up his soul. Instead of viewing Roosevelt simply as a member of the Republican Party, he should be viewed as a conservative activist political leader, despite how foreign that may sound to modern ears. The Progressive movement played an important role in Roosevelt's conception of conservatism. He sought stability and order through change which he managed, another reason he distrusted extreme factions of different reform movements. For example, Roosevelt could simultaneously embrace the idea of reform in the meatpacking industry after reading Upton Sinclair's exposé of it in *The Jungle* (1906), but admonish the author for the socialistic overtones in the book, which the president believed muted the importance of the work.

Roosevelt led the nation—pulling it along with him at times and running in front of it at others. Invoking the spirit of his cherished predecessor, Abraham Lincoln, he established the model for how an activist president should act, especially in foreign affairs and in regulating business interests. Building the Panama Canal, formulating the Roosevelt Corollary—which established America's military superiority over the Western Hemisphere—to the Monroe Doctrine, negotiating peace between Japan and Russia, and annexing strategic islands in the Pacific proved that the United States should (and would) play a major role on the world stage. Fighting monopolies, establishing consumer protection laws, and intervening in disputes between business and labor paved the way for the presidents who followed. It seems as if Roosevelt came of age at the perfect time, in sync with a nation teetering between the simpler times of the nineteenth century and the explosion that would be the twentieth. Roosevelt not only bridged that gap, he was the foundation of a new era.

Politics in the Progressive Era

In 1904 Roosevelt declared in his fourth annual message to Congress that the growth of the United States as a world power necessitated the enlargement of the national government. He recommended several expenditures the country should make, including "battleships and forts, public buildings, and improved waterways." However, the president cautioned against extravagance. "Constant care should be taken to guard against unnecessary increase of the ordinary expenses of government," he declared, "The cost of doing government business should be regulated with the same rigid scrutiny as the cost of doing a private business."[6]

Roosevelt's counsel to expand government influence cautiously, while retaining a system of controls similar to those in place at a private company, in many ways sums up the ideology of the Progressive movement at the turn of the century. The Progressives, a loosely knit group of reformers, were primarily middle-class, urban idealists who were willing to stake a claim in the political process across all levels of government. They believed that many Americans were missing out on the economic, social, and cultural opportunities presented by the new century. Given the tremendous changes people experienced as a result of the massive influx of immigrants, the changing industrial order, involvement in foreign affairs, and huge urban growth, the average person needed to believe that someone or something was working on his or her behalf.

Although the Progressives never had the kind of cohesive national organization that could effect wholesale change, they still fought against big business and for increased government intervention in the economy and social realm. Essentially, the Progressives wanted to formalize and professionalize bureaucratic institutions to ensure that government worked for the public interest. According to historian Robert H. Wiebe, "The heart of progressivism was the ambition of the new middle class to fulfill its destiny through bureaucratic means."[7]

Primarily urban reformers, Progressive leaders, including many mayors and governors, were generally economically affluent, highly educated, and upper middle-class people. They envisioned the enemy to be the alliance between business leaders and political bosses. Their first targets were the state and local bosses who had a stranglehold on government. The Tammany Hall machine, which ran New York City government, symbolized the power and arrogance of the boss system, but corruption left few towns or cities unscathed. Reformers also battled against the franchises for local utilities, such as water and sewage, gas, electricity, and public transportation, awarded to the highest bidder, usually a corrupt private company. Not surprisingly, the graft worked its way into local law enforcement circles, saloons, prostitution rings, and among civil servants.

The power of the political machines grew to such an extent that reformers fought back by attempting to pass more than 1,500 amendments to state constitutions between 1900 and 1920. Among the many reforms that passed in these years were the referendum, the recall, the primary system, women's suffrage, and popular election of U.S. senators. Recalls were especially effective in city movements. Los Angeles put a recall clause in its city charter in 1903, followed by the state of Oregon five years later. By 1914, 10 other states had followed Oregon's lead.[8]

While a large number of Progressives concentrated on political reform, countless others specialized in humanitarian relief. Settlement houses, a kind of community center for the poor run by middle-class workers, multiplied in the 1900s based on Hull-House in Chicago, reformer Jane Addams's pioneering effort at helping immigrants acclimatize to American life. Other reformers fought for improved child welfare, elementary and secondary education, and worker safety. Progressives were instrumental in passing many child labor and workman's compensation laws during the decade.[9]

President Roosevelt encouraged Progressive reformers to battle for stricter laws. "No Christian and civilized community can afford to show a happy-go-lucky lack of concern for the youth of today," he declared, "if so, the community will have to pay a terrible penalty of financial burden and social degradation in the tomorrow." Roosevelt called for strict child labor and safety laws in factories. However, as a conservative, he believed that women should stay at home, exerting themselves as housewives, and that men should be the primary breadwinners so that children would grow up healthy. "If a race does not have plenty of children, or if the children do not grow up, or if when they grow up they are unhealthy in body and stunted or vicious in mind," he explained, "then that race is decadent, and no heaping up of wealth, no splendor of momentary material prosperity, can avail in any degree as offsets."[10]

What is ironic about the Progressive Era is that many laws were passed, such as the 1906 Pure Food and Drug Act; the Meat Inspection Act; and the Hepburn Act of 1906, which regulated railroad rates and strengthened the Interstate Commerce Commission, but extreme factions in the nation grew stronger. In 1910 Wisconsin elected Socialist Party member Victor Berger to Congress, and the next several years witnessed the election of 73 Socialist mayors and 1,200 officials in 340 cities and towns.[11] And, despite his self-professed leadership of the Progressive movement, Roosevelt was not as forceful as he could have been. Senator Robert La Follette of Wisconsin, one of the nation's great liberal leaders, admonished Roosevelt whose "cannonading filled the air with noise and smoke, which confused and obscured the line of action, but when the battle cloud drifted by and the quiet was restored, it was always a matter of surprise that so little had really been accomplished." Most of the real leadership of the Progressive Era happened on the local and state level, where individual efforts equated to real results.[12]

Progressivism, in the end, comprised so many different aspects and initiatives that historians have found it difficult to define the movement. If there were overriding impulses within the Progressive Era, they seemed to center on the ideas of evolution and control. Most Progressive leaders, including Roosevelt, wanted a gradual evolution of government, not the kind of revolution advocated by socialists, anarchists, and other groups who were viewed as extreme in the 1900s. An example of this thinking is the selective regulation of corporate monopolies. Roosevelt staked his claim as a trust-buster but could have gone much farther in breaking up illegal industrial combinations. J.P. Morgan and John D. Rockefeller, who headed corporate monopolies, viewed the president's actions with disdain but regarded him as more of a nuisance than an actual threat.

As for control, Progressive leaders envisioned a government that placed control over things they believed needed to be restricted. Thus, conservatives hoped for control over immigration, which they viewed as detrimental because of long-held racist viewpoints and the fear that mass immigration would somehow debase the nation. Reformers on the frontlines wanted controls placed over housing standards, public health initiatives, and welfare. Ironically, as Progressives asked for government to control and intervene, they also warned against excessive intrusion. They

Politics were virtually for men only in the 1900s. For example, see the all-male makeup of the 1901 Florida State Democratic Convention. Courtesy of the Florida State Archives.

hoped that government would swoop in when necessary to eradicate what they saw as societal evils, but at the same time understand when involvement was too much. "Progressives recognized the need for expanded governmental power in a nation of corporate and other private power centers," according to Chambers, "but they sought only enough state power to establish the public interest as a vital counterweight to more parochial private interests."[13] The Progressives believed the answer lay with strong leaders, such as Roosevelt, La Follette, and mayors such as Cleveland's Tom L. Johnson and Toledo's Samuel M. Jones.

Diplomacy: Carrying a Big Stick

The United States not only showed off its military readiness in the 1900s, but also pushed its way into foreign markets in search for new selling avenues. The hungry maw had to be fed twice, with overseas expansion (the Philippines, Hawaii, Puerto Rico), and with access to new markets. American political leaders realized that they would benefit from a healthy dose of economic and diplomatic stability overseas. Discarding Washington's call for isolationism, the nation searched for partners that would uphold its sense of diplomatic hegemony. As with domestic reform, diplomatic leaders wanted to institute a systematic foreign policy, essentially making foreign affairs "wonkish."

The victory over Spain in 1898 catapulted the United States to a more central role and convinced its citizens that an activist foreign policy was in the nation's best interests. The Spanish-American War (1898) also symbolized the melding of diplomatic and economic initiatives, since the United States intervened at least in part to protect American sugar and tobacco interests in Cuba. The difficulty in overcoming the public's reticence regarding diplomatic maneuverings can be seen in the final count of the vote to ratify the Treaty of Paris with Spain in late 1898, which ended the war. Although the United States gained the Philippines, Puerto Rico, and Guam in exchange for $20 million, the final Senate vote was only 57 to 27, which was only two votes more than the two-thirds necessary for ratification. The Philippines rebelled against U.S. occupation and it took three years to squelch the rebellion. In all, nearly 130,000 American troops went to battle in the Philippines; 4,000 were killed and 2,800 were wounded in action. In their fight for independence, the Filipinos lost 18,000 soldiers, and between 100,000 to 200,000 noncombatants died.[14] The United States quickly learned that it was harder to govern a territory than to acquire it.

The United States did not have a cohesive strategy in East Asia. The primary goal was to keep an interest in the region and not allow the European powers or Japan to intervene and divide the spoils among themselves. Secretary of State John Hay outlined an Open Door policy in 1899 and 1900 which would allow the Western powers to enter China peacefully. Basically, the United States hoped to avoid military operations in China and settle disputes amicably. The policy aspired to take advantage of perceived economic markets in China.

Soon, Japan and Russia went to war over China, Manchuria, Korea, and other interests in the Far East. Although Japan emerged with a stunning victory over Russia, both sides overextended themselves and were ready for peace in 1905. Roosevelt stepped in as moderator and negotiated the Treaty of Portsmouth, which ended the war on September 5, 1905. Serving as negotiator gave Roosevelt a bit more swagger on the international stage, but it hardly made up for America's lack of power in China. Hay's successor as secretary of state, Elihu Root, reinforced the Open Door policy in 1908. The Open Door policy had a far-reaching impact. One historian explained that Roosevelt's "philosophy and practice of the imperialism that was embodied in the Open Door Notes became the central feature of American foreign policy in the twentieth century."[15]

While U.S. actions in the Far East were more or less a carryover from the McKinley days, the country's actions in the Western Hemisphere were stamped by Roosevelt's brand of cowboy bravado: "Speak Softly and Carry a Big Stick." Amazingly, for all his bluster, Roosevelt elevated the nation to the status of a world leader without engaging in any protracted wars or overly messy quagmires. "It was the availability of power, rather than its use, that made for effective diplomacy," claimed another historian.[16]

Toward this end, Roosevelt promoted a program to increase vastly the size of the navy by building at least two battleships per year. "The American people must either build and maintain an adequate navy or else make up their minds definitely to accept a secondary position in international affairs, not merely in political, but in commercial, matters," the president exclaimed.[17] In an extravagant display of power, Roosevelt sent a fleet of 16 battleships and 12,000 men around the world from December 1907 to February 1909. The message was clear and aimed directly at Germany and Japan: America would fight to protect its interests.

As excavation began on a canal across the Isthmus of Panama, the United States surveyed its neighbors in Latin America and decided that it should ensure that they were, in Roosevelt's words, "stable, orderly, and prosperous." However, if a nation stepped out of line, it may "ultimately require intervention by some civilized nation, and in the Western Hemisphere the adherence of the United States to the Monroe Doctrine may force the United States, however reluctantly, in flagrant cases of such wrongdoing or impotence, to the exercise of an international police power."[18] This sanction, dubbed the Roosevelt corollary to the Monroe Doctrine, ensured that the United States would intervene whenever it saw fit to preserve an orderly system. The Roosevelt corollary set in place a policy that soon made the United States the unofficial colonial master of its neighbors to the south and laid the foundation for relations between the United States and Latin America for the rest of the century.

THE ECONOMY

The Rise of Big Business

Many of American history's most prominent businessmen, including financiers John D. Rockefeller and J.P. Morgan, steel magnate Andrew Carnegie, and automobile manufacturer Henry Ford, dominated industry in the 1900s. Both admired and despised, these men set the tone for the way in which business leaders conducted themselves in the era. They could be merciless in dealing with a competitor or small business that stood in their way, but frequently they acted in the nation's best interests; for example, Morgan intervened in the financial crisis of 1907, stepping into a bleak situation and saving Wall Street.

The decade gave rise to moguls and dominant corporations and, on a more fundamental level, it also changed the prevailing social order. The corporation enabled a new white-collar managerial class to emerge, reshaped the relationship between labor and capital, and, in the words of one historian, signaled "the enshrinement of technology and science as the new American gods."[19] The rise of big business reached even further into the fabric of the nation by changing the way people looked at education as a career-building institution, by putting farmers at the mercy of fluctuating world markets, and by impacting government at all levels.

The guiding lights of corporate America in the 1900s were John D. Rockefeller and J.P. Morgan. They changed the way people viewed big business and became modern-day demigods, both feared and admired by the thronging masses. Neither man had much use for the age-old idea of business competition, so they set out to eliminate it by building what they called trusts, which Rockefeller believed were necessary and safe. Those trusts were in fact monopolies. The financiers felt that corporate combinations were in the best interests of the nation because they provided stability to the economy. If some smaller concerns had to be swallowed up in the process, so be it, but they would be sacrificed for the good of the national economy. The corporate system flourished and led to a stronger, economically dominant nation.

From 1895 to 1904, more than 2,000 companies were consolidated into large enterprises which wielded a great deal of power. For example, the United States Steel company, America's first billion-dollar corporation, consisted of 213 different manufacturing concerns, included 41 mines, and owned more than 1,000 miles of railroad track and 112 ore ships. All told, this company accounted for 60 percent of the nation's steel-making output and 43 percent of the pig-iron capacity. These large business consolidations occurred for many reasons, but the primary reason was to dampen price wars and allow one company to determine rates.[20]

Despite the preference for combines, small businesses also thrived during this period, especially in the manufacturing industries that did not require intricate production processes or advanced marketing skills, including lumber, publishing, and clothing manufacturing. Whenever big business saw no real benefit from taking over a small business, it ignored it and allowed it to continue. Small owners could protect themselves to some degree by obtaining patents over their manufacturing processes. What these small companies lacked in control over the national markets they made up for in entrepreneurial verve. They became extremely good at one area that had not been centralized by corporations and carved out a niche to remain successful.[21]

Rockefeller and the Modern Corporation

John D. Rockefeller grew up in upstate New York, but made Cleveland, Ohio, a thriving industrial manufacturing and port city on the banks of Lake Erie, his adopted hometown.

Rockefeller built a mini-empire in oil refining as a young man, which grew as advances in technology and transportation lowered overhead costs. In 1870 Rockefeller rolled all of his interests into the newly founded Standard Oil Company and headquartered the company in Cleveland, the nation's principal refining center. After his early attempt to form a cartel failed, Rockefeller spent from 1872 to 1879 buying up competing refineries. Noted for his fairness, the up-and-coming magnate paid honest prices for the companies as he gobbled them up. Refineries that did not sell out soon found that they could not compete with Rockefeller's machine.

Along the way, Rockefeller squeezed every cent out of the process by maximizing efficiencies, but he did not micromanage his empire. He trusted his lieutenants to work hard. Ultimately, they benefited from the largesse of Standard Oil. His treatment of workers was markedly different from that of the industrial leaders in railroads, steel, and coal. "Every head of a department in the Standard Oil has explicit instructions to treat all employees with absolute fairness," Rockefeller explained. "When that policy is carried out there will never be any danger of strikes."[22] By the late 1870s, Rockefeller controlled from 90 to 95 percent of the nation's refining power.

The hegemony Rockefeller established in the refinery industry carried over into feeder business segments, such as big railroads and kerosene markets. His command over the railroads forced them to pay him draw-backs on Standard's shipments and even those of his competitors. For example, if Rockefeller paid $1.20 to ship over a route, the railroad re-bated the shipment 20 cents. The few remaining competitors also paid $1.20, but the railroads paid the 20-cent kickback to Rockefeller, not the shipper. The harder Rockefeller's competitors worked, the more he prof-ited through these secret deals, giving Standard a 40-cent head start from the outset.[23]

Even the concerted efforts of oil producers could not slow down Rock-efeller. Gradually, however, public opinion turned against the titan. Ed-itorial cartoons appeared showing Rockefeller and Standard Oil as a giant octopus, with its tentacles spread out around the world. Rockefeller became the richest man in the world, but disgruntled competitors filed lawsuits and, in Pennsylvania, an indictment against Standard Oil ex-ecutives for criminal conspiracy. The latter forced Rockefeller to abolish the system of rebates and other shady practices. To combat the loss of competitive advantage, Rockefeller moved quickly to create the Standard Oil Trust, which centered the collective power of the subsidiaries into one overarching company directed by nine trustees.

But the formation of the trust was a short-lived victory. The federal and state governments were moving against monopolies, bolstered by the Sherman Anti-Trust Act, which outlawed monopolistic combinations in restraint of trade, they brought suit against Standard Oil. The attorney general of Ohio won a case against Rockefeller, and the trust was dis-solved in 1892. Rockefeller used the corporate-friendly laws of New Jer-sey to reorganize Standard. He increased the capital of the company from $10 million to $110 million and turned New Jersey Standard into the corporate headquarters for the new Standard Oil empire. In 1900 Stan-dard Oil profits reached $56 million, but six years later, climbed to $83 million.

The government again reacted against the power of Standard Oil and Rockefeller. Again, several states and the federal government brought suits against the oil giant. The company endured a $29 million fine in 1907 but could not withstand the U.S. Supreme Court decision in 1911 that required New Jersey Standard to divest itself of all subsidiaries. With much foresight, or perhaps just luck, Rockefeller realized that oil would be the basis of power in the twentieth century, fueling two world wars and the worldwide development of the automobile. After the Su-preme Court's decision, Rockefeller asked a friend, "Have you some money?" Then the cagey tycoon exclaimed, "Buy Standard Oil."[24]

By 1913 Rockefeller's fortune reached $900 million. He devoted much of his life from the 1890s onward to philanthropic activities. He endowed the University of Chicago in 1892 and established a foundation to give money to education and health organizations around the world. The breakup of Standard Oil actually increased Rockefeller's wealth, since he gained shares in numerous oil-related industries. He continued giving money away and spent the final 20 years of his long life at his two estates in Florida, playing golf and gardening. He died in 1937 at the age of 97.

Remarkably, today there is little hint left that the great Rockefeller lived much of his long life in Cleveland, despite the fact that he is buried there. In a rather shortsighted battle, Cleveland officials decided to send Rockefeller a tax bill of $1.5 million in 1913 when he stayed in the city to care for his ailing wife past the February 3 tax cut-off day. The bitter episode, especially given his wife's illness, forced Rockefeller to boycott the state. Cleveland paid the price later. Rockefeller began the largest philanthropic campaign ever seen and the city received relatively little. "Cleveland ought to be ashamed to look herself in the face when she thinks of how she treated us," he remarked. "New York has always treated me more fairly than Cleveland, much more." Cleveland's loss truly was New York's gain. Although Rockefeller gave Cleveland more than $3 million and several fine parks, New York received treasures far and wide.[25]

Morgan: America's Financier

The mid-1900s were prosperous times for American businessmen. They borrowed money at an alarming rate to gobble up stocks. When a failed takeover bid at United Copper Company happened in the fall of 1907, two brokerage houses collapsed, and worried financiers started pulling money from their banks. Money and credit dried up and even large institutions, such as the New York Stock Exchange, had trouble funding daily operations. The nation stood at the brink of financial ruin. The government in the period had no real authority to step into the crisis. As a matter of fact, only one man could save the day—J.P. Morgan.

Born into a Hartford, Connecticut, banking family in 1837, Morgan used his experience in financial services to build an empire which included vast railroad holdings and just about every other American industry. Morgan instilled fear in those around him, which he used to his advantage. Even his business associates and partners feared him.

A whiz with numbers and business deals, Morgan made more than $50,000 in 1864, when he was only 27 years old. By the 1870s, he garnered upward of $500,000 annually and recognition as one of the nation's up-and-coming financial leaders. Morgan realized the power of railroads and constructed a transcontinental network that would link together disparate financial centers and put them at Morgan's beck and call. Morgan connected the necessary investors to the railroads and took his piece out of the transaction. The financier also relied heavily on research and his own intelligence to determine the best course of action. Often, after studying a business topic, Morgan was more of an expert than the men who had spent years working in the industry.[26]

Much of the nation, especially the West and South, considered Morgan the devil incarnate. He represented the money and power of the Eastern establishment and New York City. In 1893, however, when British investors began removing their money from the American market, President Grover Cleveland realized a crisis was brewing ahead. The nation's treasury supply of gold dwindled down below $50 million, about half the amount that officials considered the bare minimum. In the midst of possible financial chaos, Cleveland reached out to Morgan, the single man who could calm the fears. Acting quickly, Morgan organized a group of investors to buy $50 million in government bonds, with an option on an additional $50 million. Cool and calculating on the surface, Morgan realized that a collapse of the dollar would threaten his empire, but he also knew a profit could be made off the government's fiscal challenges. "We all have large interests dependent upon maintenance of the sound currency of the United States," Morgan cabled to his London office. "If this negotiation can be made, it will be most creditable to all parties and pay a good profit."[27]

As word leaked of Morgan's bailout effort, the drain on the gold reserve allowed Cleveland time to reconsider his alliance with Morgan. The president suggested a public sale of bonds, but both he and Morgan knew that the United States and Europe would stop the financial bloodletting only if Morgan stepped in. They struck a deal and the crisis was averted. Estimates suggest that Morgan made anywhere from $250,000 to $16 million by rescuing the treasury. Morgan felt it was fair, even though he was criticized by government officials for "profiteering," since the financier restored the credit of the federal government. The plan worked so well that Morgan's power increased even more. Less than a decade later, Morgan bought out venerable industrialist Andrew Carnegie and formed the world's largest company, United States Steel, with a market capitalization of $1.4 billion.

Theodore Roosevelt, however, realized he could gain quite a bit of publicity and support by taking on the big corporate monopolies of the day. In 1902 he went after Northern Securities, a railroad trust controlled by Morgan. Morgan personally visited the president, attempting to work out their differences diplomatically, but Roosevelt rebuked the great financier. The president also warned that others would be in jeopardy if they did not obey the law. Roosevelt took great pride in standing up to Morgan, but before long the businessman would be called on, yet again, to save the nation financially.

The 70-year-old Morgan blamed the volatile business climate on Roosevelt, who criticized men like Morgan, whom he called "malefactors of great wealth." Although a lifelong Republican, Morgan mused that he would vote Democratic just to get rid of him. The animosity ran deep between the two, and as Roosevelt prepared for an African safari in 1909, Morgan told an associate, "I hope the first lion he meets does his duty."[28]

The prosecution of Rockefeller's Standard Oil Company on antitrust violations and increased regulation in the railroad industry put pressure on companies to find money to cover their exposure on Wall Street. A study revealed that 8,090 companies with liabilities of $116 million went bankrupt in the first nine months of 1907. The collapse of F. Augustus Heinze's attempt to take over the United Copper Company Trust caused a widespread panic on Wall Street. The falling stock prices cut cash reserves to a dangerous level. Morgan, who was attending an Episcopalian convention in Richmond, Virginia, did not return to New York. He believed that if the public saw him rushing back to New York, it would cause a deeper panic.[29]

Once again, as during the Cleveland administration, no government agency existed that could step in to provide safeguards for the economy. In the past, when banking crises erupted, reformers called for greater governmental control, but the uproar subsided when the tumult ended. As the 1907 panic unfolded, Morgan had to get back to New York. He immediately assembled an ad hoc financial swat team to combat the downturn. It included Rockefeller, James Stillman of the National City Bank, George F. Baker of the First National Bank, railroad titan Edward Harriman, and an assortment of banking and finance experts.

After closing the Knickerbocker Trust Company, a venerable bank in the heart of New York's financial district on October 21, 1907, Morgan grappled with a solution to the panic. No simple solution existed, as it had in 1895. Instead of allowing the Trust Company of America to falter, Morgan gave it a $2.5 million loan to keep it going. He disliked the financial trusts, but he knew that if more of them went under it would make his job of stabilizing the economy more difficult. The venerable financier organized a group of banks to loan money to the trust and buoyed the public's spirits to a degree. After Morgan's display of strength, the national government deposited $25 million in select New York City banks to help out the troubled trusts and banks.[30]

Over the next several days, several more banks crumbled, and the New York Stock Exchange (NYSE) suffered from depleting credit. NYSE President Ransom H. Thomas personally visited Morgan and told him that he did not have the funds to stay open. Realizing this would be a fatal blow to public confidence, Morgan called the leaders of the city's most powerful banks and persuaded them, in ten minutes, to ante up $25 million. The move brought about a round of applause on the trading floor and kudos from the *Wall Street Journal*. Over the weekend, the notoriously gruff Morgan took on a statesman-like role. He reassured the public, "If people will keep their money in the banks, everything will be all right." The city's clergy pounded this message home in church pulpits all over New York. Still, on Sunday night, around 118 patrons waited all night in the rain outside the Lincoln Trust Company to withdraw their funds.[31]

The next challenge Morgan faced occurred on Monday and Tuesday, when New York City threatened to go into default. Morgan again acted quickly to raise the millions of dollars it took to pay the city's employees. Over the following weekend, Morgan decided to organize all the remaining trust companies and force them into saving their ailing brethren. The financier made the presidents of the trusts, who had gathered together in Morgan's palatial library, band together to give the others a $25 million loan. By the following Wednesday, November 6, 1907, the panic had ended. The federal government issued low-interest bonds and gave the proceeds to the various banks. "Nothing in Wall Street history has been more important or dramatic than the day and night conference in Mr. Morgan's library of the leading financiers of Wall Street," exclaimed the *Wall Street Journal*, quite a turn for the prim daily. "He has been distinctly the man of the hour, the undisputed leader who has stood between the business of the country and disaster."[32]

Morgan retired after the crisis, but significant achievement came about as a result of Morgan's handling of the affair. In May 1908, Congress passed a currency law that guarded against money shortages by allowing banks to issue money secured by the federal government. The bill also created the National Monetary Commission, but the crowning achievement was the development of the Federal Reserve System, led by the Federal Reserve Board, in 1913. The board, known as the Fed, monitors the availability of capital to banks and gives the country a blanket of security that Morgan provided in the 1900s. Under the provisions of the Federal Reserve Act, money could be delivered quickly to local banks in times of crisis to avoid future panics. Despite the monetary power given to the Fed, it failed dramatically during the Wall Street collapse leading to the Great Depression in 1929.

LABOR AND THE WORKPLACE

The ongoing battle between the working class and business had haunted the United States from its earliest days. The issues gripping working life in the 1900s exposed the very heart of Progressivism—the fight between private power and public welfare. To be sure, each side dealt with delicate sensitivities. For business owners, where is the line drawn between maximizing profits and exploiting workers? For laborers, what rights are retained inside the enterprise and how should one go about asserting them in the workplace? These specific issues and a myriad of others set the tone for the relationship between businesses and

Workers at the Antioch Paper Mill, Antioch, California (1900). Courtesy of the Contra Costa County Historical Society.

workers. Nearly always contentious, the challenge for politicians, judges, labor organizers, business leaders, and the workingman was to find an acceptable compromise in an arena of constant conflict.

At a basic level, organized labor threatened the country's governing class because labor challenged many basic assumptions Americans held dear: the rights of private property holders, the sanctity of business, and the power of democratic institutions. Throughout history, workers had very little leverage over business. When labor organized it was viewed as a threat by business. Socialists and other radicals in the labor movement were a minority of the total membership, but their activism prompted business to be ruthless in its attempts to stop unionization. "Employers waged bloody battles with even the most 'responsible' and 'conservative' of trade unions," explained labor historian Melvyn Dubofsky. "Let there be no mistake about it, American business *never* willingly conceded any of its prerogatives to workers and unions or to political reformers."[33]

Like most other areas of life in the Progressive Era, workplaces were changing. Factories became larger and a new type of middle management focused on efficiency, stability, and solidifying its own power over workers. By 1900, more than 1,000 factories had more than 500 workers; only a handful of factories this size had existed in the 1870s. Swift & Co., a meatpacking company, employed 23,000 workers in 1903, up from 1,600 in 1886. The use of new technology centered on making manufacturing more efficient, which also disrupted the lives of workers. Glass, chemicals, steel, and coal workers were all forced to change processes to maximize production, regardless of how the pace impacted workers. With a steady supply of immigrant labor, managers could replace anyone who could not keep pace or complained about the "modern" workplace.

Although most Progressives talked about being pro-labor, more often than actually doing anything to help labor leaders directly, unions became more cohesive in the 1900s. Between 1897 and 1903, membership in the American Federation of Labor (AFL) jumped from 400,000 to almost 3 million. Perhaps more important, labor withstood the counterattacks made by big business and the periodic economic downturns that gave employers more of an upper hand, such as the fluctuation of 1907.

Labor relations were relatively quiet until 1903, but the rest of the decade witnessed a virtual war between unions and employers. From 1903 to 1905, a battle raged in the mining fields of Colorado. The governor there declared martial law and sent the militia to thwart a strike by the Western Federation of Miners, whose workers demanded the right to organize and be represented by the union, closely tying the government to the interests of big business. Fights broke out on the streets of Chicago in 1905, and the decade culminated in the bombing of the Los Angeles Times building.[34]

The rise of a new managerial class that emphasized efficiency and focused on production numbers affected workers' lives, but on the shop-floor workers still fought to retain control. Foremen still held great influence, often determining who was hired and fired, setting pay rates, and ultimately, establishing production levels. Workers fought against management's directives to raise production levels and control personnel. The battle over control at such a minute level caused great animosity between workers and capital. Employers wanted to dictate production rates and pay standards, while workers stood their ground where they could. With the benefit of hindsight, it is easy to see why workers were willing to fight corporations: working conditions were dangerous, workers routinely worked long hours, no such thing as job security existed for most workers, and the pay was abysmally low.

For all its technological superiority, the United States still had one of the highest workplace accident rates in the world. For example, from 1907 to 1910, in one Pittsburgh steel mill, 3,723 new immigrant workers were injured or killed. A 1913 study revealed that 25,000 workers were killed on the job, while 700,000 were injured. From the clothing manu-

Women working at the local phone company in Martinez, California
(1907). Courtesy of the Contra Costa County Historical Society.

facturers of New York City to the textile mills of the South, workers
toiled under unsafe conditions for pay that barely met the poverty line.[35]

The efforts of Slavic workers at the Carnegie Steel mill to form lodges
to combat workplace injury in Homestead, Pennsylvania, were reported
by sociologist Margaret F. Byington:

There are many accidents among the Slavs. The hazards are accentuated by their
ignorance of these dangers and by their difficulty in understanding the orders
of English-speaking "bosses." Given the constant peril of accident or death, and
a community which takes little interest in the immigrant's welfare, the extent to
which the lodge has been developed is not surprising.[36]

In return for weekly dues, usually ranging between $1 and $6, Slav workers were eligible for death, disability, and sick pay from among nine
Slavic societies in Homestead. Death benefits paid between $500 and
$1,000; sick pay averaged approximately $5 a week for 13 weeks and
$2.50 for the next 13 weeks. These payouts would enable families to
avoid catastrophe if the primary breadwinner was killed or disabled, but

average weekly household budgets in the mill town ran from $10 to $20. A disability or lengthy sickness could be disastrous.[37]

Exploitation and the Rise of the Wobblies

Violence was the Progressives' worst nightmare—they wanted orderly change, and labor was not willing to play along. Workers had a long memory and had only to look back to the brutality of the 1892 Homestead strike at Carnegie Steel to see how the deck was stacked against them. In 1905 a group of 200 radical labor activists met in Chicago and formed the Industrial Workers of the World (IWW), nicknamed the "Wobblies." The IWW was committed to empowering all workers, especially the nonskilled laborers excluded from the American Federation of Labor (AFL). Believing that the nation's most exploited and poorest workers deserved a voice, the Wobblies called for "One Big Union" that would challenge the capitalist system first in the United States and later worldwide.[38]

The Wobblies' rise to national prominence can be understood only within the context of the vast changes taking place in America in the early twentieth century. The influx of immigrants transformed society and provided the workforce coveted by corporations. Poverty was a way of life, however, for most working-class families. The IWW was overwhelmingly leftist and called for the ultimate overthrow of capitalism worldwide. Immediately feared by most and despised by AFL leader Samuel Gompers, the Wobblies challenged the status quo and fought for the rights of America's working poor. The Wobblies planned to do what no union had tried before: unite blacks, immigrants, and assembly-line workers into one powerful force. One IWW pamphlet outlined the union's goal, "Shall I tell you what direct action means? The worker on the job shall tell the boss when and where he shall work, how long and for what wages and under what conditions."[39] This kind of thinking rocked the Progressive ideas regarding orderly change.

IWW leaders included some of the most famous names in American labor history—Big Bill Haywood, head of the Western Federation of Miners; Mary "Mother" Jones, a longtime union advocate; and Eugene Debs, the leader of the Socialist Party. The Wobblies called for a revolution from below and began organizing strikes around the nation as a prelude to a general worldwide strike among the working class. Long before the rise of the Bolsheviks in Russia, the Wobblies were calling for a socialist revolution. Initially, the ranks of the IWW were filled with Western miners under Haywood's control. These individuals became increasingly militant when they were marginalized by the AFL. Traveling hobo-like by train, IWW organizers fanned out across the nation. Wobbly songwriters, such as Joe Hill, immortalized the union through humorous folk songs. The simple call for an inclusive union representing all workers took hold. IWW membership approached 150,000, although only 5,000 to 10,000 were full-time members.[40]

The Wobblies were courageous and militant. Wobblies mixed Marxism and Darwinism with American ideals to produce a unique brand of radicalism. They led strikes that often turned bloody, but they continued to fight. The newspapers, the courts, and the police attacked them, and "goon squads" were formed to protect the interests of corporations. The Wobblies battled for free speech and higher wages across the nation. A legendary folklore developed regarding the union since it seemed that violence and mayhem followed them everywhere. The Wobblies became the scourge of middle-class America.

As the Wobbly "menace" became more influential, American leaders took action to limit the union's power. World War I provided the diversion the government needed to crush the IWW once and for all. Anti-labor forces labeled the IWW subversive allies of both Germany and Bolshevik Russia, one senator called the group "Imperial Wilhelm's Warriors." President Woodrow Wilson and his attorney general believed the Wobblies should be suppressed. On September 5, 1917, Justice Department agents raided every IWW headquarters in the country, seizing five tons of written material. By the end of September nearly 200 Wobbly leaders had been arrested on sedition and espionage charges. In April 1918, 101 IWW activists went on trial, which lasted five months and was the nation's longest criminal trial to date. All the defendants were found guilty and 15 were sentenced to 20 years in prison, including Haywood, who jumped bail and fled to the Soviet Union where he died a decade later.

The lasting importance of the IWW was bringing unskilled workers into labor's mainstream. After the demise of the Wobblies, the AFL gradually became more inclusive and political. The Congress of Industrial Organizations (CIO) founded in 1935 by another mining leader, John L. Lewis, successfully organized unskilled workers. In 1955 the AFL and CIO merged to form the AFL-CIO, America's leading trade union throughout the second half of the century. Although the Wobblies are nearly forgotten today, the organization played a pivotal role in America's labor history. The heyday of the IWW lasted less than 20 years, but in that short span they took hold of the nation's conscience. The Wobbly spirit can be found in novels written by John Dos Passos and Wallace Stegner, as well as numerous plays and movies. In the 1950s and 1960s, IWW songs, collected in the famous *Little Red Song Book*, were rediscovered by a new generation of activists fighting for civil rights and an end to the Vietnam War.

LIVING CONDITIONS

Life and Death

The United States was a vicious place to live in the 1900s. According to most estimates, more than two blacks were lynched each week between 1889 and 1903. Union men died in state-sanctioned acts of brutality, such as those carried out by the Pennsylvania State Constabulary of 1905, a mounted police force called the "Cossacks," and by company-sponsored thugs breaking up a strike by the Teamsters in Chicago the same year. On the other side of the globe, in the battle to subdue the Philippines, American soldiers fought a moral battle against charges of brutality. In Manila, a major in the Marine Corps stood trial for shooting 11 defenseless Filipinos on the island of Samar. Littletown Waller testified that he was "instructed to kill and burn, and said that the more he killed and burned the better pleased he would be; that it was no time to take prisoners, and that he was to make Samar a howling wilderness." When asked the age of those he targeted, Waller replied, "Everything over ten." A British officer, after witnessing American atrocities in the Philippines, concluded, "This is not war; it is simply massacre and murderous butchery."[41]

Disease and unsafe living conditions in overcrowded cities took many lives, predominantly those of immigrants. Simply getting enough fresh breathing air into living spaces challenged cramped families in close quarters. Bathrooms, often shared among multiple families, or open in the streets also led to a germ-ridden society with high mortality rates. In one Polish ghetto in Chicago, more than 7,300 children lived in a three-block radius and trash, manure, and garbage lined the streets. Pittsburgh had the highest mortality rate for typhoid in the world with 1.3 deaths per 1,000 people. Disease was a major cause of death, but if fire broke out, no real escape existed for most apartment dwellers. More than 250 people died in apartment fires in Manhattan between 1902 and 1909.[42]

In 1904 the *New York Times Magazine* ran a feature article on people around the city who risked death on a regular basis, instigated by a Department of Health report that revealed nearly 8,000 people had died from accidental causes the previous year. The anonymous writer felt that "peace is far more dangerous than war in the matter of earning a daily living." To prove this point, he traveled around the city's boroughs examining the variety of dangerous professions, beginning with bridge builders over the East River, who lost seven men while they worked high above the city. Describing the fear among workers, the paper reported, "Only when one of them overbalances and with a trailing cry plunges into the air and water below are those bridge builders made aware of their danger long enough to entertain a momentary sickening fear that passes away almost as soon as it comes."[43]

Next the reporter visited the subway contractors building between City Hall and Harlem, where "there has been a victim for every square of ground above our remarkable tunnel." Others among the professions profiled included fireworks manufacturers, firemen, police officers, railway engineers, even musicians. "Strange as it may seem, the mortality among musicians is very high in this city . . . their comparative mortality is 1,214, or more than twice that of agriculturists, and exceeding by one-third that of general laborers," the paper noted. Musicians were said to die from "diseases of the nervous, circulatory, and digestive organs."[44]

While the article makes no bones about trying to prove a particular point, the accidental deaths of countless victims across the nation can be tied directly to the wave of technology and progress swallowing up the nation in the 1900s. Building skyscrapers, bridges, new railway lines, and clearing forests all required that laborers take unnecessary risks. They were forced to gamble with their lives, and many lost that wager.

Infectious diseases were the leading cause of death throughout the early twentieth century. Yellow fever, cholera, and smallpox thrived in the crowded metropolises, while people constantly fought influenza, pneumonia, measles, and tuberculosis. In the South, hookworm and malaria were frequent causes of death among the poor. Mosquitoes carried malaria into unscreened homes, and being barefoot led to acquiring the hookworm parasite. Of all these diseases, however, tuberculosis was the most deadly prior to 1915. In addition to the lives it took, it had a profound impact on society. Colorado and California attracted those suffering from the disease because of their abundance of clean air and sunshine, and legislators passed laws requiring teachers, nurses, and public health officials to submit to regular tuberculosis tests. Even the "dipper," a crude tin water fountain popular in public areas was removed and replaced by glass-lined water coolers and paper cups.[45]

Mary Mallon, or "Typhoid Mary" as she was better known, was the first carrier of typhoid to be identified in the United States. An immigrant from Northern Ireland, Mallon worked as a cook for many wealthy families in New York City in a seven-year span. As a carrier, Mallon never caught the disease herself, but she spread the disease from household to household. At least three deaths and 53 cases of typhoid can be directly attributed to Typhoid Mary. Some observers believe she may also have been responsible for an outbreak in Ithaca, New York, in 1903, which led to 1,400 cases. Mallon entered a hospital in the Bronx in 1907 and was held there until 1910. She dropped out of sight but reappeared four years later and was quarantined for life at Riverside Hospital in New York. She died there in 1938.

Suicide was a common way to die in the 1900s, and the front pages of daily newspapers across the nation, including the *New York Times*, blared with gruesome accounts of suicides, double suicides, and murder-suicides. Little formal study has been conducted on suicide rates in the 1900s, but an examination of several papers from the decade indicates a shocking number of reported suicides. Perhaps much of this fascination with suicide can be credited to the sensational nature of the press, but it also speaks to the way in which people viewed death in the 1900s. People dealt with a number of calamities, from financial ruin to terminal illness, by ending their lives. Perhaps suicide was regarded as an honorable alternative to living as a pauper or an invalid. Another answer may lie in the wave of neurasthenia, or "American nervousness," which swept the nation in the 1900s. This disease, reportedly caused by the agitation and stress of modern life, could have driven many people to act out their rage, especially given the number of husband and wife murder-suicides that occurred. According to journalist Mark Sullivan, the suicide rate was 11.5 per 100,000 in 1900, which compares with the murder rate of 2.1 per 100,000 citizens. Sullivan also reported, for example, that cancer had a death rate of 63; tuberculosis reached 201.9 per 100,000.[46]

Even the nation's literature contained characters that decided to kill themselves, rather than continue confronting a frustrating world. Beginning with Kate Chopin's *The Awakening* (1899) all the way through Jack London's *Martin Eden* (1909), authors dealt with the angst of the modern world by having their characters make the ultimate sacrifice. Other authors that used suicide in their work included Stephen Crane, Theodore Dreiser, Frank Norris, Willa Cather, and Edith Wharton. Their characters, from Wharton's look at upper-class life, to the seedy worlds of Dreiser and Norris, are unable to overcome the stresses of their age, whether it deals with their social status, financial well-being, or marital happiness.[47]

Disaster

In the 1900s, it seemed that natural and man-made disasters were a constant way of life. The decade experienced hurricanes, tornadoes, earthquakes, floods, shipwrecks, fires, and automobile accidents. Many of these disasters can be attributed to a new way of life which clashed with the old; for example, trains and cars smashing into horse-drawn carriages and hitting pedestrians. In Berkeley, California, at the turn of the century, people had a terrible time with trains. Since the main line traveled directly through the center of town, trains frequently hit horses, cows, milk wagons, people, and other trains. Oddly enough, people found it difficult to judge the speed of steam trains and electric street cars as they passed over the tracks, even though the liners were only moving at 15 miles per hour. On January 3, 1900, an unknown man

The first fire station in Crochett, California (1909). Courtesy of the
Contra Costa County Historical Society.

stepped in front of a northbound train and, according to a report published in the *Berkeley Daily Gazette*, "was ground to pieces under the
swiftly moving train." Others made dashing escapes just in the knick of
time.[48]

More horrific were the natural disasters that destroyed America's little
tinderbox cities. So many urban areas were still predominantly wooden
that the smallest spark could lead to widespread destruction.

One of the first cataclysmic events of the decade occurred on the island
city of Galveston, Texas, on September 7, 1900. On Labor Day weekend,
as Galveston filled with tourists and revelers, a hurricane approached
the region. Gale-force winds reaching 102 miles per hour and rain
smashed into the city, and a storm surge carried away the bridges that
linked Galveston with the mainland. Soon, telegraph poles and homes
were ripped from the ground and tossed in the air like matchboxes. Tidal
waves repeatedly washed over the city and, at one point, the sea rose
four feet in four seconds. At dawn, people thanked the heavens for sur-
viving the night—a thousand people wandered the city naked and in a
daze; the storm had ripped the very clothes from their bodies. In one
strip four blocks wide and three miles long, every single house and

building had been destroyed. Nothing remained but fallen timber and dead bodies.[49]

In the end, more than 6,000 people died in Galveston. It was the greatest natural disaster the nation had ever experienced. More than 5,000 others were injured in the hurricane, and 10,000 were left homeless. The 32,000 survivors had no food, shelter, clothing, light, or power. The number of dead bodies overwhelmed gravediggers, and every available man was put on duty to bury the victims.[50]

As news of the destruction of Galveston blared across the front pages of newspapers across the country, relief poured in. Millions of Americans contributed to the effort. In just over a month, more than $1.5 million had been raised to help the survivors. Newspaper magnate William Randolph Hearst, who led the charity effort in New York, organized fund-raising events featuring Broadway stars. Led by Winifred Sweet Black, a Hearst reporter writing under the name Annie Laurie, the money raised was used to build a hospital and given to other relief efforts. Black was so moved by the tragedy that she personally helped find permanent homes for 48 children left orphans by the destruction.[51]

Built in the 1880s to serve as the county seat of DeSoto County in Southwest Florida, the city of Arcadia quickly grew to more than 1,000 residents and became the center of the state's cattle industry. Like most swelling cities at the turn of the century, Arcadia's downtown area was a mish-mash of cypress and pine-framed buildings that housed numerous stores and offices. Builders could not keep up with the influx of people or businesses to the city, and as a result, residents had to go without many basic services, such as a public water system and fire fighting equipment.

On November 30, 1905, the people of Arcadia celebrated Thanksgiving, though it was an unseasonably hot day, forcing many residents indoors to avoid the hot sun. That night, for reasons that were never determined, a fire broke out in downtown Arcadia, fueled by a livery stable behind Oak Street, the main thoroughfare running through the town. A fire alarm sounded, but brisk winds that had picked up after nightfall propelled the fire. Witnesses recalled that the fire made an unbearable noise and produced thick, heavy smoke that blanketed the town.[52]

Men and women joined together to fight the fire, forming "bucket brigades," an assembly line that passed buckets of water from the source to the fire. Others tried to remove valuables from stores before they burnt to the ground. At daybreak, little remained except ruins and piles of ash. Only three brick buildings in downtown Arcadia were saved; most prominently was the town's new brick bank. In total, 43 buildings were destroyed in "the big fire," as the people of Arcadia have called it ever since. The estimated loss reached $250,000 and only about 25 percent of it was covered by insurance.

The publisher of Arcadia's newspaper lost everything in the fire, but determined to report the news, he boarded a train north to Zolfo Springs and published from there, writing: "Today Arcadia presents a scene of ruin and desolation rarely ever visited upon a city. Where yesterday stood substantial business houses well filled with merchandise now repose a bed of smoldering ashes."[53]

As a result of the devastation, Arcadia officials and citizens banded together to rebuild the city. They wanted it to be a model for others of its size. One of the first ordinances they passed was a law requiring all buildings in the business center to be built with brick, stone, or concrete. Next, streets were graded and paved, trees were planted, and water and electric plants were built. Arcadia was not going to take any more chances with fire. In 1909, *The Tampa Morning Tribune* reported that "The city of Arcadia owns one of the most complete waterworks systems in any small city in the state."[54] The new system included 55 fire hydrants distributed at all major intersections.

Supplies began arriving by railroad as soon as the next day. The people of Southwest Florida were not willing to let Arcadia die. By December 15, a dozen temporary structures had been built on or near their former sites by storeowners who wanted to return to business. By the end of the decade, Arcadia's population jumped to between 2,500 and 3,000 and it was reported that "There is little or no lawlessness in Arcadia, and it is an ideal place to live."[55]

In the morning hours of April 18, 1906, an earthquake shook Northern California on a 200-mile stretch along the San Andreas Fault. The tremor lasted for 40 seconds, then stopped for 10, then resumed for another 25 seconds. A series of smaller tremors then struck periodically. In San Francisco, the earthquake buckled streets producing great cracks, broke water pipes, tossed buildings into the air, and set off fires that raged across the hilly streets of the City by the Bay. Unsure what to do next, the survivors poured out into the streets, unaware of the complete destruction going on around them. The walls of City Hall fell in, the Valencia Hotel caved in and caught fire, gas mains broke, and telecommunications lines fell—the city was in ruins.[56]

The earthquake was intense, but the resulting fires raged on for several days after, covering 500 blocks and 2,800 acres, completely destroying the financial district and 60 percent of the homes in the city. The famous San Francisco winds propelled fires across the city, and witnesses reported that the flames stretched a mile high on the night of April 6. The loss of property reached an estimated $350 to $500 million. Despite all this, the people of the city rallied. Jack London reported that he saw "no hysteria, no disorder" and "no shouting or yelling."[57]

Arcadia, Florida, after the 1905 fire that destroyed the city. Courtesy of the Florida State Archives.

Pictures taken after the earthquake and in the following days support London's assertions. The people who gaze out from these photographs look confused but orderly. Most of the women are properly dressed, wearing the day's big, floppy hats, and the men are all wearing ties and bowlers—this decorum despite the fact that thousands of people were sleeping outside and taking all their meals from soup kitchens. The nation once again contributed heavily to the relief efforts, sending medical supplies, food, and doctors and nurses. President Roosevelt asked Congress for $2.5 million to help in the rebuilding of the region. A report from one New York newspaper summed up the determination of the city, "She's crippled, thirsty, hungry, and broke; she has a few whole churches, only half her schoolhouses . . . she is full of people without homes, jobs, or clothes; she is the worst bunged-up town that ever was. But the spirit of her is something to bring tears to an American's eyes."[58]

Legacy of the 1900s

The Progressive Era had a profound impact on the way Americans viewed government, personified by the dynamic leadership style of Theodore Roosevelt. Reflecting the basic optimism of the decade, reformers believed that they could change the nation for the better. Looking back, some of their attempts may seem naïve, but their activism set a tone that would be continued for the rest of the century. The Progressives also created private associations that helped fill the gap between what the government provided and the help the less fortunate could expect from individual philanthropists. Various agencies, such as settlement houses, tuberculosis relief organizations, the YMCA and YWCA, and the

Aftermath of the 1906 San Francisco earthquake and fire. Courtesy of the Oakland History Room of the Oakland Public Library, Oakland, California.

Sierra Club, rose up to fight the societal ills of the day. These kinds of groups rose up through grassroots activism and were an essential mechanism for social change during the Progressive Era.

For many people, the 1900s were years of chaotic change. Sons and daughters left the nation's farms in droves, relocating to the cities in search of work and new lives. What they saw upon arrival must have been overwhelming—a sensory explosion of sights, sounds, and constant movement. For the millions of immigrants coming to America, the experience had to have been as intense. What the nation faced at the turn of the century was its transformation into a multicultural, urban, industrial society. This rapid change brought: overcrowding in the cities, a society becoming more violent, strained resources, and a callousness and malaise creeping into mainstream thought. On the other hand, for many Americans the Progressive Era was a time of economic comfort, increased leisure time, and when they reaped the benefits of technological innovations.

The 1900s gave rise to new ways of thinking about old institutions.

The same way Roosevelt expanded and redefined the presidency, J.P. Morgan and John D. Rockefeller transformed big business. Roosevelt also bridged government and corporate America by emphasizing the government's right to regulate businesses through the establishment of federal agencies and direct intervention when dealing with trusts. The size of the federal government grew at a fast pace, from 95,000 employees in 1880 to 230,000 in 1900. It would continue to grow throughout the 1900s, mirroring the Progressive impetus for a bureaucratic system fostering moderate change. The ability to organize and centralize the national government would play an important role during the crises of the Great Depression and the two World Wars later in the century.

For the average American, the workplace of the 1900s was a dangerous place. For laborers, technological advances may have made the workplace safer in some respects, but the pace of work increased as well, which led to numerous calamities. Progressive leaders passed workplace reform legislation, such as outlawing child labor, mandating safety requirements, and providing worker's compensation, but their efforts fell through the cracks when it actually came to enforcing these laws. When workers took matters into their own hands, through labor unions and lodges, they were met with staunch resistance from business. Union membership grew throughout the 1900s, but the AFL did not allow unskilled workers (mainly immigrants), blacks, or women to participate in most unions.

Big business definitely established itself as a dominant force in American life during the 1900s. As a result, the gap between rich and poor was solidified as well, which may just be one of the most lasting legacies of the period. For every Rockefeller or Morgan, there were millions of Americans living in poverty, with no national welfare program to provide relief. The nation wrestled with the notion of how to get some of the vast wealth enjoyed by the rich to trickle down to the less fortunate—a problem that still plagues society today.

With hindsight it is easy to judge the actions of people in the 1900s, but keep in mind that for them the world was being transformed by the events we study today. They had to deal with the growth of cities, the move from a rural to urban society, and all the other factors that contributed to the formation of modern America without historical knowledge to guide them. They were tackling these issues on the fly, which must have seemed like chaos. The collective spirit of the 1900s could be labeled optimistic and energized, but Americans also harbored feelings of fear and uncertainty.

In moving from a rural to urban nation, the United States faced an age of upheaval, which began with the dawn of the new century and did not abate until after the horror of World War I. The 1900s were filled

with both heroes and villains—champions who fought for those less fortunate and others who wrangled every possible ounce out of the system.
We stand in judgment of them, just as will be done to us a century from
now.

2

World of Youth

When I works nights, I'se too tired to undress when I gits home, an'
so I goes to bed wif me clo's on me.
—A young girl in Georgia, exhausted from factory work (1906)

Depending on social status and circumstances, children growing up in the 1900s experienced vastly different upbringings. Some youths, regarded as vital cogs in the family economic machine, were shuttled off to the mills or factories as soon as they could produce. On farms children worked alongside their family members in the fields or barns soon after they were able to walk on their own. Other young people went to school and received a formal education, graduated from college, and pursued professional careers. Youth from wealthy families were dressed up for show at extravagant feasts; many other children went to bed hungry at night. The contrasts between children in the period varied enormously, but most often the disparity was tied directly to wealth and social class.

The nation's most famous father in the 1900s was Theodore Roosevelt, and the public followed his family and their activities avidly. Alice, his eldest daughter, was every young man's dream, and oldest son, Ted, found his every move reported while at Groton preparatory school and later Harvard. Roosevelt's attitude had no political motivations. The president tackled the role of father with all the gusto and enthusiasm he employed in other parts of his life, if not more. He believed that raising children was the most important thing parents could do, and he raised his own with as much love as imaginable. "There are many kinds of success in life worth having," Roosevelt wrote in his autobiography. "But for unflagging interest and enjoyment, a household of children, if things

Hawaiian children in traditional island
clothes, ca. 1900s. Courtesy of the
Oakland History Room of the Oakland
Public Library, Oakland, California.

go reasonably well, certainly makes all the other forms of success and achievement lose their importance by comparison."[1]

In the 1900s, children fell primarily into one of two norms. First, in farm families and among the nation's urban working class, children were viewed as part of the overall economic production machinery. These young people were vital producers within the larger unit, especially male children. Other young people, however, were raised in a protected, nurturing environment where their actions were graded against others in the same age range. These children, usually found in urban upper middle-class and wealthy families, had sheltered upbringings, marked by a distinct separation from adult concerns.

If nothing else, children across the social classes could be happy they survived childbirth—in some states, infant mortality reached 16 percent in 1900, and another 5 percent died before the age of five. Although the statistics gathered by the Census Bureau in 1901 were limited (from 10 northern states and selected cities), infant mortality still hit 124.5 per 1,000; another 57.5 died between ages one and five, and an additional 28 died up to age 15. If any good news could be drawn from these sobering statistics it is that the infant mortality rate was slowly decreasing. By the 1920s, infant mortality had dropped by nearly one-third for white babies. Rates dropped for African Americans as well, but the exact figures are unclear. Perhaps even more striking, mortality fell by almost 50 percent for children between one and four. Despite the ills that befell children in the 1900s, it is not a stretch to declare that conditions were improving for many young people as a whole at the turn of the century.[2]

Driven by Progressive Era activists, the fight for children's rights, fueled in part by a concern over high infant mortality rates, led to many reforms, such as improved health-care facilities for women and an expanded public education system. The first steps taken centered on cleaning up urban environments, which helped dramatically. Then the focus turned to increasing nutrition among children. Activists were concerned about the children who survived childbirth because the declining fertility rates among women in the United States made each life more valuable. The era of basically throwing children to the wolves once they made it through infancy gradually ended in the 1900s.

Elite Northern families worried most about declining fertility rates since they felt threatened by the influx of immigrants, who generally produced larger families. Theodore Roosevelt went so far as to label the problem of declining birthrates among white families "race suicide" and an "unpardonable crime."[3] A 1910 sample of Northern white women shows the discrepancy: wives of professional workers averaged 2.1 children; businessmen's wives, 2.2; skilled workers, 2.8; unskilled workers, 3.3; and rural and farm families, 3.8 children. Although Northerners were most concerned about immigrant family size, studies proved that second-generation immigrants had fewer children than their parents. Female children in immigrant families spent a longer time working and helping out domestically, raising younger siblings and working around the house, thus delaying marriage. The alarm set off by Progressive activists gave immigrant children in the industrial hubs much more attention than their numbers warranted, especially compared to the rest of the youth population.

Limiting the number of children gave parents the time, energy, and resources to focus on them—a version of quality over quantity, according to historian David I. Macleod. As pay increased among working-class families, parents set goals for their children that they themselves could never have attained. For example, in Buffalo, New York, high school attendance increased significantly between 1900 and 1915, while at the same time fertility rates dropped. In 1904 a fireman whose salary reached $150 a month purposefully limited his family to three, because he wanted each of his children to excel. "My youngsters are going to have a good time and lots of schooling. They must have book learning to get up in

A community Christmas celebration in rural California (1909). Courtesy
of the Contra Costa County Historical Society.

the world," he explained.[4] It is easy to see the strains of the American
Dream peeking through here—parents actively planning so that their
children have better lives then they did.

In addition to education, a "culture of play" linked youngsters,
whether they lived in rural or urban areas. According to historian Elliott
West, "Children could be seen playing the same games in vacant lots in
Brooklyn and in schoolyards in Arizona and Alabama."[5] About all children needed was an open space large enough to accommodate them.
Children in the country had no problem with space issues, but in the
cities, young people cavorted in the streets and between buildings, setting up shop in vacant lots and other public spaces. Many of these games
had been passed down for generations, such as Ring Round Rosy, which
still holds the attention of small children on playgrounds today. Boys
played stickball or baseball in the streets and fields across America, imitating their heroes in the world of professional baseball. While at play,
children were able to be independent and work at defining social roles
on their own terms.

LEGISLATING CHILDREN'S LIVES

For some scholars the twentieth century was "the century of the child."
Perhaps for the first time in the nation's history, young people became

the center of attention. The 1900s served as an important bridge between the nineteenth and twentieth centuries. If children truly played such an important role in the span, much of the credit for building the society that enabled this evolution must go to the leaders of the 1900s. Children's rights was a main tenet of the Progressive movement that was sweeping the nation.[6]

Reformers in the 1900s, however, moved slowly. Many children still died early, many performed inhumane labor in all regions of the nation, and most received a rudimentary education at best. Life for children in the 1900s could be difficult, dangerous, and often deadly. Efforts at reform were sporadic, embraced by some groups and utterly disregarded by others. People who could benefit from child labor certainly took advantage of the situation, while on the other end of the social scale, some children had to work to help support families teetering on the brink of ruin.

Progressive Era reformers coveted social justice. They believed in the righteousness of moral authority, the power of law, and its capacity for correcting social ills. Children's rights fell alongside the fight for equality for women, immigrants, minorities, and other suffering groups. The struggle for children's rights included addressing the issues of poverty, industrialism, education, tenements, tainted food products, sanitation, medical care, and parental knowledge.

Children's rights activists were shocked that child mortality rates remained so high given the technological advances made in the United States. Physicians traced the cause of many deaths to impure cow's milk. Initial efforts in this field began in 1897, when Dr. George W. Goler initiated milk experiments in Rochester, New York. Researchers soon realized that cow's milk had to be produced in sanitary conditions and that new mothers had to be educated regarding the use of cow's milk. As a result of the success of Goler's work, many other large cities began establishing milk codes in the 1900s. These codes regulated the acceptable amount of bacteria per cubic centimeter and covered the areas of sanitation and pasteurization. In its efforts to reduce infant death rates, New York City set up a division of child hygiene in 1908. The city gave clean milk to needy mothers, either at cost or below, and in some cases, free of charge. Massachusetts also set early standards for the amount of butterfat milk had to contain, and set up procedures for having cows tested for disease and allowing dairies to be inspected.[7]

The early success attained with milk pushed reformers into other realms of child rearing. Cities established baby clinics where doctors and nurses could measure infant growth and provide care. Also, visiting nurses examined young children in their homes to witness them in their natural surroundings. As one historian explained, "The extraordinary success attending the work of the visiting nurses in New York

City is indicated by the fact that during four and a half months in 1911 only 1.4 percent of the 16,987 babies under their care died, which was less than half the prevailing rate for the entire city."[8] In addition, concerned groups, such as Boston's Women's Municipal League, advocated education regarding prenatal care, control of midwifery, and legislation regulating the working environment of wage-earning mothers. Throughout the decade a combination of public and private educators, medical specialists, and activists campaigned for expecting mothers and infants.

In the early years of the twentieth century, homelessness plagued American cities as a result of the influx of immigrants and the countless number of young people moving to the cities from rural regions. A disproportionate number of these homeless people were children. The actual number of homeless youngsters is impossible to determine, given the sketchy calculations from the period, but most agree it was vast. During the Civil War, for example, one observer estimated that New York City had as many as 30,000 homeless children. The cities reacted to the problem of youth homelessness by devising ways to keep children off the streets.

One solution involved sending them to poorhouses, also called almshouses, where they were boarded with people of all ages who could not take care of themselves. Some parents who had handicapped children took their children to almshouses to be raised. As time progressed, a better solution to the problem of youth homelessness was the orphanage. For reformers and politicians concerned with costs and efficiency, the orphanage seemed to fulfill both requirements. In large buildings, a relatively small staff could oversee a large number of children, who all lived under the same common rules. The children performed much of the cleaning and upkeep themselves. To feed the youngsters, institutions bought food in bulk to reduce the overall expenses of the asylums.[9]

According to the 1910 census, there were 1,151 institutions for dependent children in the United States, housing approximately 150,000 young people.[10] Despite the efforts of reformers to improve conditions for homeless children, many of the orphanages were dilapidated. Children in the poorer asylums, who lived under harsh conditions with inadequate food supplies, were constantly put to work. Critics balked at the unhealthy and abusive conditions in many of the nation's orphanages. Reformers had high hopes for orphanages and did not want them to become like the almshouses—more like prison cells than anything else. Despite these concerns, many orphanages were like little factories: children worked hard for long periods and were given the bare necessities to get by in terms of food, clothing, and shelter.

The 1901 graduating class at Concord High School, Concord, California.
Courtesy of the Contra Costa County Historical Society.

EDUCATION

In December 1900 the California State Educational Commission assembled in San Francisco to discuss public school legislation. The most
controversial law considered by the committee would have made it mandatory for children between the ages of 8 and 14 to attend school at least
five months a year. Although the commission, which included professors
from the University of California at Berkeley and Stanford University,
believed mandatory education was a positive step, the discussion broke
down when they debated clauses to the proposed law. Some of the
clauses were vague, including a provision allowing students to circumvent the law for "unusual conditions"; others dealt directly with prohib-
iting the employment of children if it interfered with their education.[11]

Although cities like Berkeley wrestled with making education mandatory in the 1900s, much of a child's education depended on age: the
older a youth, the more earning power he or she brought to the family.
Schools achieved nearly universal schooling within a narrow age range,
usually between the ages of 9 and 14. In 1910 studies revealed that 88
percent of children between 10 and 14 attended school at some point in
the year, while 62 percent of youth between the ages of six to nine did,
up from 49 percent two decades earlier. Secondary schools increased
during the 1900s, but not as quickly as elementary schools. As late as

1920, secondary schools enrolled a paltry 2.4 million students, compared with 20.4 million attending the earlier grades. An elementary education was the most the vast majority of people could obtain.[12]

Race and regional disparities remained a problem for educators in the 1900s. In the South, only slightly more than half the black children between 10 and 14 attended school, while 78 percent of white children did. And, perhaps most striking, the Progressives did not adequately fund schools in most regions in the nation, which led to sporadic attendance and less quality when students did attend. Nationwide, the average school term lasted from 140 to 186 days. However, average attendance per student was only 121 days by 1920. The gap between North and South widened in the period because the Southern states simply did not keep up with their Northern neighbors. For African Americans the situation was worse—their school terms ranged from 9 to 51 percent shorter than school terms for whites in 1910. "For many children," explained one historian, "schooling was still a sometime thing—and for black farm children it was scarcely that."[13]

Spending rates per pupil reveal the limited resources schools had during the Progressive Era, despite the reform-minded ideology. The average spending per student in attendance was 15.1 cents in 1900, up from 12.8 cents a decade earlier. The figure actually decreased due to inflation and did not pick up again until the 1930s. These national statistics, however, hide the disparity between the North and the South. Southern states spent less than half the average per capita on education in 1900. For blacks, the situation was worse. Southern white politicians allowed blatantly unequal school facilities and would not let Northern activists help the reform movement unless they prepared black children for nothing more than menial jobs.[14]

Compounding the difficulty of universal education was a shortage of teachers in most areas. Even though it was the home of the University of California, the city of Berkeley found itself suffering from a teacher shortage in 1905. School leaders asked volunteers to fill the many openings, most common in the country schools dotting the California hills. Salaries ranged from $65 to $75 a month for these positions, according to the *Berkeley Daily Gazette*, and efforts were being made to attract more men to the profession. "Grammar school principals are in demand," the newspaper reported, "and salaries are being increased for the purpose of attracting men teachers to them." Reflecting the sexism of the 1900s, the article went on to state, "More men should fit themselves to fill these positions, as it is being found that they are more competent than women for work of this kind, and very good inducements are accordingly being made."[15]

Other actions were taken to beef up the supply of qualified teachers. Since the 1880s, "normal schools" (such as the Slippery Rock Normal

School, now Slippery Rock University, in Pennsylvania, opened in 1887) were established across the nation to train teachers to teach in public schools. However, many of the teachers had not received much of an education themselves—often only through the elementary years, especially in rural areas. In the 1900s and later decades, colleges and universities began studying education systems, which led to efforts to raise the qualifications of elementary school teachers. Many states passed ordinances regarding teacher qualifications, and teacher training classes were added to many high school curriculums.[16]

Legislators and education experts were not involved only in deciding qualifications, they also impacted the subjects taught. William T. Harris, U.S. Commissioner of Education from 1889 to 1906, pushed for grammar, literature, mathematics, geography, and history to be the primary subjects. Emphasizing the need for an educated workforce, Theodore Roosevelt himself urged "practical training for daily life and work."[17] Although this idea won favor among many scholars, racists used the notion to support the training of nonwhites exclusively for menial positions. Federal officials wanted to use this idea to train Native American children for wage labor and domestic service, while Southerners lauded efforts to train blacks for basic industrial jobs.

For youngsters entering school for the first time (anywhere from five to seven years old), the ordeal could be traumatic. Many were physically constrained for the first time. They had to sit still and quiet at desks bolted to the floors in urban schools; country schools were often small, one-room buildings with insufficient space and few amenities. Language was a barrier for many immigrant children. These children were often forced to learn English in a total immersion environment. Religious differences also played a part in the school environment. Teachers unversed in Judaism forced Jewish students to recite the Lord's Prayer. Other students had their given names—too ethnic sounding for school officials— changed to an American version, whether they wanted it or not. For example, Herschele Golden began school as "Harry" at his teacher's request.[18]

College and university students in the 1900s concentrated on many of the same things today's students find important—classes, fraternity life, sports, clubs, and mixing and mingling with friends of both sexes. Stanford University, in Palo Alto, California, was a fledgling school of 1,500 students in 1905, and approximately one-third of the student body consisted of women. Size and cost are probably the two greatest differences in student life then and now, but there were many of the same amenities, such as fraternities and sororities, a credit-based program which allowed students to pick a major, and a central "quad" where students could gather. According to Folkstom Wallace, writing in the *Overland Monthly*

Rural schoolchildren outside their schoolhouse in Clayton,
California (1903). Courtesy of the Contra Costa County
Historical Society.

in 1905, college life at Stanford cost approximately $50 a month, half of
that amount going for room and board.[19]

Across the country at the University of Pittsburgh, young Presbyterian
minister and practicing attorney Samuel Black McCormick accepted the
chancellorship (presidency) of the school on June 4, 1904. He outlined
his goals to transform the school into a university and set out on a course
so that "there can be no question that in time one of the finest institutions
in the land can be built up in Pittsburgh."[20] Over the rest of the decade
and into the next, McCormick acquired or established departments and
schools which catapulted the university into the upper echelon of academic institutions in the nation. In short order, he bought a dental college and a medical department, founded the School of Economics and
the School of Education, bought a 43-acre site for the university, and
held a nationwide architectural contest for the design of the new campus.

McCormick's administration also dealt with issues that faced colleges
and universities all over the nation. He intervened in the battle between

proponents of technical training and those who pushed for a liberal arts–based education. McCormick saved the College of Liberal Arts, despite the vast popularity of the university's scientific and engineering studies. In reply to those who thought the school should eliminate liberal arts courses, McCormick replied, "Pittsburgh needs a University. . . . Not a little, dwarfed, imperfect University, but one finely equipped, largely endowed, splendid in all its departments."[21] Other schools fought similar battles nationwide, a fight that often rears its head in today's arguments regarding higher education and its purpose, especially given the movement toward professional education and the use of online resources.

Mirroring Ivy League schools, such as Harvard and Yale, and Midwestern powerhouse the University of Michigan, Pitt officials raised the school's national reputation through sports prowess. The McCormick administration focused on building a winning football team first then moved on to other sports. After a disastrous 1903 season, which included a season-ending loss to arch rival Penn State 59–0, the newly formed football association raised $2,000 to fund the team. Pitt then hired the University of Kansas's head coach, Arthur St. Leger Mosse, and raided players from nearby Geneva College.

In 1904 the team played 10 games, scored 406 points, and held its opposition to a mere 5 points. In the next decade, Pitt turned the football program over to the legendary Glenn (Pop) Warner, who won national championships in 1915, 1916, and 1918. Most important, the plan to raise the school's reputation worked, as well as a campaign to raise additional funds. By 1908, Pitt's enrollment topped 1,000 students and had endowments of more than $500,000. In just a few short years, McCormick and his staff had built the University of Pittsburgh into one of the nation's finest academic institutions.[22]

LABOR

Countless "breaker boys" littered the coal mines of Pennsylvania and West Virginia in the 1900s. Breaker boys were as young as 9 or 10 years old. Crouching over coal chutes 10 hours a day, they picked slate and other waste from the coal as it rushed by them on conveyor belts. Sharp edges often resulted in cut flesh and broken, pulverized fingers. More often than anyone cared to admit, workers got caught up in the machinery. When this happened, the machines were not turned off; the body would be recovered later. Those "lucky" enough to survive the endless rush were rewarded with a permanent hunchback from bending over day after day in the mines. Asthma and black lung, caused by the coal dust which constantly filled the air, plagued other workers.

A 1905 study made by the National Child Labor Committee revealed that, in one small, coal-mining village in Pennsylvania (population

Miners (including child workers) in Somersville, California, in 1898. The mine closed in 1906. Courtesy of the Contra Costa County Historical Society.

7,000), more than 150 boys were working illegally in the mines. Because the legal age for employment was 14, mine operators doctored claims to show the children were older. In many coal regions, parents manipulated the forms to allow children to go to work as many as five years too soon. The extra income helped the family make ends meet, despite the adverse effect the mines had on growing bodies.[23]

The detailed description of children working in coal mines and other dangerous occupations came from John Spargo's *The Bitter Cry of the Children* (1906), produced the same year Upton Sinclair published *The Jungle*. Like Sinclair's graphic polemic against capitalism and the meat-packing industry, Spargo supplied horrifying detail about conditions faced by children in the workplace (including the real possibility of death). Spargo's book, like *The Jungle*, sparked nationwide debate and forced government action. The U.S. Bureau of Labor investigated the issue and published the 19-volume *Report on Conditions of Women and Child Wage Earners in the United States*, which supported Spargo's assertions.

Marie Van Vorst, another crusading journalist, went undercover in the

1900s, posing as a worker to gain firsthand knowledge of conditions in factories all over the country. In a cotton mill in South Carolina, Van Vorst and the young girls around her worked 13 hours a day. The children (as young as six) who taught her to spool—attach yarn to spools—chewed tobacco, went barefoot year round, and got into vicious fights to break the monotony of life in the mill. Van Vorst reported that the air was white with cotton, which led to the constant threat of tuberculosis and pneumonia. She reported that the children in the mills were underfed, filthy, and perpetually exhausted.[24]

The work of reformers was realized between 1905 and 1907 when two-thirds of the states either strengthened existing child labor laws or passed legislation restricting child labor. By 1914 every state but one had some kind of law regulating child labor for children from 12 to 16 years of age. The states imposed laws that limited the work children could do in dangerous environments, and most states tied work to literacy efforts, ensuring a young person could read and write before entering the workforce. In Berkeley, California, the town newspaper reported that many young people working in the canneries were let go when they were unable to prove their ages. Children between the ages of 14 and 16 had to have the written consent of their parents to work during vacations; those 12 to 14 had to have a certificate proving that they attended school the prior term, in addition to documentation from their parents.[25]

Even though towns like Berkeley occasionally cracked down on child labor, most states could not actively enforce the regulations, especially when parents connived to evade them. As late as 1919, a bill imposing a 10 percent tax on the net profits of factories that employed youngsters under the age of 14 was declared unconstitutional in spite of widespread support in Congress. Although many advances occurred in the 1900s, the child labor problem persisted for years.[26]

In many cities, especially in New York, immigrant children labored with their parents in home-based commercial operations. The 1910 census estimated that more than 13,000 tenements in New York had some type of commercial component. Historians believe that at least half and perhaps as many as three-fourths of children working at home were female, since boys would have more economic value outside the home. Working at home had many disadvantages, including long hours. Furthermore, most tenements were breeding grounds for a multitude of diseases. In addition, the children who worked at home had no escape from the daily grind and little or no social interaction. Since parents and extended family members slaved together, little could be done legally to limit the hours worked or the conditions.[27]

The tasks performed in "tenement trades" included sewing cheap clothing, making artificial flowers, and piecing together beads. Some children also learned to roll cigars, which could be made at home alongside one's parents. More often, youngsters performed the final task related to cigar making, licking the wrap to hold it together, which they would do up to 1,000 times a day. It is impossible to estimate the damage this practice had on young children, but combined with the filth of the tenements themselves, it no doubt led to the death of many children.[28]

COUNTRY LIFE

Although the opportunity for schooling increased in the 1900s, farm children spent much of their time at work or play. Half of America's young people lived on farms in the first decade of the twentieth century. For the most part, their lives were filled with hard work.

Farm children began doing chores at an early age, usually by the time they were between four and six years old. They helped feed and water the chicken and livestock, gathered eggs, took water to the men working in the fields, and performed other "light" tasks. Anyone who has ever spent time on a farm knows these jobs are vital but certainly not easy for children so young to perform. With a heavy reliance on farming and manpower, Southern children were expected to toil in the field during peak seasons planting and harvesting cotton, tobacco, and corn. Even the children of wealthy planters often plugged away in the fields alongside the hired help, with the idea that these youngsters, regardless of privilege, needed to understand the value of hard work.[29]

Some analysts have criticized Progressive reformers for concentrating so much energy on the relatively small number of child workers who were exploited in mills and factories. Perhaps in straight percentages, children working on farms worked much longer hours and received far less schooling than their cohorts in urban areas. Work for farm youngsters began early and intensified—by their early teens, both boys and girls were fully acclimated to adult farmwork. Somewhere between the ages of 8 and 11 the daily tasks of farm children solidified into morning and evening chores. During these years gender differences began taking shape as well. Girls did "women's work," such as cooking, cleaning, preserving food, and caring for younger siblings, among others.[30]

Farm children faced a life of never-ending tasks in a relentless battle against nature, the seasons, and the one early frost or storm that could destroy an entire year's output. Like small farmers today, rural families in the 1900s worked around the clock against the cyclical nature of farming. The end of one chore merely meant the beginning of another. For youngsters, this led to laboring from sunup to sundown, regardless of the weather. One Texas woman recalled working in the fields of east Texas as a child, remembering the rows of cotton which faced her "like a monster." "Sometimes I would lie down on my sack and want to die," she said, thinking back to the hot August and September days of re-

The men (including a young boy) of a farming family in Antioch, California, ca. 1900. Courtesy of the Contra Costa County Historical Society.

lentless heat. "Sometimes they would pour water over my head to relieve me."[31]

At 12 to 14 years of age, boys started doing heavier fieldwork, including plowing fields—even if they could barely reach the handlebars. In West Virginia, farm boys considered themselves full "farm hands" by the age of 14. On many Midwestern farms, taking part in the threshing party was a major rite of passage and considered the final step to manhood. On the other hand, older girls on farms also stepped up their tasks. As they grew, farm girls would drive teams, husk corn, and take part in other physical tasks. Alternately, young women on farms found that a life of household duties meant a virtually nonstop workday that could stretch from predawn hours well into the late night. During threshing season on wheat farms, some farm girls cooked meals for the men from 4 A.M. until 10 P.M.[32]

CITY LIFE

In Margaret F. Byington's sociological and economic study of Homestead, Pennsylvania, she took careful note of the mill town's children. She understood the debate raging over child labor and actively searched for answers in Homestead. Although her study was limited, she concluded, "The working people of Homestead when talking of their chil-

dren show a distinct recognition of the value of education and wages."
Byington's work, which primarily examined English-speaking working-
class families, reported that many girls between the ages of 14 and 21
stayed at home helping their mothers with household duties, rather than
working to supplement their father's income. However, 15 of 17 boys in
the same age group worked outside the home.[33]

Most sons in Homestead worked to supplement the family's income,
particularly in the teenage years, before they left home to get married.
Byington found that male children contributed 29 percent of the income
in English-speaking European families having a total weekly income of
more than $20. Many sons earned as much in the mills at 19 or 20 as
their fathers, and the family reaped the financial benefit. Some of that
windfall was used to purchase homes. The father in one family visited
by Byington earned moderate wages, but these were supplemented by
those of two grown sons. They were able to upgrade their home and
furnishings, and purchase luxurious furniture and a music box. When
the boys left home to get married, the parents continued to enjoy the
fruits of a three-income family.[34]

The Slav families in Homestead counted on their children's wages
even more than the families higher up the social scale. The Slavs made
up most of the unskilled labor in the steel mills. They performed the
most difficult and dangerous tasks, including handling steel bars, toiling
in cinder pits, and loading trains.[35]

For Slav children and families, living conditions in the ghettoes of
Homestead afforded virtually no creature comforts. Many families lived
in one-room tenements with little ventilation, no running water, and
constant overcrowding. In three different sections of the ghetto, more
than 110 people were dependent on one hydrant for water. Outdoor
toilet facilities were used, on the average, by two families, better than
the numbers for water, but hardly an adequate or sanitary situation.

Despite nationwide efforts to curb infant mortality, immigrant families
in Homestead were far behind the times in that category. Among Slavs,
nearly 33 percent died before age two, compared with 14 percent among
English-speaking immigrants of European descent. The cause of most
deaths, according to physicians, was "malnutrition due to poor food and
overcrowding."[36]

Technological innovations in housing played a part in declining infant
mortality rates among some segments of the population. Central heat
became more commonplace, including the use of steam radiators and
floor furnaces, a huge improvement over the home stoves which had
warmed houses throughout most of American history. Plumbing also
contributed to improved conditions for youngsters. Although plumbing
is taken for granted today, in the 1900s it was a revolutionary innovation.
Doctors realized how important it was to have fresh (or relatively clean)

drinking water and sewage removal. These improvements, implemented first by the wealthy, gradually became available to the masses. In the first decade of the twentieth century, there were still tens of thousands of outhouses in the city streets, many of which filtered into the water system.[37]

Urban children formed a new consumer market. Youngsters were willing purchasers of candy, soda, and other sweets, and they went to movie houses when they became more prevalent. Critics lambasted the movie theater owners who, they claimed, pandered to children to increase their profits. Picture shows, in their estimation, were too violent, glamorized criminals, and featured risqué scenes. Perhaps more important, critics did not like that young boys and girls were together in close quarters at theaters. In a 1909 report, the Society for the Prevention of Cruelty to Children claimed, "Boys and girls are darkened in the room together while the pictures are on, and . . . indecent assaults upon the girls follow, often with their acquiescence. Depraved adults with candies and pennies beguile children with the inevitable result." Summing up the influence, the report exclaimed, "GOD alone knows how many are leading dissolute lives begun at the 'moving picture.' "[38]

Movie houses and penny arcades had a pervasive effect on children's lives. A 1911 study showed that one child of eight watched at least one movie a day. In Portland, Oregon, 90 percent of the children went to the movies, while one-third went to two or more a week. "As much as the films themselves, the appeal seems to have been the chance to get together, romp, and flirt beyond the gaze and control of adults," asserted one historian. "That was exactly what alarmed many reformers, moralists, and social critics of the day."[39]

Part Two

Popular Culture of the 1900s

3

Advertising

Why is the merchant who doesn't advertise like a man in a rowboat?
Because he goes backward, I suppose.
No, because he has to get along without sales.
—Advertising Joke (1901)

In the 1900s industrialism and consumerism converged to form a culture of consumption in the United States and elsewhere. The more consumer goods businesses produced, the more they required a buying public. Consequently, corporations developed innovative means to encourage wide-scale shopping. Advertising emerged as the most pervasive technique for promoting the budding consumer culture. As a matter of fact, the advertising industry was as innovative and clever in developing new ways to get people to buy things as the manufacturing industry was in creating modern production practices.

In its earliest form, advertising meant simply placing announcements in newspapers and magazines. However, as the medium evolved and the avenues for reaching the public expanded, the everyday world seemed covered in ads. Photographs from the period reveal how quickly advertising became all-encompassing. There were ads everywhere—signs appeared on billboards, in store windows, the outside of buildings, and on public transportation. They urged people to validate their self-worth through the products they accumulated.

Advertising became embedded in people's daily consciousness and its messages constantly continued the bombardment. As a result, class and social status even more clearly marked the difference between the "haves" and the "have-nots" in American culture. Blatant displays of newly acquired wealth permeated the land, especially in the urban centers, where the rich congregated and tried to outdo one another through displays of wealth.

The rich, however, were not the only ones to prosper in the new century. The nation's climb to economic and industrial superpower status by the end of the nineteenth century gave ordinary people the ability to buy goods at an unprecedented rate as well. Americans purchased increasing numbers of machine made goods because the rising middle class acquired more disposable income than in past generations. The upward mobility of the middle class was guaranteed by the millions of immigrants who moved to the United States and took their place in factories and other points of production, virtually pushing those ahead of them up the social ladder. The immigrants themselves formed another buying class targeted by advertisers.

Advertising actually helped bring the immigrants to America in the first place. Agents working for the railroads and businesses that needed a steady flow of labor went to Europe to recruit. They took out ads and handed out leaflets urging Europeans to go to the United States. In 1904 steerage prices dropped, which allowed Europeans to board ships bound for America and be there a month later for as little as $10. Usually guaranteed a job upon arrival in the United States, they worked the fare off quickly.[1]

As the quantity of consumer goods increased, the outlets to purchase them expanded as well. Urban department stores, chain retail stores, and mail-order catalogs granted greater access to the goods people felt they needed. Advertisers embraced the idea of progress and adopted methods to use it to sell goods. In the 1900s, science, technology, and health care were consistent themes in advertising campaigns.

For example, Philadelphia-based Scott Paper capitalized on the demand for improved hygiene by manufacturing and selling assorted brands of toilet paper. In the 1900s the company, which sold more toilet paper than any other company in the world, essentially invented the market themselves. Later in the decade, Scott Paper introduced the world's first paper towels, first called Sani-Towels, but later renamed ScotTissue, its more widely known brand name. Again, Scott Paper took advantage of society's demand for enhanced cleanliness and brought a product to market to fill that need. They used advertising to convince the public that they needed these products.

The first paper towels were actually made by accident, when one of Scott's mills made a tissue that was too thick to use as toilet paper. Always looking to expand Scott's product line, company managers decided to use some to make experiments. Company founder Arthur Scott had heard about a Philadelphia schoolteacher who cut up copy paper for her students to use to wipe their hands, instead of using a communal

The Davis General Store in Crochett, California (1902). Courtesy of the
Contra Costa County Historical Society.

cloth towel, which spread germs. Scott realized a use for his absorbent
tissue, and paper towel was born. Soon hundreds of health institutions
used paper towels, as well as businesses, railroad stations, hotels,
schools, and other public facilities.[2]

The quick adoption of paper towels mirrors how advertisers persuaded the nation to view toothpaste, deodorant, and other products as
daily essentials. Other items were initially driven by health benefits, then
later transitioned to wider audiences, which meant increased sales. Coca-
Cola's soft drink is perhaps the foremost example since it began life as
a medicinal tonic, with "curative powers." Advertising played an important role in these decisions. The industry helped define what was
necessary and determined how products should be viewed by the general public.

Advertisers targeted their ads to women, who were the nation's primary shoppers. Advertising agencies, run primarily by men, believed
that women made 85 percent of the purchases, since, according to some,
they were the "weaker sex" and could not engage in serious topics or
endeavors during the day. Many books advanced this notion in the
1900s, including one written by Professor W.I. Thomas, *Sex and Society*

Interior of the S.S. Coachman & Sons General Store, Clearwater, Florida (1902). Courtesy of the Florida State Archives.

(1907). The fact that advertisers believed that women made the majority of purchases had a significant impact on the way advertising developed in the twentieth century. It could be argued today that little has changed regarding the way in which advertisers view women and their purchasing power, even as more women have become involved in the business.[3]

The creation of a modern consumer culture required the introduction of new products in innovative ways, which persuaded people to buy them. On the surface, advertising came into being to give consumers information about products; however, in the 1900s, advertising became much more complex. In many respects, advertisers needed to establish new domestic habits which people would pick up and practice daily. For instance, advertisers had to convince people to buy boxed, wax paper–wrapped crackers instead of crackers scooped out of a big, open air crate at the general store. Advertisers linked packaging and product presentation to an emerging lifestyle which focused on saving time and improving the quality of life.

As the United States transformed from a rural country of small towns and villages, into a nation filled with bustling cities, advertising played a critical role in redefining what the new urban way of life would mean for people on a daily basis. The idea of convenience, whether at work or in one's own kitchen, meant installing electric lighting and gas and electric stoves and buying foods that cut down on preparation time, since time given to household tasks increased in value. With an increase in leisure time, people wanted to spend their valuable free time doing enjoyable activities.

These ideas became practical realities; for example, the Colgate company taught consumers about the benefits of brushing one's teeth. Colgate booklets, such as *ABC of the Teeth*, driven by advertising agencies, were distributed at county fairs and other places where people congregated. The process had two goals: to inform people about performing basic dental hygiene on a daily basis and to sell Colgate toothpaste.[4]

The same forces combined to deliver similar ideas about shaving and other areas of personal grooming. The Gillette razor, in advertisements featuring company founder King Gillette himself, convinced male consumers that they needed to shave daily and that his product was the ultimate tool for the purpose. Gillette's "shaving lessons" ads made his product the one to long for, even when the typical Gillette razor cost $5, certainly a luxury in an age when industrial workers usually brought home between $10 and $15 a week.[5]

Even a pure luxury item, like the newly invented line of Kodak cameras, could be incorporated into everyday life. Through an aggressive ad campaign, targeting both upper- and middle-class audiences, the Eastman Kodak Company made taking pictures a normal part of life. As one of the company's copywriters explained, the idea for the camera was "that every man can write the outline of his own history, and that the outline will be a hundredfold more interesting if it is illustrated." Next, Kodak convinced the public that photography was so easy that a child could do it and introduced the Brownie line, an inexpensive camera which fit in one's pocket. By linking the camera to major holidays (picture-taking opportunities), primarily Christmas, Kodak achieved great success and the company name became virtually synonymous with cameras as a whole.[6]

MERCHANDISING

The fact that the public developed a relationship with companies, products, and sellers through advertising validated the use of advertising. With companies manufacturing more consumer goods and more shoppers willing to buy them, retail outlets flourished. At the same time, mail-order catalog companies used improvements in transportation, packaging, and the national postal service to expand their services.

The transformation of packaging became an interesting phenomenon in its own right. Cans, bottles, and other devices were designed to be both practical and appealing to customers. Wax-sealed cartons kept many foods, such as breakfast cereals and snacks, fresh for longer periods. Other innovations included sealed glass jars and bottles, cans, tins,

Ben Scheline's general store in Richmond, California (1903). Courtesy of the Contra Costa County Historical Society.

and metal tubes. However, the advances in the actual packaging itself paralleled what occurred on the outside wrapper covering the product. Advertisers realized that designing packages that appealed to customers visually and stood out against the competition on store shelves developed brand recognition. Brand identification and loyalty drove sales, especially as shoppers (primarily women) had more time to hunt for the best price at many different stores.[7]

Taken as a group, the mass merchandisers worked to change America's shopping experience and, in the process, solidified the unwritten rules that still govern the process to this day. Retailers set the price of goods. The art of haggling for the best price, a common practice in nineteenth-century America, ended—no one argued with Macy's or Marshall Field's over the price of its wares. The outcome of the new pricing policy enabled the department stores and chains to hire large numbers of low-paid, young salespeople. For many American teenagers and young adults, working "in retail" became a rite of passage which still endures. Workers were just another form of overhead to the owners. To make up for their wages, rent, electricity, shipping, and other costs the goal became to move merchandise as quickly as possible. Selling quickly required that shoppers be able to find what they needed as fast as possible. The retailers solved this dilemma by setting up stores with different departments that catered to one's needs. A man who wanted suits could now go directly to that area and find what he desired. Placing goods in departments gave management the ability to track what items sold the best and also how individual employees performed. Numbers-based reporting gave retail a pseudo-scientific feel which Frederick Taylor was just beginning to use in the heavy manufacturing arena.[8]

Mass merchandisers realized the importance of establishing new policies for consumers, even if they were unwritten, but just as important was giving shoppers a place to buy things, where people would want to spend time. Luring people into the cities to shop, especially middle-class suburban women, was a key element in forming the consumer culture. On the other hand, the large catalog retailers fulfilled the needs of people in rural areas. People who wanted to stay at home were catered to by such stores as Philadelphia's John Wanamaker's department store, which took telephone orders around the clock beginning in 1907.

At the end of the 1800s, department stores offered a wider array of services to draw people to the stores and keep them there longer. At first they built soda fountains and lunchrooms for patrons. Gradually they added other conveniences, such as post offices, women's parlors, and child-care facilities. The most common way to describe the largest department stores at the turn of the century was to liken them to palaces. Not only did department stores offer just about any product under the sun, they also offered lectures, live music performances, beauty shops, and even libraries to help people in their quest for personal improvement—a favorite theme in the 1900s.[9]

In 1902 both Marshall Field's and Macy's built cavernous new stores with more than a million square feet of floor space. In the process, they became important employers. Marshall Field's had 10,000 employees and estimated that 250,000 customers passed through its doors during the busy holiday seasons. The thousands of smaller department stores learned from the large players and instituted similar ideas, just scaled down to a manageable level. They all used advertising specialists and filled local newspapers with ads emphasizing price and quality. To get slow-moving goods off the shelf, retailers offered deep discounts on the merchandise, thus beginning the phenomenon of clearance sales and bargain shopping.[10]

Chain stores, which stood between the small mom-and-pop general stores and the large department stores, became the next development in mass merchandising. Chain stores began when local entrepreneurs expanded their businesses outward, while at the same time adopting the economies of scale—low prices, low profit margins, and high volume—which characterized bigger stores. Moving from the local market to the regional and national required detailed central management and an emphasis on low prices. Directly competing with local general stores, the chains had to offer something different to make people want to switch their shopping routines. Usually the differentiation came in the form of less expensive goods and a wider variety of products. Two of the more recognizable names, Woolworth's and J.C. Penney's, reached great heights in the following decades, with Woolworth's hitting the 600 store mark in 1913 and Penney's opening 300 stores by 1920.[11]

The first mail-order firm, Montgomery Ward, catered to the needs of the Grange, the nation's leading farmers' organization, when it began operation in 1872. Two decades later, the Montgomery Ward catalog listed 24,000 items. Customers paid cash on delivery and paid only if they were satisfied with what they received. Grangers were extended a 10-day grace period. Richard Sears began his business by selling watches in 1886. The company grew quickly. Just before the turn of the century, the Sears catalog contained nearly 800 pages. By 1900 it had passed rival Montgomery Ward as the nation's largest mail-order company.[12]

Sears revolutionized the mail-order business by expanding its operations into manufacturing and bringing its auxiliary services, including transportation, mail sorting, and billing procedures, into modern times. In 1906 Sears moved into a 40-acre plant, with buildings connected by underground tunnels, railroad tracks, and wiring. The Sears empire grew to include owning or partial ownership of 16 manufacturing facilities. The Merchandise Building looked like an ant colony—workers labored around the clock to fulfill the Sears goal of providing "nearly everything in merchandise." On a daily basis, more than 2,000 Sears employees processed 900 sacks of mail, while the express companies, railroads, post office, and telegraph company all operated branches on the complex. To run the operations, Sears owned its own printing plant and controlled the second largest power plant in Chicago, right after the Edison Company itself.[13]

The success of Sears depended heavily on advertising because the Sears Catalog is actually one long ad, for both the products and the company itself. Sears combined a keen understanding of advertising, with the budding field of marketing, to establish innovative methods of selling goods. The company collected card indexes showing all the goods ever bought by every single customer. Also contained on the card were details about address changes, preferences, and family information. Sears used the card index to further segment its customer base. According to one historian, America's largest mail-order firm collected files on 4 to 6 million people.[14]

Arguably, no product has used advertising better in its history than Coca-Cola. Asa Candler bought the rights to the product in 1888 after the death of its inventor, John S. Pemberton, an Atlanta chemist. By most accounts, Candler wasn't sure what to make of the drink. Originally conceived as a possible headache remedy, the company's advertising was ambiguous on the issue into the 1890s. At one point, it alternated between portraying Coke as a "nerve and brain tonic" and a "remarkable therapeutic agent."[15]

Despite the rumors that Coke actually contained trace quantities of cocaine and that the company pumped it full of excessive amounts of caffeine, it caught on as a fountain drink, then as a bottled drink. By 1909 the company had more than 375 bottling plants. In the early 1900s, the company manufactured other products, including cigars, razor blades, and chewing gum. Heavy advertising for the soft drink began in 1902. Several years later, the company installed an animated sign on the Penn railroad tracks between Philadelphia and New York. In 1909 a blimp with the famous Coca-Cola script lettering flew over Washington, D.C. At that time, the Associated Advertising Clubs of America reported that Coke was "the best advertised article in America."[16]

ADVERTISING AGENCIES

Over the course of the decade, advertising agencies evolved into entities quite similar to today's firms, though on a much smaller scale since globalization was many decades away. Large agencies hired copywriters who specialized in the text and slogans contained within an advertisement. Artists and designers took over the look and feel of the ad, which in earlier times had been left to the whims of the printer. Designers insisted that the look of an ad exceed the reliance on text. The position of account executive gained importance as a middle ground between the creative types at the agency and the clients, who focused on the bottom line and the return on investment. The account exec also played mediator in the battle of wills within the agency—the copywriters on one side and the artists on the other.[17]

Over time advertising agencies took control of complete campaigns and developed into highly professional firms to keep control over the process. Clients demanded coordination, a necessity considering the number of new products introduced by companies. Advertising campaigns commanded synchronization between the strategic planners, copywriters, designers, media placement experts, and clients. Some critics were not impressed with the results, especially the impact copywriters brought into the profession. "They came from newspaper offices, studios, the bar, and the pulpit," exclaimed Nathaniel Fowler, an early advertising leader as a writer, agency owner, and teacher, "and they literally poured into the advertising arena a stream of delicious nonsense which, if it could have been hardened, might have served for the decoration of afternoon tea cups."[18]

Achieving the coordination necessary for national campaigns required

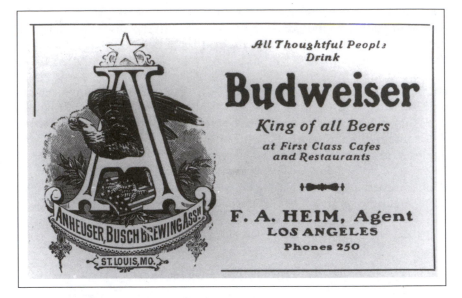

Budweiser advertisement. *Grizzly Bear* magazine, October 1907.
Courtesy of the Oakland History Room of the Oakland Public Library,
Oakland, California.

advertising firms to rely on teamwork, where each person performed a subset of tasks which contributed to the project as a whole. This idea fit perfectly with the transformation taking place in society and in the business world. Catering to the needs of large corporations, advertising agencies were part of the "service sector," which began to appear in twentieth-century America.[19]

Early advertising agencies employed a trial-by-fire mentality. The leaders conscientiously tried to lay the ground rules for the budding industry and debated over the place of advertising in the twentieth-century world. At various intervals, art took precedent over text and slogans; at other times, the copywriter's message held sway. One of the earliest uses of advertising was preparing jingles to adorn streetcars to amuse commuters. Realizing the power of pictures early on and as the use of colorful illustrations spread, advertising companies hired gallery artists to work on accounts. Famous artists, including N.C. Wyeth and Norman Rockwell, were among the many who lent their talents to advertising campaigns.

With little of the outside stimuli provided by today's multimedia gadgets, advertising ditties stuck in people's minds. One copywriter prepared weekly jingles for the streetcars in 80 cities. Others used the jingles to tell linked stories, so the public clamored for the next week's installment like people turn to modern-era situation comedies. The most popular advertising ditties had carryover powers and were used for toys, plays, political cartoons, and other marketing avenues.[20]

While jingles caught the public's imagination, seeing familiar characters over and over again in advertising media gave consumers a warm feeling about the company and its products. Technological innovations in printing contributed to the use of characters and art in advertising campaigns. At the turn of the century, printers were able to produce varying shades of light and dark tones and print in color. The result turned advertising art upside down—color art looked as magnificent as if painted with oil colors. In 1900 four-color front and back covers and one- or two-color interior ads became standard in the magazine industry. Increasingly, the look of ads gained importance—as the old saying goes "a picture is worth a thousand words."[21]

The National Biscuit Company, then known as NBC, produced and marketed a cracker in a distinctive package, sealed in a wax paper lining (dubbed the "In-Er-Seal") to keep the crackers fresh. This method of selling crackers was totally different from the traditional way of letting customers take their own from open barrels, with no concern for sanitation or freshness.

NBC leader Adolphus W. Green insisted on the low price of five cents a box for his crackers, so everyone could afford them—which meant an extremely low profit margin. The company would have to sell tremendous numbers of crackers to make any money. Advertising became a critical concern for Green. Looking for a likable name and symbol for the cracker, NBC turned to N.W. Ayer and Son advertising agency in New York. The agency recommended "Uneeda" (pronounced "You Need A") and, in a stroke of genius, Ayer created the biscuit slicker boy, a young child posed in a hat and raincoat, with the phrase, "Lest you forget, we say it yet, Uneeda biscuit."[22]

After winning the client's approval, Ayer launched the first multimillion-dollar ad campaign in 1899. The success of the slicker boy fueled NBC's other products, including Fig Newtons, Barnum's Animal Crackers, and Oysterettes crackers. In its first decade (1890–1900) NBC spent $7 million on advertising, which included outdoor billboards which were constantly updated. Almost immediately, NBC realized the return on the advertising expenditure. In 1900 it sold 10 million boxes of Uneeda crackers a month, and in 1907 alone NBC made $4 million in profits. After Green's death in 1917, Uneeda fell to the wayside, but the impact it had on the advertising industry reverberated long past its demise. NBC's ideas regarding sanitation and packaging, which paralleled the company's use of advertising and a finely orchestrated national campaign, were ahead of its time.[23]

Corporate Innovators

William Wrigley

Another company that experienced great success with advertising was the William Wrigley Company, famous worldwide for its chewing gum. During his lifetime, William Wrigley Jr. was widely regarded as "the world's greatest salesman." Almost by force of will, he transformed a small soap business into the top chewing gum manufacturer in the world. Although he did not invent chewing gum, it was his company that made it an international phenomenon. Relying heavily on various forms of advertising, Wrigley pushed his company to the top, making his name virtually synonymous with chewing gum.

In 1891, after working in his father's soap business for 20 years, Wrigley moved to Chicago at age 29 with his wife, Ada, and young daughter, Dorothy, to go into business for himself. He planned to sell soap in Chicago for his father's company and offer baking powder as a premium. For the rest of his business life, Wrigley advocated giving a bonus with each purchase. "Everybody likes something extra, for nothing," he often said.[24]

Wrigley's success in Chicago was hardly guaranteed. He arrived in the city with a meager 32 dollars in his pocket, but the young entrepreneur was able to secure a $5,000 loan from an uncle on the condition that his cousin serve as Wrigley's business partner. It did not take long for Wrigley to see that customers were more interested in the baking powder than his soap. Using his customers' wishes as his guide, Wrigley quickly switched to the baking powder business.

Looking for another premium to offer, Wrigley next turned to chewing gum, which had become popular in the 1860s after New York inventor Thomas Adams introduced chicle to the United States after visiting with former Mexican dictator Santa Anna, who chewed the stuff while they spoke. Wrigley gave away two packages of chewing gum with each baking soda purchase until he once again grasped that the premium was more popular than the product. In 1892, Wrigley Chewing Gum offered its first two brands: Lotta Gum and Vassar. Gradually he phased out baking powder and soap and concentrated on chewing gum.[25]

The chewing gum business was highly competitive in the late 1800s. There were at least a dozen companies pushing their wares and in 1899 the six largest merged to form a chewing gum trust. Although a newcomer to the industry, Wrigley was offered a place in the monopoly, but he refused. The young businessman ploughed ahead, despite the relentless competition, often teetering on the verge of bankruptcy.

A natural salesman, Wrigley realized the power of advertising early in his career. Much of the company's budget focused on selling the prod-

A farmer in Martinez, California, with a Wrigley's ad painted on a building in the background, ca. 1900. Courtesy of the Contra Costa County Historical Society.

uct through advertisements and gimmicks. Wrigley himself did much of the selling and had a knack for understanding the customer needs. He expanded his premium offers, giving away items ranging from lamps and razors to cookbooks and fishing tackle. The premium system worked so well that Wrigley even published premium catalogs to help customers choose what they wanted.

Wrigley used every form of advertising at his disposal. In his company's ads, Wrigley repeatedly told people about the benefits of the product. He bought space in newspapers, magazines, and even outdoor posters. His motto was "tell 'em quick and tell 'em often." In 1893 and 1894, Wrigley introduced the flavors that would make the company timeless: Juicy Fruit and Wrigley's Spearmint. The enterprising Wrigley even designed the logo on the Spearmint package. He decided that the company would concentrate on popularizing Spearmint, which no company had been able to achieve.

The general public did not accept Spearmint right away, but Wrigley believed in it and pushed it relentlessly. In 1907, a depression year, Wrigley spent $284,000 in advertising, mostly on Spearmint and with that much was able to buy over $1.5 million worth of advertising in cash-strapped New York. The gamble paid off when sales jumped dramatically. Company revenue topped $1.3 million in 1909 and a year later, Wrigley's Spearmint was the top selling gum in the United States.

Wrigley soon became the largest chewing gum manufacturer in the world. He bought Zero Company in 1911, which had been making Wrigley's gum since 1892. From that point forward, the newly named William Wrigley Jr. Company manufactured its own products. Even as the company grew into a major corporation, Wrigley emphasized quality. He often recited his basic philosophy: "Even in a little thing like a stick of gum, quality is important." By the time of Wrigley's death in 1932, global sales pushed company revenues to $75 million with a profit of $12 million.

Albert Lasker

Every new industry needs a kingpin to propel it forward through frequently murky waters. Albert Lasker served that role in advertising in the 1900s. Working for the Chicago advertising firm of Lord & Thomas, Lasker paraded around like a lord, controlling his workers with artificial deadlines that were ahead of schedule, the constant threat of firings, and a colossal ego. Unlike most men with his authority, Lasker stayed out of the public eye, wielding power behind the lines, where he could, as he explained, "cover more territory—I could be a free lance, a lone wolf, and I liked that."[26]

Beginning his career at Lord & Thomas as an office boy, sweeping up after the principals and cleaning spittoons, he later became a salesman in the Midwest. His success there, bringing in $50,000 in new business after just a few months, sent him down the path to prominence. By 1902 Lasker was the firm's star salesman, and his salary reached $10,000 a year. Two years later, Lasker made $50,000 and bought 25 percent of the firm after Lord retired. At the age of 24, Lasker became a partner. Lasker's innovations included a card system that allowed the agency to determine which outlets (newspapers, magazines, and so on) were most successful for their clients. The system gave Lord & Thomas a strategic edge over other firms. The results gave Lasker hard data which impressed clients, resulting in higher budgets for campaigns.[27]

Lasker was also revolutionary in his thinking about writers. He liked advertising copy to resemble news pieces. He had trained as a reporter and later in life regretted that he never pursued his first love as a livelihood. Lasker paid writers extremely well, but if they did not produce quickly or stumbled, he fired them in the blink of an eye. Explaining Lord & Thomas's emphasis on copy, Lasker said, "Ninety percent of the thought, energy and cost of running our agency goes into copy. We have stated that our copy staff costs us four times as much as that of any other agency. No one has disproved this statement." Lasker's overall success can be appreciated in the revenues generated by the firm, shooting up from $800,000 in 1898 to $3 million in 1905 and then doubling to $6 million seven years later.[28]

By 1912 Lasker had bought out his partners and ran the largest advertising agency in the world. If there was any regret in his life, it centered on his longing for affection from his father and the feelings of doubt fostered by the relationship. Even when the son was at his peak, the father admonished him for not achieving enough for "humanity at large." In his later years, Lasker dabbled in Republican politics and various hobbies, including cultural affairs, but he could never get beyond his love for advertising. The "uncrowned king of Chicago" continued to work tirelessly, never slowing down, even through a series of nervous breakdowns.[29]

Under Lasker's leadership, Lord & Thomas transformed agency work in the early years of the twentieth century. Lasker himself, although behind the scenes, set the tone for what advertising should be. Many of Lasker's innovations are taken for granted today, but in the 1900s people were still struggling to understand how to advertise successfully.

MAKING ADVERTISING PROGRESSIVE

The reform movement sweeping America in the 1900s looked at the advertising industry with a wary eye. Many firms made unsubstantiated claims about products and, as soon as they could lash out, consumers retaliated. Patent medicines, cure-alls, wonder pills, and health devices were all targeted by critics of advertising. The movement began when the influential editor of the *Ladies' Home Journal*, Edward W. Bok, began to crusade against unsubstantiated claims in medical advertising in the early 1890s. Other magazines joined Bok's crusade. The effort culminated in a muckraking article, which appeared in *Collier's* in 1904, which published a chemical breakdown of the ingredients of several advertised products. Later available in a book, *The Great American Fraud* (1906) compiled by Samuel Hopkins Adams, the articles proved that such supposed "remedies" contained no secret ingredient and, as a matter of fact, contained many harmful additives which were either addictive or unhealthy. Even more frightening in the eyes of reformers were the chemical additives put into foods to extend shelf life. Scientists developing these preservatives worried more about effectiveness than the long-term consequences of consumption on customers.[30]

The consumer movement spurred by Bok's efforts and the muckraking novel *The Jungle*, written by Upton Sinclair, which investigated the grotesque conditions of Chicago's meatpacking plants, led to government regulation. In 1906 strong federal laws such as the Meat Inspection Act and the Pure Food and Drug Act forced companies to change the way they manufactured goods. Laws required businesses to list ingredients on food containers, medicine bottles, and pill holders. Advertising had to adhere to the new rules.

Henry J. Heinz, born in Pittsburgh, founded the company that bore his name, advocated health standards, even though his stance put him in contention with many of his colleagues. After launching the H.J. Heinz Company in 1888, Heinz used advertising to build brand recognition. The famous slogan "57 Varieties," describing Heinz's pickles, was actually a made-up number that sounded good to consumers and Heinz. At the turn of the century, the company already produced close to 200 products. For product distribution, Heinz used brightly painted wagons and freight cars painted bright yellow and decorated with the Heinz pickle emblem. The Heinz Company participated in world's fairs, markets, and expositions. At the World's Columbian Exposition in Chicago (1893), Heinz had the largest space designated for a food manufacturer. The company hired pretty girls to hand out samples and little mementos, such as a green pickle, labeled "Heinz" which could be worn as a charm. The company gave away more than a million at the exposition. Officials had to enforce crowd regulation for fear that the floor would cave in around the Heinz booth.[31]

Heinz's next ploy involved establishing the Crystal Palace by the Sea on the Heinz Ocean Pier in Atlantic City. Visitors walked under an arch to a glass-encased Sun Parlor, which had comfortable furnishings and a full kitchen where hot and cold Heinz products were demonstrated. Next, adventurous guests could walk 900 feet undersea to the Glass Pavilion, which had a 70-foot-tall electric sign, "57." The pavilion contained an art gallery, lecture hall, and display of all the products manufactured by Heinz. In Pittsburgh, Heinz used his industrial complex as a living museum, where visitors could witness the cleanly scrubbed "Heinz girls" working in spotless surroundings. By 1900, more than 20,000 people visited the plant a year.[32]

Heinz became one of the first industrial firms to hire women, mostly German, Polish, and Italian immigrants from Pittsburgh. The girls had to wear clean uniforms to impress the many visitors passing through the complex, and they were spotless themselves, a far cry from the unsanitary sweatshop conditions other immigrant women faced in the 1900s. Like many firms of the period and throughout the early part of the century, Heinz watched over the moral and physical welfare of workers. They were given cultural and recreational facilities to provide outside activities, and the company paid each worker's medical and dental bills. Other companies, Ford is a notable example, employed cultural and sociological means to control workers and attempt in many ways to "Americanize" them, especially if the company relied heavily on an immigrant workforce.

Heinz was an authoritarian and did not allow unions in his plants, but he also realized that a great company could not cheat its customers and still be considered an outstanding business. Consequently, Heinz took a public stance against the preservatives and additives used and supported by many of his colleagues. Heinz fought the pure food fight "so enthusiastically that many other processors regarded him as a traitor to his class." Dr. Harvey W. Wiley, a crusader who drafted the 1906 Pure Food and Drug Act, always remarked that he would have lost many battles without Heinz's support.[33]

The entire campaign to improve sanitation standards, both at home and in business, greatly improved the health and welfare of citizens in the early twentieth century. Advertising played a fundamental role in bringing the issue to the attention of a national audience. Schools, organizations, boards of health, and concerned citizens groups all combined to focus on education and used advertising.

Metropolitan Insurance joined the fight for sanitation through advertising campaigns directed at the immigrants who bought insurance policies at the firm. The company sent agents into the homes of people new to the country, who then extolled the virtues of cleanliness (at a time when a "clean" person bathed once a week on average). Agents handed out pamphlets that explained how diseases were transferred. Metropolitan then installed disposable drinking cups on many railroad lines and gave away flyswatters with the message "Clean Homes, Pure Food, Clean Milk, No Flies, and No Mosquitoes."[34]

In this health-conscious framework, many entrepreneurs, including those at Scott Paper, produced goods that helped fight disease. In 1908 Hugh Moore used disposable drinking cups, but the idea did not catch on until health activists published a study proving the dangers of using publicly shared drinking containers. Moore then promoted the cups heavily through advertising. One ad, which incorporated the tagline "Spare the Children," pulled on America's heartstrings by showing a diseased man drinking from a public basin, while a young girl waited in line behind him. Advertisements like these seem more than a little heavy-handed, but they were effective and served the public's own best interest. Moore's Dixie Cups became the most famous, best-selling disposable cups in history.

At the beginning of the twenty-first century, the advertising methodologies introduced 100 years ago have become part of everyday life, but in 1900 these techniques had a revolutionary impact. Legacies from that age include promotions to get people to buy certain items over others, such as frequent flier programs and toys in cereal boxes, similar to Wrigley's promotional program; and segmenting consumers into buying categories, a derivative of the way advertisers and corporations broke down buying groups in the 1900s.

Albert Lasker's descendants, though they may rely on technological

innovations in computer-driven design and special effects, still compel
the public to choose one product over another every time a buying decision is made. Today's critics may find advertisers and their techniques
too pervasive, but the fact remains that modern advertising took much
of its shape in the 1900s, after serving as merely an information conduit
when the era began. The decade laid the groundwork for successors to
build an even greater structure, for better or worse, which invades every
aspect of people's lives.

4

Architecture

> The machine is here to stay. It is the forerunner of the democracy that is our dearest hope. There is no more important work before the architect now than to use this normal tool of civilization to the best advantage instead of prostituting it as he has hitherto done in reproducing with murderous ubiquity forms born of other times . . . which can only serve to destroy.
>
> —Frank Lloyd Wright

American architects in the 1900s were more than simply builders or designers; they considered themselves artists, as did the public. As such, architects faced many of the same challenges artists experienced in other disciplines: overcoming European influences, dealing with modernity, and finding their way in an age dominated by industrialism and machinery. For the period's greatest architects, like Louis Sullivan and his protégé Frank Lloyd Wright, the answer was to find an essentially American soul and allow that spirit to personify their work.

On many fronts, the nation attempted to show that it belonged on the world's stage as the lead actor with the great powers of Europe in tow. While the country demonstrated its clout with displays of industrial might and military supremacy, it was more difficult to prove its superiority in the artistic realm. Continental artists enjoyed a head start that stretched thousands of years. Despite the lack of history on their side, American artists rose to the challenge and many vanguards across the arts rose up to defend the honor of the brash, young nation.

Architecture was one art form where the United States could challenge European achievements, especially in the area of commercial buildings.

Since the discipline combined artistic value with science, engineering, and technological innovations, architecture served the needs of growing corporations. If businesses could turn the thin air formerly above their roofs into revenue-generating floor space by building skyward, they could maximize the potential of each parcel of land they purchased. This point became especially important in such growing cities as Chicago, New York, and San Francisco, where prime office space became harder to obtain.

In the late 1800s, American architects built great castles and large, imposing buildings which celebrated the increasing wealth and might of the nation. Because they used a variety of styles from the past (Gothic, Romanesque, Renaissance, and Baroque), there was little uniformity. Sometimes several styles made it into the design of a single building. As time advanced, however, architects adopted specific styles to meet the needs of the growing nation.

Building materials had advanced throughout the nineteenth century, which allowed designers in the 1900s to be more adventurous and daring in their work. Architects used standardized sizes of prefabricated lumber (called "balloon framing" for its lightness in comparison with older structures) to build wooden skeletons for housing, offices, and other buildings, using wire nails to piece them together. This method reduced the cost of building and set off a growth spurt around the country. The success of the wooden balloon frame, although highly susceptible to fire, led architects and engineers to consider other sources of structural framing. Using technology developed in Europe, American designers experimented with iron. They achieved early success with the metal but took the innovation one step further by using cast iron to build multistory structures, first in the SoHo section of New York City in the 1850s.[1]

Chicago and New York were the hotbeds of the building movement. Most important firms were headquartered in one of these two cities, and much of the innovative design and building occurred there. The challenge of multistory buildings came not from the design work itself but rather in convincing business leaders (in an age when corpulence was a virtue) that they should climb multiple floors. Elisha Otis solved the problem with the safety elevator, which ran on a ratchet system that locked the carriage in place at each floor. Art and architecture critic Robert Hughes called the elevator "the most crucial business invention until the computer. It changed everything, not least the American skyline." Otis's innovation debuted in the Old Haughwout Building at 490 Broadway in New York, a five-story iron monolith dubbed "the Parthenon of American iron."[2]

The next innovation in architecture transpired as steel gradually replaced iron as the metal of choice for builders. The Brooklyn Bridge (1883), the greatest engineering achievement of the nineteenth century, proved the utility of steel. More important, John and Washington Roe-blings' (father and son) bridge set the stage for the scope of New York. The bridge guaranteed that the city would be colossal, to match the great power of the bridge. As the longest suspension bridge in the world, the Brooklyn Bridge inspired awe. It symbolized both the country's unity after the horrors of the Civil War and the promise of the industrialized future.

In Chicago, architect William LeBaron Jenney designed the 11-story Home Insurance Building, considered by most observers to be America's first skyscraper. Jenney's building was the first to use steel girders. Later, his student, Louis Henri Sullivan (1856–1924), became the nation's first great modern architect. With the construction of the Brooklyn Bridge and the Home Insurance Building, the race began between Chicago and New York for architectural superiority.

Building tall structures was not the only innovative design work tak-ing place at the turn of the century. Residential homes, mansions, fac-tories, government offices, and the like were being built all over the country. Architects were crafting a new America, represented by its tall buildings and magnificent structures on one hand, and homes and fac-tories on the other. The building craze had a profound impact on the nation. The influence of architects from the last half of the nineteenth and early twentieth centuries is still seen today. In fact, many people look back on various forms of buildings and feel pride if they live or work in a place that is 100 years old or more. These buildings, many designed and built by architects of the 1900s, are still used every day to house businesses, organizations, and families.

CLASSICISM AND REVIVALS

Between the Civil War and World War I, various styles of architecture gained popularity with the changing times and were influenced by the divergent climates across the nation. In successive waves, new styles became popular and then were replaced by another. Few fashions en-dured throughout the entire decade, although some became staples and remain so today. Living in a house built at the beginning of the new century is so commonplace in some areas that most people do not con-sider the structures particularly old. The technological advances made in building homes in the 1900s, combined with the spiritual innovations made by the decade's architects, have fueled housing growth and styles into our own times.

Not only did housing styles alter, but the actual infrastructures changed as well. Technological innovations like electricity, central heat-ing, and plumbing made homes more livable. Building materials, like stucco and tile, were used to make houses built in warm climates, such

as California and Florida, more bearable. Mass customization of the construction industry also played a significant role in housing styles. As the
decade wore on, necessities like doors, windows, roofing shingles, and
other items were mass-produced and could be transported to all areas
around the nation. This led to a more uniform look in cities and suburbs
where building houses quickly to meet the demand was essential.

One approach architects instituted, which recalled the classical forms
of Europe, was spread by Americans who trained in Europe and returned to America to practice their profession. Many Americans studied
at the Ecole des Beaux Arts in Paris, the foremost architectural school in
the world. The Americans who studied there, led by Richard Morris
Hunt (the first American graduate), brought its techniques and theories
back to the United States. The style centered on lavish ornamentation,
low-pitched roofs, exaggerated stonework, masonry walls, and arched
windows.[3]

The Beaux Arts–influenced designers built mansions in this style,
which gave an air of royalty and power to America's new industrial rich.
The New York firm of McKim, Mead and White designed the mansion
Rosecliff (1902) in fashionable Newport, Rhode Island, a summer get-
away for the wealthy, along with many other mansions along the East
Coast. Stanford White designed Rosecliff with Louis XIV's Versailles in
mind, built by the great Jules Hardouin-Mansart. At the end of the last
century, the firm of McKim, Mead and White built numerous remarkable
houses in Newport, including the Colman House (1882–1883) and the
Tilton House (1881–1882). The firm also designed shingle-style houses at
the resort community, each of which contained an array of porches, ga-
bles, and chimneys all wrapped up in different types of shingles.

The firm, led by Charles Follen McKim, William Rutherford Mead, and
Stanford White, developed into the leading architectural firm in the nation in the 1900s. The accomplishments achieved by the firm included
Penn Station, Madison Square Garden, the Brooklyn Museum, the Boston
Symphony Hall and Public Library, and Low Library at Columbia University. The firm remodeled the White House, adding additional executive offices. McKim, Mead and White carried out traditional designs,
primarily centered on Renaissance and Romanesque styles. Although
modernists scorned this type of architecture, it remained popular for
much of the twentieth century.[4]

Between 1880 and 1910, the château style flourished, based on
sixteenth-century French châteaus that combined Gothic elements and
Renaissance detailing in stone masonry. The style, adopted primarily for
wealthy patrons in the United States, included steeply pitched roofs and
high spires. In the public realm, this style found its way into many
churches and government buildings. It was also favored by the industrial
titans of the era. The most famous example of the château style is George
W. Vanderbilt's Biltmore estate in Asheville, North Carolina (1895). At

one time, the estate, landscaped by Frederick Law Olmsted who designed New York's Central Park, was a retreat. Today open to the public, it highlights the architecture and decorative arts of the period.[5]

The Beaux Arts influence continued into the 1900s, even as a more modern style began taking shape. People enjoyed being taken back to earlier periods through design and architecture. The love affair with Renaissance, Greek, Roman, and Baroque architecture can be seen on almost any college campus in America and in many of the nation's public buildings.

A Tudor revival (modeled after English country homes) grew in popularity, first among the wealthy suburbanites of New York, Chicago, and other large cities, then gradually as designers built less expensive models for average home buyers. Tudors feature tall, narrow windows; large chimneys; and Renaissance detailing on doors and windows. Tudors remain one of the most popular home designs in the nation. The only rival of the Tudor is the Colonial revival, which dominated domestic design in the United States until the 1930s, then regained popularity in the second half of the century.[6]

The Colonial revival stood as the symbolic rebirth of early English, Dutch, Spanish, and French designs, adapted to conditions in the United States with modern materials. Different styles of Colonial dominated different regions: in California, one found Spanish and Pueblo revivals; on the East Coast, Georgian and Dutch houses were common. McKim, Mead and White made fortunes by building Georgian and Adam Colonials for wealthy patrons. Later, the Colonial form underwent a slimming process, down to a single story, which resulted in the Cape Cod style.[7]

The unassuming bungalow made its appearance, setting off a national bungalow craze up to 1910. Designers modeled bungalows after the single-story houses used by the British in India. In fact, a Hindustani term was used to derive the name "bungalow" itself. In the United States, bungalows, appropriate for a warm climate, were first built in Southern California. Builders in other regions, in spite of harsh weather conditions, adopted the style for low-income and lower middle-class families. The craze for bungalows stretched into Vancouver, Canada, and even as far as Australia. In the end, the structures were simply cheaper to build than traditional suburban middle-class homes. Because of their low cost they began to appear in industrial neighborhoods, such as the small steel mill town of Clairton, Pennsylvania, and large sections of Cleveland, Ohio, which sprang up around Republic Steel.[8]

INTERIOR DESIGN

The turn of the century brought changes to the interior of residential homes as well. Begun in England and accentuated at the Philadelphia Centennial Exposition of 1876, the Colonial revival influenced the way in which people decorated the insides of their houses. Dubbed the Arts and Crafts movement, the philosophy hinged on a general rejection of the excesses of the Industrial Revolution and machine-made products. Looking back with nostalgia at the Colonial period, interior designers discarded wallpaper and heavy carpeting and returned to hardwood floors and simple styles of furniture. The movement turned into a crusade for simple living. In 1904 there were 25 Arts and Crafts societies in the United States, whose purpose was to stifle the chaotic lifestyle of urban dwellers and bring them back to a simpler way of life. As the nation wrangled with its budding superpower status, fueled by industrialism, people searched for an escape behind the closed doors of their homes.[9]

The women of the 1900s rejected the Victorian interiors so popular a decade before in exchange for simpler designs. A typical Victorian home was dark and cluttered with antiques, sculptures, and paintings mixed together with heavy draperies, embroidered tablecloths, and various lace curtains and doilies. Elsie de Wolfe, the self-proclaimed first professional interior designer in America, made it her intention to get people to adopt brighter colors and minimal decorations.

The main proponent of the style in the United States was Gustav Stickley (1858–1942), founder of *The Craftsman* (1901), a magazine trumpeting the movement. He advised that home decorating be unadorned, with paneled walls and small windows with groups of square panes. Stickley used many built-in corner seats, fireplace nooks, and other cozy touches. He also advocated a sensible variety of furniture, labeled Mission style. These pieces used rough-hewn timber and no nails or glue to hold them together. Mission carpenters used oak as the standard material and finished it until it turned a golden brown. The educated members of the middle class were Stickley's devotees. They enjoyed the emphasis on comfort and practicality. Somewhat similar to a modern-day Martha Stewart, Stickley used *The Craftsman* to fuel the movement and comment on other areas that touched his readers' lives, including art, education, politics, and urban planning.[10]

The Arts and Crafts movement was especially popular in California. A group of architects, including Joseph Worcester, Irving J. Gill, and Julia Morgan, among others, built structures which underscored practicality. They used native materials and color schemes to boost natural living. The Arts and Crafts movement had a profound influence on the nation as a whole. Sears offered craftsman home kits and matching Mission furniture in its mail-order catalogs. By mid-century, the company boasted that enough of its materials had been purchased to build a city containing 25,000 people.[11]

The craze for natural-looking furnishings helped drive the bungalow rage, which featured exposed wood and heavy, organic fittings. Many firms responded to the Colonial revival by designing handcrafted furniture, pottery, and glasswork. Frank Lloyd Wright, destined to become the nation's foremost architect, used this style in his own designs. He emphasized large fireplaces where the family could gather together, exposed wooden beams in ceilings, and stained wood detailing.

For many women, as the country transitioned from a rural to an urban nation, the home ceased to be a place of production and women, at least married women, became full-time homemakers. Single women, usually between the ages of 16 and 20, worked outside the home and accounted for nearly 60 percent of the female workforce in the early 1900s. Many women worked in the years they spent between school and marriage. Wives, on the other hand, were confined to the home—they had fewer opportunities for outside work, although these opportunities increased as the decade progressed.[12]

For women both on the farm and in the suburbs and cities, however, domestic life changed quickly. They may have rejected industrialism in decorating, but women quickly adopted the most innovative laborsaving devices. Even the means for acquiring such goods became simpler. Women could turn to mail-order catalogues to fulfill just about every need: from a coffee grinder (49 cents), to a rocking chair ($2.95) or a full-sized wood-burning stove ($17.48), to a hair-waving iron (11 cents). Women's domestic lives were altered by the availability of household and personal goods.[13]

The 1900s proved to be an interesting decade for designers of furniture and crafts. The industrial age seemed to inspire them, either to move ahead with modern ideas or to revert back to an earlier era. Overall, the idea of functional design inspired the builders of the age. Architects and craftsmen exhibited a unified connection between the structure of a building and the interior contents. They also attempted to link buildings themselves with their natural surroundings. Architect Frank Lloyd Wright became the most famed practitioner of this idea.

FRANK LLOYD WRIGHT

America's greatest architectural genius was Frank Lloyd Wright (1867–1959), the son of a preacher father and a schoolteacher mother. His long career spanned nearly seven decades. During the 1900s, Wright established much of his early reputation. While growing up in Wisconsin, Wright developed dual loves—music and architecture—which combined to heighten his sense of feeling and led him later to exclaim, "form became feeling."[14] Wright's designs, especially the houses that seem tucked into the surrounding land or flowing from it, look almost musical, the way a cartoonist would draw musical notes floating together in the air.

After finding his mentor in Louis Sullivan, considered the father of modern American architecture, Wright helped the firm of Adler and Sullivan design the Wainwright Building in Saint Louis, the Garrick Theater in Chicago's Schiller Building, and many other buildings. Wright referred to Sullivan as "Lieber Master," or beloved master, although the two men had a falling out over Wright's accepting private commissions to design houses (later in life they renewed their friendship). Wright resigned from the firm and set up his own shop in Oak Park, Illinois, a suburb of Chicago. Being on his own fueled the young architect, and Wright's fame grew as he began designing homes. The first masterpiece he designed was the Winslow House (1893) in River Forest, Illinois. Observers labeled Wright's designs the Prairie style, although they were nowhere near the prairie—for the most part in and around suburban Chicago—because of Wright's nostalgic feelings for the Western plains.[15]

Wright's Prairie style houses reflected horizontal, rather than vertical, lines. Wright wanted his residential homes to be simple, relaxing, and promote harmony and quiet domesticity. There were no basements or attics in Wright's Prairie homes, and the wood was always stained, never painted, to emphasize the material's natural beauty. The outside of the buildings featured wide, overhanging eaves; the interiors were somewhat sparse and lit primarily with outside light.

The houses were supposed to adapt to the natural surroundings. Wright did not consciously attempt to be controversial with his designs. In fact, he relied on somewhat conservative patrons for his living, so he could not be outrageous in his plans. However, Wright was striking out against the ornamentation and overwrought structures that dominated the American scene. In a Wright Prairie style home, it is not uncommon to see the landscape meld with the walls and to find built-in planter boxes, meshed together perfectly with the overall rectangular design.

The Robie House (1909) in Chicago is arguably Wright's most powerful design of the decade. Rather than building a great homage skyward, Wright widened and flattened his houses, bringing them closer to the ground to interact with the environment. Fred Robie, an ideal client for Wright, wanted a modern house that emphasized ease of life. The Robie House was built with brick, stone, concrete, glass, and tile with efficient electric lighting, telephone, and burglar alarm systems. Robie, an engineer and efficiency nut, wanted his house to be free from "curvatures and doodads" which did little but collect dust. In total, Robie paid about $60,000 for the house and its interior decorations—a bargain, even if that figure equals ten times more in today's money.[16]

Another of Wright's famous Prairie Style homes was built for wealthy heiress Susan Lawrence Dana in Springfield, Illinois. In the Dana House, Wright rejected the idea that individual rooms had to be a series of boxes and positioned his rooms diagonally, achieving his goal of "destroying

Exterior of Frank Lloyd Wright's Frederick C. Robie House (1909).
Courtesy of the Frank Lloyd Wright Archives, Scottsdale, Arizona.

the box." The Dana House was Wright's first to be built with a two-story living room.[17]

Then, Wright moved on to the exterior, expanding the number and size of windows. He also invented a way of wrapping windows around corners, making the corners of the house look like they vanished into thin air. Next, he made the roof longer and wider, extending it 20 feet past the last masonry support.

In the Dana House and others of the 1900s, Wright made artistic changes that were both admired and advanced. Wright's roofs were angled to protect inhabitants from harsh sunlight, but still allowing it to come in during the winter. He also built central heating systems with hot-water pipes, thus keeping the architectural masterpieces artistic and livable. He even took into consideration cross-ventilation in the summer to cool the houses, especially important in the days before air conditioning.

When the Dana House opened, the socialite owner invited 1,000 guests to two receptions that were the talk of the social season. Later, in the

Exterior of Frank Lloyd Wright's Dana-Thomas House (1903). Courtesy of the Frank Lloyd Wright Archives, Scottsdale, Arizona.

1930s, Dana fell upon bad times and ill health. The house was abandoned and her fortune depleted. In 1943, an auction was held to sell off Dana's belongings. Onlookers swarmed to the house, forcing officials to charge a one dollar admission price, but few people actually bought items, even Wright originals. Reportedly, some people got Wright furniture for less than the admission charge.[18]

Throughout the decade, Wright designed dozens of homes, primarily in and around Chicago and part of Wisconsin. In 1904 Wright designed his first corporate building, the Larkin Building in Buffalo, New York. The Larkin Company, a thriving national mail-order business, was separate from its competition, such as Sears Roebuck, because it manufactured its own products. Although the edifice Wright built was demolished in 1950 and was never fully appreciated by its owners, the building held a lofty place in the annals of architectural history.

The Larkin Building, in downtown Buffalo, was adjacent to train tracks on one side and busy city streets on the other. The plot was a trapezoidal nightmare of noise, chaos, and confusion. Wright decided that the building must be grand, lending an air of dignity to the otherwise drab Larkin complex, which consisted mainly of bland factories. The building also had to be sealed off from its environment, which is routine today, but virtually impossible in Wright's day. The list of innovations Wright achieved with the Larkin facility includes double-glazed windows to reduce noise, heat, and cold; subfloor electric light and telephone connections; the use of magnesite, a synthetic fireproof material as durable as concrete but softer; and wall-hung toilets with ceiling-hung stall partitions. The interior of the building featured a five-story-high atrium, topped by a huge skylight. Although some observers have likened the building to a closed society or church of work, Wright designed it to be worker friendly, providing fresh air (a rarity next to the coal-burning railroad cars) and an early form of air-conditioning. Ultimately, in his words, it was "a restful, harmonious environment . . . under conditions ideal for body and mind."[19]

Later in life, Wright built his most famous structures: Fallingwater (1936–1939) in Bear Run, Pennsylvania, and the Solomon R. Guggenheim Museum in New York City (1956), his only design in that city. Wright designed Fallingwater for department store mogul Edgar J. Kaufmann Sr. as a secluded home in the hills south of Pittsburgh. In one of the greatest displays of modern architecture, Wright sited the house to hang out over the Bear Run stream and accompanying waterfall. When Kaufmann asked why the house was not located across the creek, so they could see the waterfall, Wright characteristically replied, "E.J., I want you to live with the waterfall, not just to look at it."[20]

As a result of his daring, Wright found himself on the cover of *Time* magazine with a drawing of Fallingwater imposed behind him. The house became his signature work, much like the Larkin Building had in the 1900s, and the Guggenheim Museum did later. Kaufmann's son, Edgar Jr., became a famed architecture historian and critic. In his book, *Fallingwater*, Kaufmann explained "that the architect and his client knew the design of Fallingwater was an exploration beyond the limits of conventional practice." With the structure, Wright found near perfection in his melding of nature with man-made materials. He used concrete to decorate walkways playfully, contrasted the cool stream with walls of glass, used both rock ledges and cut masonry, and made the balconies jut out of thin air that seemed to defy gravity. No one would have even considered building a house over a waterfall at the time and that Wright pulled it off with his typical aplomb attests to his genius.[21]

SKYSCRAPERS

The skyscraper is one of the most impressive tributes to the twentieth century. Since America came of age in the industrial age, these structures celebrated modern technology, materials, and innovation. On one hand, they were viewed with awe as artistic pieces, but also served a utilitarian role as offices, headquarters, etc. On the other hand, Skyscrapers also performed a more pedestrian role: coping with zoning and tax laws, political squabbles, and real estate battles for control of prime locales.

Skyscrapers have been an awe-inspiring part of American culture. Most people gaze skyward in wonder at their beauty, power, and size.

The development of iron and steel as structural materials fueled the idea of the tall building in the early nineteenth century. These materials allowed architects to design buildings beyond the limitations of masonry and brick.

Steel allowed architects to move skyward with a minimum of bulk, thus enabling larger windows and more flexible interior spaces. Actually, the work of bridge builders inspired architects to apply metal technology to buildings. The development of a safe passenger elevator in 1857 eliminated the final obstacle to erecting tall structures. Before the elevator, the traditional limit had been five stories.

Many of the early advances in skyscrapers can be directly attributed to the devastating fire that wiped out most of Chicago in 1871. City planners and architects in the Windy City turned to fireproof iron and steel instead of wood and masonry. Modern business also demanded large working spaces so, combined with high real estate costs, the skyscraper took shape in Chicago. William LeBaron Jenney is considered the founder of the Chicago School of architecture. His firm built an entirely metal nine-story structure in 1885. He used Bessemer steel, which reduced the price, allowed mass production, and increased the use of metal framework.

The men behind the rebuilding of Chicago were Boston financiers. Their main interest, not surprisingly, revolved around money. They urged Chicago architects to build tall buildings to maximize profits and encouraged designers to keep the structures simple by eliminating unessential ornament. The resulting approach, renowned for its minimalism, became known as the Chicago style. Louis Sullivan, in particular, realized the necessity of recognizing height, not just magnitude, in structures. Sullivan viewed himself as a poet first, and an artist second. The materials he worked with were his words. He wanted to turn tall buildings into "proud and soaring things."[22]

The Wainwright Building (1890–1891) in Saint Louis was Sullivan's first step in redefining tall buildings in the United States. Sullivan immortalized his ideology when he coined the simple term "form follows function" in an 1896 essay written for *Lippincott's* magazine. In the work, Sullivan articulated his thoughts that skyscrapers must be lofty and tall, "every inch of it tall . . . every inch a proud and soaring thing, rising in sheer exultation." Sullivan believed that everything in nature had an exterior shape and form that separated it from other things. In Darwinian fashion, he explained, according to biographer Robert Twombly, that life takes on forms in response to needs and that the life and form are indivisible; thus, function dictates a thing's natural form.[23]

Sullivan's theories and work transformed architecture in the twentieth

The Arata Building in Antioch, California (1909). The architectural style is influenced by Louis Sullivan. Courtesy of the Contra Costa County Historical Society.

century. The architect regarded skyscrapers as "the characteristically American edifice, as the prototypical cultural manifestation of a business civilization, loaded with social meanings, not the least important being entrepreneurial ruthlessness in accumulating the money to build it." In addition, Sullivan realized the structures offered "cultural salvation." Nature served as the guide for the young architect. Unlocking the mystery contained within a building revealed the resulting social solution. Sullivan's essay, which traveled beyond architecture, also served as his "manifesto on the role of art in social transformation."[24]

Sullivan soared to the top of the profession in the late 1800s, building great structures in Chicago and the Prudential Building (1895) in Buffalo. The Bayard Building in New York was his only work in the rival city to the east. It has been called a "spiritual ancestor" to the towering skyscrapers that line the streets of the city in modern times. After his partnership with Dankmar Adler broke up, Sullivan had fewer and fewer commissions. His prickly personality and righteous attitude about his work drove away many potential clients.

Despite Sullivan's eccentricities, his reputation won him new projects. He designed what many consider his best work in the early 1900s: the Schlesinger & Mayer Store (later sold to the Carson Pirie Scott Company) in Chicago. Although certainly not a tall building (the functions of a department store meant its form had to be somewhat blocky), Sullivan nonetheless used innovative techniques in the structural design so that the department store could remain open during the busy Christmas holiday season. Under his direction, workers put in a new foundation under the old one while shoppers strolled among the luxuries above them. Sullivan's delicate decoration made the department store a popular place for middle-class women to shop and get away from their everyday routines at home. Every aspect of department stores at the turn of the century had to reinforce the notion that shopping was a delightful experience.[25]

As the decade progressed and in the remaining working days of his career, Sullivan turned to other types of buildings to express his "democratic" style of architecture. He secured commissions to design rural banks to serve primarily farming customers. Perhaps the most impressive bank built by Sullivan was the National Farmers' Bank in Owatonna, Minnesota (1906–1907). The structure showcased a 68-foot square banking area and had 38-foot-high arched windows on the two sides facing the street which were divided into vertical stripes of green glass. Sullivan paid a great deal of attention to interior design, where people actually interacted with the building—his democratic theories applied to design. He chose Stickley furniture pieces and others of his own design. Critics cheered the bank enthusiastically. One observer remarked on the effects of the bank on the sleepy farming town, "Owatonna suddenly found itself famous and became the Mecca of architectural pilgrimages. At the last report, twenty-five strangers a day were visiting Owatonna expressly to inspect it."[26]

Sullivan's ideas about building tall structures served as the guide for a stunning display of construction over the next several decades. However, the stage moved from his beloved Chicago to the city that would become known around the world for its massive skyscrapers—New York. Fueled by what they had witnessed in Chicago, New York architects pulled out all the stops to surpass their Midwestern rivals. In the mid-1890s, New York skyscrapers already pushed past 20 stories. Even more critical than the shortage of suitable office space in New York (since Manhattan is an island), the necessity of using land wisely pushed architects to build taller and taller buildings.

Ironically, the architect who showed New York what a skyscraper could be was Chicagoan Daniel Burnham (1846–1912). Burnham joined with another famous Windy City architect, John Wellborn Root, in the nineteenth century to form one of the nation's most revered firms. They built a number of Chicago's most famous structures from that period: the Montauk Block (1882), the Rookery (1886), and the Rand-McNally Building (1890).

After Root's early death in 1891 at age 41, Burnham took over the agency and continued plying his trade. The newly renamed D.H. Burnham and Company grew into Chicago's largest firm and then opened offices in New York and San Francisco. Later in his career, Burnham designed the Wannamaker department store in New York (1903), Chicago's Orchestra Hall (1904), and Union Station in Washington, D.C. (1907). Burnham also gained international renown as an urban planner. He played a major role in the redevelopment of Chicago, which resulted in Grand Park, throughout the 1900s. Burnham helped design urban plans for other cities, including one for San Francisco after the earthquake and fire of 1906.

Although Burnham achieved great fame with many projects, it was his design of the Flatiron Building (1902) that has been described as the ideal skyscraper. A joking reference to the shape that stuck, the Flatiron Building has a steel frame covered in terra cotta and stone. The building is a product of its strange position in New York. Situated on a relatively narrow triangular site at the intersection of three streets, it faces Madison Square Park. Under Burnham's steady leadership, however, the Fuller Building (the official name of the site) became a sensation in New York. The Flatiron, along with the Statue of Liberty and the Brooklyn Bridge, shortly became a major tourist attraction and adorned countless postcards.[27]

The Flatiron, still as remarkable today as it was in 1902, looks more like an alien craft cutting through space than a 22-storied office building. The head of the triangle, which comes to a dizzying point, is accentuated by a single row of windows fronting the structure. The building's most famous photographer, the modernist Alfred Stieglitz, described the Flatiron as "the bow of a monster ocean steamer—a picture of a new America still in the making." Stieglitz captured the building, towering over the trees in the adjacent park, in a magnificent black-and-white photograph which depicts the remarkable thinness of the structure. It looks impossibly slender, like it could be teetering just before falling over. Stieglitz's photograph juxtaposes the man-made Flatiron with a slightly crooked tree in the foreground, contrasting nature with fabrication, a key theme of architects and artists in the 1900s.[28]

The most revolutionary aspect of Burnham's structure was not its unique shape or even its impressive height. Actually, the Flatiron Building transformed the way in which people viewed office towers. More than just a place to work and maximize space, Burnham's design made tall buildings a source of corporate pride. Skyscrapers, in essence, defined corporate America, showed off the accumulating wealth of the nation, and helped solidify the burgeoning "corporate culture" engulfing American workers. For corporate leaders, it was not enough to have a thriving business: a skyscraper with the company's name emblazoned on it became the new corporate symbol of power.

From 1900 until the Great Depression hit in 1929, one or more new skyscrapers appeared every year in New York. Each year, the city's designers pushed the envelope a bit farther in their yearning to maximize the space above. Tall buildings had an even more sweeping effect on the psyche of the nation. In many respects, skyscrapers marked a rite of passage for cities around the world. On one hand, they were perpetual advertisements for their owners; on the other, skyscrapers catered to the romanticism of the masses. They reflected the power of the United States and the modern technological age. People often look to a city's skyline as a determining factor in assessing its prestige and popularity, whether it's from the cavernous streets of Manhattan or the standing at the mouth of the three rivers in Pittsburgh. Skyscrapers define the American city and, in that regard, what it means to be an American.

5

Fashion

Now the Summer Girl, she packs her ducks,
(It's beautiful weather for them!)
And puts on a skirt with a thousand tucks,
Three hundred ruffles and eighty pucks,
Some darts and gores and a hem.

—C.R. Bacon, *Life* magazine (1901)

In the 1900s, fashion and design melded together into one seemingly cohesive movement (though definitely an informal one) that swept through clothing styles, art, furniture, and architecture. The same pattern occurred over and over in each field—a decided movement away from European traditions, with subsequent attempts to define the subject from an American point of view. In fashion, upper and middle-class men and women were still tied closely to European and Victorian styles from the 1890s. However, as industrialism sparked urban growth, working men and women dressed in styles appropriate for their jobs. Young women working in factories or workshops could hardly layer themselves in frilly lace or don hats trimmed with flowers or fruit. Fashion took on a utilitarian look that did not hinder work-related tasks. Conversely, a proper "lady" would never leave the house without a tight corset or the right makeup, and aristocratic men always donned a top hat and carried a walking stick.

Industrialism had another profound effect on fashion in the decade. As corporations mass-produced goods, they either fueled or created markets to purchase them, and advertisers pushed the message that the accumulation of goods equaled status. Searching for ways to get merchandise into the hands of consumers, companies like Sears flooded the countryside with mail-order catalogs, while department stores and chain stores fed the machine in urban centers. Fashion took on a whole new meaning when women in small towns and villages could buy the same clothes that were available in cities. Industrialism brought democracy to fashion, although, like its political counterpart, those with the money held the power and ultimately influenced future styles. The rich looked overseas or to the finest boutiques for their inspiration; the middle class and their poorer cousins got secondhand permutations via department stores and catalogs.

Clothing served as yet another measure in the widening gap between the rich and poor. While urban immigrants and rural farmers struggled to keep clothing on the backs of their families, wealthy families regarded clothing as a status symbol, merely another commodity. An immigrant girl working 12-hour days over a sewing machine in a New York sweatshop had absolutely nothing in common with the daughters of high society who were attending afternoon tea parties and summering in Newport.

A great clothing industry rose up to provide men and women with the mass-produced and handmade clothes they desired. In the 1900s, women spent more than $1 billion a year on clothes and accessories. In fact, they spent more than $14 million on corsets alone. The 1905 Sears, Roebuck catalogue offered 150 styles of the new shirtwaist blouse, ranging from 39 cents for a plain shirt to $6.95 for a fancy taffeta version. New York city factories alone churned out more than $60 million worth of the blouses in 1910.[1]

When the 1900s began, fashion hinged on smallness—tiny waists, "clasped with two hands," shoes a size or two too small, and small hats.[2] As the decade advanced, fashion rules became less rigid, but most people still adhered to ideas and styles developed earlier. Both men and women were status conscious and, in the words of one observer, were "perfectly willing to forfeit comfort if in so doing he looked like a more prosperous and proper citizen." In fact, upper- and middle-class men and women both changed clothes several times a day. They treated the evening dinner as a formal occasion and each changed for dinner, even if they had no guests and were dining at home.[3]

Styles in the 1900s centered largely on padding—the woman in layers of ruffles and the man in large, boxy suits. Even casual events were governed by strict guidelines, such as linen or flannel trousers in the summer for men and the ever-present corset for women. Both sexes wore hats just about everywhere, whether at work, on vacation, or at formal functions. Although glimmers of style emerged in the first decade, it would take World War I and the heady days of the 1920s before a sense of fashion wholeheartedly took hold. As many of the stringent fashion rules of the decade fell to the wayside, people experimented with looser styles and more functional clothing, which came to symbolize the American spirit. European fashion designers scoffed at American incarnations of modern styles in the first several decades of the twentieth century, but over time these changes added up to a uniquely national fashion.[4]

THE GIBSON GIRL

The ideal woman in the United States from 1890 to World War I was not Theodore Roosevelt's teenage daughter, Alice (although her every move was followed by the press), or a star of the fledgling movie industry. Instead, the image every female idolized was illustrator Charles Dana Gibson's "Gibson girl"—an elegant, graceful, romanticized female of the age. Women imitated the style and fashions of the Gibson girl; men tried to be like her dashing suitors. The power of Gibson's illustrations rested in the air of dignity he conveyed and the detachment he captured in the Gibson girl's eyes.

For society at large, the Gibson girl was the ideal "new woman." The new woman broke through the barriers that had plagued women in earlier times. Generally, she had a college education, supported herself, and did not marry young like her mother's generation. Gibson encapsulated all the intrigue of the new woman in his illustrations and even the fear many people experienced regarding women's empowerment. Conservative traditionalists lashed out against the new woman movement. They attributed many social ills, such as soaring divorce rates, to the new woman.

Gibson's popularity, however, never wavered. The Gibson girl played golf and tennis, rode bicycles, made men swoon, and dressed in a simpler style. Typically, she wore a long skirt and a blouse, or "shirtwaist" as they were known in the era. Actually, the Gibson girl helped widen the appeal of the blouse over the frilly layers of heavy petticoats normally worn by women.[5] Gibson licensed the image of his drawings, so one could find her adorning china, silverware, pillows, or even whiskbroom holders. Many young men decorated their apartments with Gibson girl wallpaper, the height of chic for bachelor pads.[6]

By serializing his drawings in *Life* magazine, Gibson found a way to encapsulate the new woman in elegant pen-and-ink sketches which appealed to women across class lines. Women from working-class families aspired to be like the Gibson girl and achieved a certain level of independence perhaps as a telephone operator or social worker. Women from wealthy families certainly did not concern themselves with working, but found inspiration to do something meaningful, which the Gibson girl aspired to do.

The men in Gibson's drawings are almost as telling as the Gibson girl

A Charles Dana Gibson picture used as a cover
for sheet music: "A Girl Like You Would Do For a
Boy Like Me To Woo," words by C. P. McDonald,
music by Percy Wenrich (1907). Courtesy of the
Oakland Public Library, Oakland, California.

herself. Men hover over her, and older women scorn her for grabbing
the men's attention. Almost embarrassed to be the focal point, she presents an air of supreme indifference. One young man—a dark-haired,
square-jawed fellow—is usually depicted. His sadness is palpable. He
knows he will never win the girl's hand, but he cannot keep himself
from being near her.

The Gibson girl swept the nation. Her image could be found everywhere, from pinups on college campuses to the Alaskan Klondike. Gibson's male characters papered the walls of many female boarding
schools. According to journalist and historian Mark Sullivan, "Gibson's
characters, always clean and fine, composed the models for the manners
of a whole generation of Americans, their dress, their pose, their attitude
toward life."[7] The New York *World* summed up Gibson's influence: "As

soon as the world saw Gibson's ideal it bowed down in adoration, saying: 'Lo, at last the typical American girl.' Not only did the susceptible American men acknowledge her their queen, but the girls themselves held her as their own portrait." In fact, the *World* critic stated, "It was Gibson's pen which sent mustaches out of fashion and made the tailors pad the shoulders of well-cut coats."[8]

Alice Roosevelt was the closest incarnation of a real-life Gibson girl. Spirited and boisterous like her father, Alice flaunted many of the notions about "proper" behavior. She smoked in public, danced until dawn at social gatherings, and even danced the hula in Hawaii, a nearly immoral act at the time. She so exasperated the president that he remarked, "I can do one of two things. I can be President of the United States, or I can control Alice. I cannot possibly do both." However, one can sense the tone of playfulness and delight in that statement. Roosevelt surely took a great deal of pride in having a daughter routinely labeled a "chip off the old block." Like a modern-day movie star or musician, the more outlandish Alice acted, the more popular she became. There were songs written for her ("Alice, Where Art Thou?"), countless newborns named after her, and she even had her own color (Alice blue).[9]

Alice's popularity stretched around the world. European magazines followed her every move and published her picture on the cover of magazines. The British government offered to confer royal status on her so she could attend the coronation of King Edward VII (her father refused); the Japanese lined the streets of Tokyo, shouting "Bonzai!" as she passed; and the Empress of China invited her to spend the night at the Imperial Palance in Peking. When she married Ohio Congressman Nicholas Longworth, it was the event of the year and followed by millions. She truly held the title of "America's Princess" in the 1900s.

FASHION IN THE FACTORY

Most women who worked in the 1900s found employment in department stores, factories, and offices—symbols of America's rise as an industrial leader. As a group, they were young, primarily urban, and single. For example, in New York City, 80 percent of the 343,000 working women in 1900 were single, and one-third were between the ages of 16 and 20. These women had quite a different set of jobs from those who had worked just a decade earlier, who usually labored as domestic servants or worked in small sweatshops. For young working women, clothing served many functions and allowed them to express themselves and push beyond the limitations of urban, working-class life.[10]

Dressing up gave working women the ability to present themselves in a guise that took them out of the realm of the factories or department store floors, whether they were parading in the streets or enjoying a night on the town with a group of friends. Clothing allowed one to assert one's identity, even if that meant bending the supposed "rules" of fashion by dressing like upper-class women and putting on airs of wealth. Some observers believed women dressed like their wealthier counterparts in order to marry into a higher social class. There is some truth to this notion; however, the way working-class women dressed and the implications it entailed went beyond looking for a rich husband.[11]

Working women used clothing to define respectability. Because of their dual roles in the workplace and in society, they separated their clothes into work clothes and Sunday clothes, their nicer articles. What women wore to work depended on the job. A waitress might wear a white apron and matching cap, but a seamstress would wear older clothes that would not be ruined by sweat or grime from the shop floor. Sunday clothes, however, played an important social role. Women engaged in social activities in the community on Sundays. Without an acceptable set of Sunday clothes, women did not feel they could participate in these identity-building events. When new immigrants arrived in the United States, they acquired a set of nice clothes to help assimilate them to American culture.[12]

Although lumped together into one large group by the outside world, working-class females differentiated themselves through fashion, speech patterns, levels of schooling, and other yardsticks. Fashion served as a measurement in forming an unofficial hierarchy among workingwomen from different ethnic groups and religious backgrounds. Some women gained an air of aristocracy from the Sunday clothes they wore at social gatherings. Women in New York bought cheap versions of the latest fashions from the clothing stores located on Grand Street. They also avidly read the fashion pages in the newspapers and saw upper-class women in department stores and modeled their own dress on the basis of these encounters. The working class adopted other aspects of elite culture, such as calling other women "lady friends." They even used romance novels as a kind of guide to look inside the lives of women from the upper classes. "To be stunningly attired at the movies, balls, or entertainments often counted more in the working woman's calculations than having comfortable clothes and shoes for the daily round of toil," explained one historian.[13]

The most important fashion development for women at the turn of the century was the shirtwaist, a simple, yet attractive blouse worn with a skirt. The shirtwaist, which allowed a full range of motion, did not restrict a worker's movement like cumbersome formal wear did, and it could be worn all day, a requirement for long hours at work. Both shirtwaist blouses and suits (usually called tailor-mades) gained momentum as a result of mass production. Companies produced both articles at prices workers could afford. The shirtwaist cost around $1.50; suits

ranged from $10 to $20. According to fashion historian Caroline Rennolds Milbank, the importance of the two styles cannot be underesti-
mated: they "established America's reputation for a well-dressed
'average woman' . . . established America's superiority in the field of
ready-to-wear. And that they continued to be popular, despite the efforts
of couturiers to supplant them with more ornate styles, established
American women as having a mind, and a style, of their own."[14]

FASHION AT HOME

Most working-class females did not work outside the home. They took
care of the household and served as money managers, relying on the
husband (and children) for the family's entire income. For these women,
fashion and clothing served a different purpose than for young, single
factory workers, but it was still an important part of everyday life. In
fact, as wages rose for average workers, their wives became the target
audience for department stores and advertisers. For women living in
rural areas or on farms, the same was true for mail-order catalogs. By
some accounts, the Sears or Montgomery Ward catalog was more prevalent in farming houses than the Bible in the 1900s.

In her seminal work *Homestead: The Households of a Mill Town*, Margaret
F. Byington examined Homestead households in 1908. In the smoky city,
only seven miles from downtown Pittsburgh, life revolved around the
former Carnegie Steel Company, now a part of the United States Steel
Corporation.

Homestead was also the site, in 1892, of one of the nation's most infamous labor battles, in which union steelworkers in Homestead clashed
with Pinkerton security company strikebreakers. It was a dark day for
labor in the United States, and the legacy of the strike still shaped Homestead 16 years later when Byington visited.

Working-class wives had responsibilities beyond cleaning and cooking
in Homestead. They also had the burden of balancing the household
budget. Thus women were more aware of the needs of the family, especially what it took to feed, clothe, and maintain the unit. One of her
responsibilities was to keep her husband on the straight and narrow.
One woman explained how she kept her husband home at night: "I
always put on a clean dress and do my hair before he comes home, and
have the kitchen tidy so he will enjoy staying."[15] In this situation, fashion
was more than ornamental; it was a key feature of interfamily politics.

According to Byington, households making the most money per week
spent the most on clothing; poorer families spent less. However, the
amount the better off families spent is surprising. Families with expenditures of $20 or more a week spent $3.36 a week on clothing, which is
almost as much as they paid for rent ($3.73). Households with weekly

costs under $12, the lowest figure in the study, spent only 94 cents a week on clothing, about half what they paid for rent ($1.88).[16]

Families in Homestead were aware of social status and the roles their homes and appearance played in the larger social dynamic. People bought fancy furniture, mainly on the installment plan to show off their front rooms, giving the façade of status, even if they struggled to make the payments. One woman Byington interviewed did not save any money for the future because she wanted her children to dress as well as their friends. Women with growing daughters were pressed to clothe them well. A woman who ran her house on a mere $2 a day bought fabric from the sales bin and made clothes for her three daughters. Although they were nice dresses and made her daughters happy, "the strain of overwork in the long run wore her out, mind and body."[17] Providing clothing was a struggle for most families, not just in the gritty steel town of Homestead, but all over the nation. According to estimates made in the late 1900s, it took $100 a year minimum to clothe a family sufficiently, but families in Homestead spent less than half that amount.[18] Ideas about social status played an important role in clothing decisions, touching upon a family's thoughts about fitting into American culture and individual niches within one's own neighborhood or city.

MEN AT WORK

Working-class men wore sturdy, durable clothes that stood up against long hours and sweat-filled days. Mass production required men to work longer hours and toil at monotonous tasks, but it also made clothing less expensive. Other workers wore uniforms or clothing suited to their jobs. Workers on the railroads, construction crews, and those who worked primarily outdoors needed outerwear that kept them warm, but fit into their limited budgets.

Since price served as a sticking point for most workers, cheap materials, such as canvas, duck, corduroy, and leather, were the primary materials used in their clothes. In the 1900s, corduroy cost from five to ten cents per yard, and leather sold for five cents per square foot. Clothes made from these materials had two prerequisites: to keep workers warm and be roomy enough to permit the range of motion necessary to perform tasks. Often included in a workingman's uniform was a sheepskin vest, which provided another layer of protection against the elements.[19]

Workers in factories wore clothing that mirrored their counterparts in high society, except that the workers' clothes were obviously less-expensive imitations. Photographs from the 1900s reveal workers on the shop floor wearing white, high-collared shirts and bow ties, vests, and hats, indicating the formal nature of the workplace. Even if the task at hand was not physical labor, men still had to have clothing that allowed them to labor at least 10 hours a day, six days a week. The rigorous formality of men's clothing on the shop floor indicates that strict rules were instituted regarding clothing and status in the factory.

Men who owned general stores or worked in the budding retail industry wore work aprons, which had developed over the years to feature various straps and pockets depending on one's occupation. Heavy-duty aprons had extra stitching and leather patches to increase durability. With the formality of clothing in a variety of professions, men donned aprons to protect their clothes against dirt and grime. They also used sleeve garters to keep extra fabric out of the way or cuff protectors to keep their white garments clean.[20]

THE BEST FASHION MONEY CAN BUY

Women who could afford to follow fashion looked to Paris and London for the latest styles. Moving slightly away from the tight-laced look of pre-twentieth century, women in the era donned corsets that produced S-shaped figures by pulling in the waist as tightly as possible and accentuating the bosom upward and the backend outward. Women looked as though their waists were pitched forward, while the rest of the body tilted backward. Topped off with a wildly exaggerated hat, women in the era looked uncomfortable in their formal garb. According to one scholar, "the finished effect is of a human lampstand rather than a woman's body."[21]

Regardless of the pain or agony of wearing them, corsets defined the look of affluent women in the 1900s. Meant to draw attention to the curve of the back, corsets used whalebone stays to force the body into this S-position. They were made from cotton or linen and worn over a vest of silky material, probably to absorb some of the chafing from the contraption. Corsets then went over the lace and required help to put on. The corset laced in the back, which tied the body into the S-shape. Women added another layer with a corset cover, also made of fine material.

Women's dresses and petticoats were frilly; accentuated with lace, ribbon, or cord; and expensive. The petticoats were stiff and worn over high-necked shirts which covered the entire neck area. Skirts were usually bell-shaped and had a slight train effect. Well-dressed women wore leather boots or suede shoes that fastened with buttons.

Hats literally topped women's fashion in the period. As the decade progressed, women's hats got larger and larger. By the end of the decade, hats had gigantic brims featuring ornate trains of feathers which hung down to the middle of the back and sometimes included lace to cover

A woman posing in front of the Oakland
Orpheum theater billboard in her theater
clothes (ca. 1900s). Courtesy of the
Oakland History Room of the Oakland
Public Library, Oakland, California.

the woman's face. Hats were artworks and fashion statements all in one. In 1905 Sears offered 75 different types of ostrich feathers to adorn women's hats. Milliners used a wide variety of bird feathers to decorate hats, including egrets, orioles, pigeons, doves, and wrens. Precariously balanced on the head or tilted to one side, the monster hats required countless hatpins to keep them in place. There was probably enough metal, in the form of pins, at one New York high society function to build a block's worth of skyscrapers.

COSMETICS

The use of cosmetics grew over the course of the 1900s, but makeup did not play a large role in women's lives. As late as 1916, one magazine estimated that only one in five people used toiletries, and the average spending per capita reached just 50 cents per year. Magazines and mail-order catalog companies did not feel women should "buy their way to beauty," so they did not feature cosmetics as they did clothing, hairpins, and other beautifying products. Gradually, however, women's interest in makeup grew, bolstered by the department stores and chain stores that carried cosmetics.[22]

Despite the supposedly low number of women using makeup in the early 1900s, a growing legion of women defied public opinion and began applying rouge and powder. The issue was contentious because up until that time, the only women who openly flaunted makeup were prostitutes and "sporting" women, urban dandies who frequented the dance halls, clubs, and cafés. The rise of urbanization, however, put more women out in public at night, and they began decorating their faces, just as they did the rest of themselves with different styles of dress. Wealthy women followed the lead of French women who were using makeup regularly. Working women in urban centers wore makeup as an inexpensive means to distinguish themselves. However, there were downsides to such notions. In 1913 a manager at Macy's fired a salesgirl who wore makeup, exclaiming, "he was not running a theatrical troupe but a department store."[23] Until World War I women simply did not have the freedom to wear makeup as they pleased. Societal norms excluded cosmetics, and women who wore makeup were treated as spectacles.

Although cosmetics took some time to catch on, the industry provided women with an opportunity to build their own businesses in the 1900s—one of the few entrepreneurial outlets available to them. Two famous African American entrepreneurs, Annie Turnbo and Sarah Breedlove, more commonly known as Madam C.J. Walker, built thriving cosmetics businesses in the 1900s. Turnbo started her business in Illinois, but later relocated to booming Saint Louis, which had a vibrant black community, before going national. The orphaned daughter of former slaves, Walker built a hair-care empire, eventually running national advertising campaigns and starting a mail-order business.

Their empires extended beyond the cosmetics industry and spoke directly to the experiences and aspirations of black women. "New visions of economic self-sufficiency, personal autonomy, and social participation, spreading through African-American communities, arose to combat the deepening privations and assaults of everyday life." Beauty culture, for Walker and Turnbo "became an economic and aesthetic form that spoke to black women's collective experiences and aspirations."[24]

PUTTING ON THE RITZ

Men's fashion in the 1900s relied heavily on styles carried over from the Victorian era of the 1890s. Designers introduced innovative styles in the new century, but for the most part, men's clothes were dark and conservative, the style made popular in the preceding decades. Men's clothes, as well as women's, served as a status symbol. Men from the upper classes adhered to fairly rigid standards and rules about how they should dress and act in public.

Everyday wear centered on the suit, almost always three-piece and buttoned high up the chest. Suits from the 1900s were cut in an oversized style. An average sized man required five yards of cloth per suit. Since oversized designs ruled the day, men's suits were basically long and loose, resulting in a bulky appearance. Narrow, high lapels accentuated the boxy look, which made men look as though their shoulders were being held back against gravity's wont to slump them forward. No suit could be complete without a vest. Men carried heavy gold pocket watches in their vests, connected to the other pocket with a watch fob, a gold chain draped in front of and across the vest.

Men's trousers were also cut large around the hips and waist, most likely to account for the portly stature of most wealthy men in the previous decades. Girth was a symbol of wealth in the Victorian era. Many politicians, lawyers, and civic leaders were immense by today's standards. Pants, called "peg-top" slacks, were pleated and cut to taper in sharply at the bottom. The British introduced cuffs at the bottom of their pants to keep their trouser bottoms dry at sporting events. Supposedly, an English noble was on his way to a wedding in New York on a rainy day and, to save the bottom of his pants, he turned them up. Arriving late to the church, he forgot to fix his pants. American men noticed the style and quickly adopted it. By 1905 cuffs were standard on most trousers in America.[25]

If a person could afford only one suit, he bought a sack suit in dark blue serge, a smooth twill fabric. Named for the formless shape of the jacket, with no waist line seam giving it a shapeless look, it came in three- or four-button styles, single-breasted, with high, short lapels. By 1907 fashionable men wore sack suits of varying colors and adopted a more youthful look by having the suit shaped at the hips and waist. The sack suit adapted to the changing ideals of masculinity and strength exemplified by Theodore Roosevelt. The paunch of the 1890s was being pushed aside by the vigorous, energetic twentieth-century man. "The goal of the well-dressed man in this decade was to look genteel, prosperous, and athletic in the broad-chested fashion of Theodore Roosevelt," noted fashion historians. "A sack suit of dark blue, dark gray, or black all but guaranteed this look."[26]

The growing legion of businessmen in the United States forced designers to make a suit more formal than the sack variety. For this look, the coat extended down to just above the knees, an adaptation of the English walking coat suit. The proper accessories, such as a high silk hat, leather gloves, and walking stick, emphasized the formality of the suit. Also known as the business frock suit, the style quickly gained acceptance in the banking world, a contrast to the ultraconservative attire worn by today's banking executives. The importance of the suit, however, is that it signaled a move toward suits that were less bulky and more in line with current trends emanating from the Continent.[27]

Formal evening attire for men included the tailcoat, which unlike the everyday suit, fit snuggly against the body. The main feature of the coat, the tails, stretched below the break in the knee. The only thing the tailcoat had in common with a business suit was the heavy cloth, weighing between 16 and 18 ounces a yard. When attending the theater or dinner on the town, men wore stiff, attached or unattached collars. One version of the collar, called the poke, had a slight curve in the front. The other style, the winged collar, came into fashion during the decade and is still the customary collar on men's tuxedo shirts today. Shirt studs were usually made of pearl, but they were spaced out on the shirtfront more than current styles. In addition to a heavy overcoat, formal wear called for high silk hats and a fashionable walking stick.

HAIRSTYLES

Women wore their hair long in the 1900s. As a matter of fact, to balance their gargantuan hats, which could hold an entire family of stuffed birds or enough feathers to make a down comforter, women added artificial hair as padding. A commentary in the *Ladies' Home Journal* published in 1909 declared that men would be puzzled to see "the hair of womankind increase amazingly in quantity."[28] Critics of female hairpieces called them "rats" or "puffs."

The *Ladies' Home Journal*, under the guidance of Edward Bok, served as a monthly Bible of fashion for women in the 1900s. Bok counseled them on everything from proper decorum to home furnishing and decoration. Bok's influence on American women grew so pervasive that newspaper comedians targeted him with jokes. His only rival in that department was Henry Ford, who introduced the Model T.

While doing women a great service by consulting physicians, nurses, and other authorities for the magazine, Bok had a bit of teacher/crusader in him, which led him down a path contrary to his readers. Bok led a campaign to have fashion based on styles emanating from New York, not Paris or London. He instituted the slogan "American Fashion for American Women" and pushed it heavily in the magazine. Despite the great deal of energy he expended, Bok found little success. His defeat came about on the grounds of "commercial forces and feminine nature."[29] He also tried to get women to stop decorating their hats with egret plumes, which necessitated the slaughter of millions of the birds.

Eventually, after his magazine campaign failed but quadrupled sales, he championed legislation in Congress that was later adopted.

At formal occasions, women teased their hair into a pompadour, in which the hair was primped up on the side, with a bun at the crown. This style helped balance a woman's hat. As hats got bigger, women moved the bun from the top of the head to the back as an extra pin holder. Sometimes, women accentuated their femininity by allowing tiny ringlets to hang down from the sides in front of the ears. Women used curling irons, waving irons, and other tools to manipulate their hair in the 1900s. To keep it all in place, various hairpins, combs, and hairpieces were utilized.[30]

Men's hair care, whether on the face or on top of the head, went through many changes in the 1900s. Full beards were in style from the 1850s until 1901, but then they went out quickly. Moustaches were popular for most of the decade, spurred by Roosevelt's own walrus-like look, but even then, many women disliked them. Many heroes of romantic novels wore long, blonde mustaches which they stroked, seemingly on every page. The clean-shaven look served as an egalitarian symbol for men of all classes. A reporter for the Chicago *Chronicle*, Edith Sessions Tupper, commented on the shaved face: "There is a certain distinction about the clean-shaven man which the wearer of whiskers can never possess. Moreover, a smooth face is a stimulant to high thoughts."[31]

Hairstyles varied for men in the 1900s, but the fact that they paid attention to their hair at all proved that hair had become a status symbol as well. Some wore their hair with a part on the side and a curled effect on top. Crew cuts were also popular, with short sides and varying lengths on the top. Sideburns were an option, especially on college campuses where men experimented with ways to distinguish themselves. Most men put some kind of tonic in their hair to accentuate their natural waves or to slick it back. The thinking behind slick hair was that it brought an air of sophistication, especially to the newly clean-shaven man.

Facial hair and hairstyle categorized the men in Charles Gibson's illustrations. The older men were portly, usually combing what little remaining hair they had over a bald spot, and they sported waxed mustaches with the ends curled up. Most of the younger dandies in Gibson's drawings, modeled after novelist, journalist, and adventurer Richard Harding Davis, were clean-shaven with hair parted down the middle or on one side, slicked back to emphasize high cheekbones and square jaws.

Fashion in the 1900s did not change as dramatically as in the 1920s or 1960s, but the decade gradually loosened many of the severe rules weighing style down. Americans in the decade still primarily looked to Europe for design cues, but adapted those trends to fit into American

Typical swimming attire at Daytona Beach, Florida (1909). Courtesy of the Florida State Archives.

life. Thus, the shirtwaist—providing a wider range of motion and increased comfort—became the standard uniform for many women workers. Men's fashions also became slightly less rigid, though it still hinged on heavy, dark fabrics. A breezy style put forth by Gibson's male characters steadily took hold, although it did not catch on fully until the glitzy days of the 1920s.

If anything, people across both racial and class divides grew more style conscious in the 1900s. People down the economic scale looked to those above them for fashion cues. Mass production allowed people to dress well without spending huge sums on clothing. On a daily basis, formality ruled the day, though its grip weakened as the nation moved toward the later decades—skirts rose to above the ankle, while men adopted lighter tweed jackets. The shirtwaist, worn by both female factory workers and wealthy wives and daughters of the wealthy, helped usher in a looser style, based on functionality, rather than class status.

With the rise of department stores, chain stores, and mail-order businesses, fashion grew into a nationwide phenomenon. Department stores were a place to be seen (for the wealthy) and a place to get a firsthand look at all the goods one could aspire to (for the working- and middle-classes). Magazines and advertisers trumpeted the importance of fashion as well. Taken as a whole, these influences combined to make fashion a part of people's daily lives.

Looking back, style mavens from the 1900s were not much different from the ones we see today. While today's supermodels and designers have more outlets for attracting the public eye, ideas regarding fashion and style were sold to the public the same way 100 years ago. It took an entire industry working together to spread the notion that fashion could and should be a daily concern. Fashion and style were important parts of the expanding consumer culture in the United States. Creating concepts about style and design allowed the fashion industry to develop a captive, self-perpetuating audience which demanded new products on a regular basis. Thus, the industry played a major role in establishing the idea that buying and acquiring goods were crucial aspects of being an American.

6

Food

Mary had a little lamb,
And when she saw it sicken,
She shipped it off to Packingtown,
And now it's labeled chicken.

—New York *Evening Post*

The skills farmers and food producers in the United States acquired in the decades leading up to 1900 hastened the nation's ascent to world economic and military superiority. In the first decade of the twentieth century, the combination of agriculture and technology pushed the country to even greater heights. An interesting dichotomy was underfoot. America's agricultural prowess (enhanced by technological advances in farm machinery) fueled its industrial strength by providing the foodstuffs to feed the growing urban centers, even as agriculture's overall importance as part of the national economy lessened. More important, heightened technology gave farmers the ability to grow more food with less manpower. Thus, the sons and daughters of the farm were freed to move to the cities and provide the brute force needed to staff the growing factories.

According to one historian, "the Agricultural Revolution hastened the Industrial Revolution in various ways," including the increase in production per farmer which allowed rural workers to move into industry without diminishing the food supply. Furthermore, "the profits derived from agriculture could be used for buying manufactured goods, thereby further stimulating industry and manufacturing."[1] Although historically farm families had been nearly self-sufficient, advertisers and manufac-

turers included them in the equation as they established a national consumer culture, based on purchasing mass-produced goods that would
have been made by hand decades earlier or done without. The Sears and
Roebuck mail-order catalog was a staple in the homes of America's farmers, propelling the consumer culture by reaching out even to those unable to go to the shopping meccas in the cities. Farm families, especially
wives, were spared many hours of backbreaking labor by the affordable
commodities offered in the catalogs, including sewing machines, cream
separators, and inexpensive clothing.[2]

The food industry, along with machinery and tobacco, played an important role in the development of the modern corporation. Prior to
World War I, the United States had 39 major corporations in machinery
and 35 in food production. The first successful large-scale food producers
processed perishable items. Meatpacking corporations, including Ar-
mour, Swift, Wilson, Morris, and Cudahay, were early examples of that
national corporation and were followed closely by breweries, such as
Anheuser Busch and Schlitz. Other leading food producers made cheap
packaged goods using continuous-process machinery (Quaker Oats,
Heinz, Borden's, Libby, and Coca-Cola).[3] Not only did these corporations
establish business processes, they stimulated the budding advertising
and public relations industries.

American corporations fueled an increase in food production, but
shortcomings came to light regarding the health and safety standards
used in the manufacturing process. Muckraking author Upton Sinclair
published *The Jungle* in 1906, which examined the horrendous conditions
in Chicago's meatpacking industry. He described the unsanitary methods used to make sausage and even insinuated that workers had fallen
into the vats and become part of the product. While other industries were
not as flagrant in their violation of the public's trust, most food producers used some form of additives to enhance the flavor, smell, or coloring
of products. Many adulterants turned out to be harmful, such as acids
used to mask spoiled beef or hallucinogenic drugs added to headache
remedies.

The food-producing corporations grew powerful in the decades leading up to the twentieth century and solidified their growing power in
the early 1900s. When congressional members first introduced pure food
legislation, the food trusts derailed the bills by using their collective lob-
bying skills and money to thwart any such attempts. It took a polemic
tract like *The Jungle* and the subsequent full support of President Theodore Roosevelt to best the combined efforts of the food producers. In the
end, the public outcry against unhealthy production methods and chemical additions rose to such a deafening roar that legislation could no
longer be blocked.

Although legislators passed pure food and drug laws in 1906, food

Two female sugar factory workers in Crochett, California (1905).
Courtesy of the Contra Costa County Historical Society.

producers did not comply with the new regulations overnight. Nevertheless, awareness of the need to clean up the food-preparation industry attests to the level of sophistication of the pure food activists of the 1900s. They were extremely perceptive in fighting for pure food laws, even in the face of the opposition of powerful corporate trusts.

WORKING UP AN APPETITE

When Margaret Byington conducted her study of families and household budgets in Homestead, Pennsylvania, in 1908, she soon learned that knocking on the front door failed to get a response. To get the attention of the woman who ran the house, she needed to go to the back door, which opened in to the kitchen. Here one could feel the warmth of the hearth and smell the aromas of cooking vegetables and meats.

The planning involved with purchasing food and preparing it was mentally taxing and physically demanding for working-class women. Harsh conditions surrounded these women. "In spite of the high wages among steel workers, the problem Homestead housewives face in trying to provide food and a good home on a man's earnings is no easy one." It took determination to make ends meet. "Excellent management is required to secure a really adequate food supply with the amount that can be set aside for this purpose."[4]

Whether it was oatmeal and eggs for breakfast or sweet potatoes and roast beef for supper, food preparation was "economically her [working-class housewives] most important task." Food accounted for nearly half the total budget and was the largest single expenditure. Women manipulated the amount spent on food to coincide with fluctuations in earnings. By using "thrift and ability," women could change the diet "without lessening the comfort of the family." Since Pittsburgh had a higher cost of living than any other city of its size in the nation, women in Homestead actively engaged in methods of balancing the budget while providing enough food to keep the family fed.[5]

The task of balancing the monthly budget grew in importance during the time Byington investigated Homestead. The United States suffered through a financial panic in 1907–1908 that crippled many industries. In Homestead, U.S. Steel responded by cutting production in half, which had not occurred in at least 15 years. The slowdown caught most workers off guard, and families, who depended on the mill for their lives, suffered a significant drop in wages. Many workers took home less than half what they made before the cutback. Because the entire city depended on the mill, people had no chance for outside employment. The slowdown at the mill caused a ripple effect throughout the community—every store, restaurant, and link in the service industry felt the effects of the reduction. Even those who took in boarders to supplement their incomes suffered when the renters could not pay the rent.

Oddly enough, the typical Homestead family responded by increasing the percentage of money they spent on food each week, while virtually eliminating every other unnecessary expense.[6] During harsh conditions, many families got loans from banks or credit accounts from individual stores, but the women running the household budgets did not cut back on food. They may have spent less each week in total, but the women running the household budgets found a way to keep their families fed. Using tact and skill, many women were able to stretch the budget by substituting less expensive foods in place of more expensive ones.

For most mill families, the lunch pail played a central role in the family eating dynamic. The husband ate at work, but the remaining members of the family unit usually ate a light midday meal. "The women take great pains to make it appetizing, especially by adding preserves in a little cup in the corner of the bucket," reported Byington. "They try to give the man what he likes the most, apparently half from pity at the cold food and hard work that fall to his lot."[7] When the man of the house worked long hours for low pay, children were often caught in the middle. Working-class children received meager lunches, often nothing more than mush and milk with bread and molasses. The household revolved around the man's needs and until children became income producers, they were kept on the periphery. The importance of the lunch pail in working-class families remained a constant throughout the twentieth century.

Sunday dinner was a festive occasion for most Homestead families. The night before an extra piece of roast was purchased and married sons and daughters were invited to share the meal. Most men worked Sunday evenings, which muted the festivity somewhat. Holidays also served as a time for family get-togethers, especially Christmas. Under normal conditions, the mill stopped only twice a year: on Christmas and on the Fourth of July. Formal guests were infrequent in Homestead on other occasions. With supper being shifted on a regular basis to meet the husband's work schedule, people in mill towns did not use the meal as a social gathering.[8]

A single female factory worker, like 16-year-old Sadie Frowne, a laborer in the Brownsville sweatshop district of Brooklyn, was less concerned about food. She lived with a roommate (Ella), and they paid a combined $1.50 a week for their room. Frowne even managed to save 25 percent of her $4.00 weekly pay. Together the two women spent just over two dollars a week on food, which included cocoa and oatmeal for breakfast, the best quality of bread at five cents a loaf, and not skimping on fresh meat or vegetables. Their main entrees consisted of chops, steaks, veal, or fish, ranging from 8 to 20 cents a pound.[9]

When Frowne moved two years later, she still managed to live on $2 a week, half of that for food. She used the extra money she accumulated to buy clothes, attend night school, and pay for entertainment. Her co-workers harassed her for spending so much on clothes. Frowne countered by arguing "a girl must have clothes if she is to go into good society at Ulmer Park or Coney Island or the theater. . . . A girl who does not dress well is stuck in a corner, even if she is pretty."[10] Food simply did not play a large role in the life of a working-class woman. She had a steady income and learned to save at an early age. Her future looked bright, as long as she could maintain an income of more than $5 a week.

Studies of nutritional habits of working-class families in the 1900s have shown that variations in diet hinged on income. For most families, meals consisted of a handful of staples, such as large loaves of bread, stewed meats, potatoes, onions, cabbage, and condiments, like pickles. In the summer months, an abundance of fresh fruits and vegetables added diversity to meals. Dietary problems set in when the family's income changed owing to unexpected variances from layoffs, unemployment, or serious injury or illness. Sociologists, nutritionists, and social workers in the 1900s studied dietary challenges from the perspective of immigrant status, usually delineating between native-born and non-native immigrants. They often overlooked the basic consideration of income and how that primary factor played into a family's ideas regarding food preparation and nutrition. Most nutritional experts felt that a remedy was to

The Davy Crockett Saloon at 868 Broadway in Oakland, California (1910).
Courtesy of the Oakland History Room of the Oakland Public Library,
Oakland, California.

teach immigrants to "Americanize" their diets, when in fact, giving them access to steady jobs that paid well would have eliminated their food-related problems.[11]

Changing the eating habits of immigrant families developed into something of a crusade in the 1900s. Immigrants were discouraged from eating spicy, mixed foods by home economists and social workers. Even the nation's most respected "experts" on these issues offered theories that would be considered idiotic today. Robert Woods, the leader of a top Boston settlement house, foolishly explained that the rise in death rates among second-generation Italians was in part due to their native diet. He felt that changing their diet was the only way to make Italians adapt to American life. Nutritionists also believed that any diet that mixed foods together was inferior, since they thought that more nutrients were expelled in the preparation.[12]

Reformers believed that something sinister was underfoot among immigrant families who openly chose to not Americanize. "The acrid smells of garlic and onions wafting through the immigrant quarters seemed to provide unpleasant evidence that their inhabitants found American ways unappealing," according to one historian, "that they continued to find foreign (and dangerous) ideas as palatable as their foreign food." Corporations undertook programs to force their foreign workers to adopt the habits of this nation. International Harvester, for instance, set up a program in its Midwestern plants which featured a "model working-man's home" to teach wives how to cook American style.[13]

These corporate initiatives continued over the next several decades, even up to World War II. Many companies, including the most famous attempt, Ford's Sociological Department, established divisions directly responsible for encouraging non-native workers to adopt an American way of life. Eventually, in striving for a middle-class lifestyle, many immigrants did become Americanized, but if there was one tie they kept to their homelands, it usually involved food. What we find so appealing about our own individual nationalities today, while retaining our feelings about being Americans, is exactly what they hoped to eliminate from immigrant cultures in the 1900s and subsequent years. Luckily, they were unsuccessful.

The status of the United States as the world's leading agricultural producer helped families in towns like Homestead and other industry-driven cities remain viable in tough economic times. In the 1900s, industrialism pushed well beyond the country's steel mills and heavy manufacturing plants. Food production played an important role in establishing the United States as the world's exporter. Factories continued to manufacture foodstuffs in recessions, and the growth of the industry forced companies to find outlets, whether that meant cutting back prices or finding other alternatives. Laborers dependent on factory work to survive were hurt by the periodic economic slowdowns, but the fact that technology invaded the food production industry actually helped them weather the hard times.

THE FARM BECOMES A CORPORATION

In the decades leading up to the twentieth century, farming in the United States changed dramatically as a result of technological innovations. As railroads spidered across the West, settlers poured into the fertile lands and began cultivating wheat on the plains. In Minnesota and the Dakotas, advances in harvesting and planting allowed farmers to increase their levels of production vastly. When the wheat belt moved west, the corn and hog belts moved to the Midwest, later followed by the rise of the dairy industry, primarily in Wisconsin and Iowa. By the 1880s, railroads made daily stops in farming areas of the Midwest to pick up fresh vegetables and fruits to be shipped to the growing urban areas. Milk production also flourished with the railroads. American farmers sold 2 billion pounds of whole milk in 1870, but more than 18 billion pounds in 1900. Technology clearly changed the way in which farmers produced their wares. As a result, people in the cities benefited from having a supply of goods that were affordable and easy to acquire.[14]

The development of a nationwide railroad system transformed farming from a regional industry to a national one. When the Illinois Central Railway linked up with New Orleans, for example, the Chicago market benefited from an influx of fresh Southern vegetables, while the Crescent City received wheat, corn, and salted pork. Later, the use of refrigerated cars allowed growers to ship perishable items over greater distances.

The mechanization occurring on the farms and in the distribution process actually hurt many farmers. They had to buy new machinery and land continually to keep up with their competitors while the prices for their crops dropped. Large-scale production, freight costs, and machinery prices hurt agrarians and forced many into tenant farming, especially in the South and Midwest. Laborers who did not own the land they tilled did 35 percent of all farming in the United States in 1900. Small farmers disappeared as the country transitioned to industrialism. The Jeffersonian idea of an agrarian nation became less of a reality. For urban dwellers, however, the results were fantastic—they had a greater variety of fresher vegetables, fruits, and meats to choose from at affordable prices. To feed the industrial machine agrarians had to embrace the ideas of conglomeration and incorporation.[15]

Commercial farmers entered into a period of unmatched prosperity in the 1900s. Theodore Roosevelt's Commission on Country Life reported in 1909, "There has never been a time when the American farmer was as well off as he is today, when we consider not only his earning power, but the comforts and advantages he may secure."[16] The victory of industrialism and the subsequent transformation of farming into big business ushered in a new era for farmers, but countless small farmers were starving to death and barely maintaining subsistence. The success of farm conglomerates gave rise to a nostalgic view of farmers and farming, but the real picture could be quite grim.

As a result of the mechanization and organization of farmers, many became specialists. They produced one crop, often specific to the particular region they farmed, and moved away from general production. This line of thinking ultimately increased the stratification between wealthy farmers (who had adopted the ideas of big business) and those who were left to their own devices. "The modern farmers' organizations," explained one historian, "have shown no sympathy for, have often indeed shown much hostility to, the interests of those farmers who were dispossessed or bypassed or displaced by the processes of prosperity."[17] After 1900 big business, upset by the antibusiness rhetoric coming from the nation's farmers, actively courted farmers into an alliance which ultimately benefited both parties. Business interests, such as bankers, merchants, and the railroads, among others, had a large stake in the success of farmers, so it was only natural to invite a common spirit among businessmen and farmers. Most farmers welcomed the alliance with business. In 1907 one farmer queried the editor of *Wallace's Farmer*, "Had you not better take up the subject of how to market our produce, rather than to tell us all the time how to produce more?"[18]

The mix of agriculture and big business remained a main theme throughout the twentieth century. Farm associations and agricultural colleges urged farmers to act like captains of industry. They hired government lobbyists and eagerly used politics to wield their newfound power. However, the elevation of farmers as a whole did not eliminate the suffering of small farmers and migratory workers who relied on seasonal work for survival. "While marginal farmers and migratory laborers live in desperate poverty and squalor," successful agriculturists have been able to respond to the canons of conspicuous consumption and the American love for luxurious gadgetry."[19]

THE PURE FOOD AND DRUG ACT

Most people associate the drive for healthy, unadulterated food in the early twentieth century with the muckraking work of socialist author Upton Sinclair and his best-selling novel *The Jungle*, published in 1906. The assumption, however, that pure food activism began with Sinclair is incorrect. Discerning citizens and watch groups lamented the state of American food production long before Sinclair's study. The chief critic of tainted food was Dr. Harvey W. Wiley, the chief chemist of the Department of Agriculture (1883–1912). Wiley waged public skirmishes against large corporations and business enterprises for the good of the common people.

In April 1900, Senator William E. Mason from Illinois wrote a long article in the *North American Review* lamenting the amount of food adulteration in the United States. Senator Mason placed the blame on the growing corporations, intent on running one another out of business. "The extent of this adulteration it is difficult to comprehend, but it grows largely, in fact almost entirely, out of excessive competition." He pointed to a Congressional investigation into the flour industry, which revealed "very dangerous and absolutely insoluble substances were being used to adulterate flour."[20] In fact, the flour producers who were not using additives pushed for the inquiry because the offending companies tarnished the reputation of the entire industry, especially in the growing overseas market. American flour manufacturers could ill afford to have Europeans doubting the quality of their products.

Senator Mason called for national legislation that would prevent unhealthy materials from finding their way into the nation's food supply.

He openly distinguished between additives that diminished the health value of the product versus adulterations that harmed consumers. "If milk is diluted by water, the only danger to health is lack of nourishment, but it is also a fraud upon the consumer," Mason explained. "If, however, it is preserved, as it is in some cases, by the use of acids, it becomes a menace to public health." Mason saw the issue in black and white—consumers should be aware of every ingredient in the foods they buy and manufacturers should be required to provide this information.[21]

Calling for the continuation of the pure food activism sweeping the nation, which led to a series of pure food congresses and investigations into additives, Mason touted the benefits of good-faith labeling. By encouraging the "honest manufacturer" and protecting them from dishonest competition, Congress would in turn offer protection to consumers, who would know what ingredients they were ingesting. Furthermore, Mason declared, the nation as a whole would prosper by establishing a reputation for high standards regarding food products, which would increase the demand for American goods all over the world. Mason also raised the bar by calling out to a higher power, explaining, "We shall raise the standard of the purity of goods that go into the human stomach, and by the use of better foods, make a better citizen. The destiny of the nations depends upon how they feed themselves."[22]

Practically every food manufactured in the 1900s contained some kind of chemical additive that was potentially harmful to consumers. Butcher shops had readily available bottles of "Freezem" or "Preservaline" on hand to deal with spoiled meat; ketchups, canned vegetables, chocolates, and skim milk all contained some kind of additive—sulphite, benzoate, and boracic acid, among others. In many respects, science served the public interest by allowing companies to mass-produce foodstuffs, thus feeding greater numbers of people. However, food producers used science to mask unhealthy additives and preservatives, which contributed to an overtly noxious diet for most people.

While activists rallied against unhealthy products, politicians were less willing to fight the food companies out of fear of retribution. On the surface, the need for legislation seemed obvious, but it took years to get legislation through Congress because the legislators were unwilling to fight big business. One of the first rallying points occurred when Edward Bok, editor of the *Ladies' Home Journal*, took up the fight against patent medicines. Bok waged the battle in the magazine, which had more than 1 million readers in the 1900s, but came up against an industry that had more than $59 million in sales in 1900. Although Bok proved many patent medicines contained opium, cocaine, alcohol, morphine, and other hallucinogenic drugs, his efforts did not produce the national legislation he hoped to see. Actually, there were some indications that patent medicine sales increased as a result of Bok's work, proving the old adage "any publicity is good publicity."

As early as 1898, farmers and chemists came together to fight unhealthy standards. They formed the National Association of State Drug and Food Departments. The group lobbied for stiffer regulations regarding food production and uniform food and drug laws across all states, so that farmers could meet one standard. Farmers who produced wholesome foods quickly realized that they were being hurt in the marketplace by doing so. One historian noted, "Properly prepared and wholesome foods were at a disadvantage in the market because they were likely to look less vivid and to cost more."[23]

Wiley, the pure food movement's greatest activist, pursued the large corporations relentlessly during the 1900s. His fight took on the tone of a moral crusade against tainted food products. Taking the skirmish to the streets, Wiley experimented on volunteers in 1903, feeding them foods to see if they were damaging. Dubbed the "poison squad," Wiley's experimentation drew others into the pure food movement, including many middle-class women, who were the ideal audience—they held the purchasing power in families and they realized the difference between healthy and unhealthy foods. For his part in the food wars, Wiley earned the nickname "Old Borax." His fight eventually included working closely with certain food companies (a clear case of each side gaining in the process), Wiley getting the publicity and funds he needed to drive the effort, while the companies, most notably Pittsburgh's Heinz, had their names associated with untainted food.

The many constituencies fighting for unadulterated food (doctors, chemists, women's groups, farmers, and so on) organized into a cohesive whole at the 1904 World's Fair held in Saint Louis. Using visual demonstrations, the pure food activists at the exposition took the fight to the big businesses duping the public in a booth nearby the corporations' exhibits. The activists took popular foods that were dyed to hide impurities and extracted the dye from the food. Then they used the coloring to dye pieces of silk and wool. It did not take much more than this visual display to get the fair's hundreds of thousands of attendees talking about the duplicity taking place among food corporations. The pure food exhibit at the World's Fair caused a national scandal, but big business still thwarted national legislation by outspending and outsmarting the activists. It took an even more pervasive event to get people incensed enough to act: the publication of *The Jungle* in 1906.[24]

Sinclair wanted *The Jungle* to open America's eyes to the evils of capitalism and big business. His grotesque depiction of the meatpacking industry—rancid by-products, acids, additives, and dead workers going into sausage-making vats—turned people's stomachs and created an outrage that could no longer be suppressed. The time had come for pure food and drug legislation, and Roosevelt turned his attention to the problem.

Outraged by the descriptions of the meatpacking industry, Roosevelt assigned Agriculture Secretary James Wilson, as well as Attorney General William Moody, to investigate the problem. Roosevelt realized that the dastardly conditions described in Sinclair's book made government look bad, especially his own administration. Barely hiding his contempt for Sinclair's socialist rants, Roosevelt wrote to the author, who had sent him a personal copy of the book. He concluded the letter by telling Sinclair "the specific evils you point out shall, if their existence be proved, and if I have the power, be eradicated."[25]

The task force Roosevelt assembled learned that meatpackers were illegally using government inspection labels giving products the seal of approval because the only real inspection occurred on the killing floors, not at any other stage of preparation. The commissioners reported back to Roosevelt, publishing a report explaining, "We saw meat shoveled from filthy wooden floors, piled on tables rarely washed, pushed from room to room in rotten box carts, in all of which processes it was in the way of gathering dirt, splinters, floor filth, and the expectoration of tuberculous and other diseased workers."[26]

Roosevelt used this report to convince legislators and the public that the time had come for national legislation. After the president released the full report, no one questioned the need for regulation. Even the staunchest members of the meat trusts realized they were beaten. With Roosevelt's full backing, various leaders in Congress introduced a series of bills that dealt with pure food and drugs, meat inspection, and labeling. Senator Albert J. Beveridge passed the first legislation in May 1906, which required government inspectors at every point in meat production, not just on the killing floors. Public uproar over the government report reached a crescendo. The Pure Food and Drug Act passed a month later by a vote of 240–17. The dissenters were Democrats who did not oppose the bill but protested under the belief that food regulation should be handled by state governments.[27]

Roosevelt's willingness to throw his weight behind pure food legislation served as a turning point. The president could clearly identify the villains and victims in the fight—he knew a winning cause when he saw one. However, Roosevelt showed a great deal of flexibility and tact while maneuvering the various bills through Congress. There were powerful forces on the side of the meatpackers, but he used his public power to circumvent the collective money and influence of the beef trusts. One powerful foe, Congressman James W. Wadsworth of New York, supported by the food corporations, introduced weakened legislation, then fought the president as he pushed amendments to it. His battle against Roosevelt ultimately cost him his seat in Congress, which he had held since 1881. His constituents were infuriated by his refusal to support Roosevelt, and they retaliated by voting him out of office. The defeat sent a chill down the backs of Roosevelt's critics who felt he had too much power.[28]

CHANGING DIETS

With a national dialogue regarding the consumption of healthy foods taking place in the 1900s, Americans adopted a simpler diet, based less on the heavy fare consumed in earlier decades. In fact, advertisers played on the consumers' desire for "pure" foods by stressing a brand's healthiness in national advertising campaigns in magazines and newspapers. The most notable example of this phenomenon occurred among breakfast foods. Breakfast food companies, such as Kellogg with Corn Flakes and Post with Grape-Nuts and Toasties, convinced consumers that they should substitute traditional meat-oriented breakfasts with highly processed grains.

One of the strangest stories in the history of American food production is the rise of ready-to-eat breakfast cereals. After many years of testing and failure, William K. Kellogg and his brother—Battle Creek, Michigan, sanatorium director Dr. John Harvey Kellogg—invented Corn Flakes as a vegetarian health food. Each later claimed to be the brains behind the creation. In turn, Battle Creek became the world capital of the Adventists, under the fiery leadership of Ellen Gould Harmon White. John Harvey Kellogg transformed the Battle Creek sanatorium into a thriving health resort catering to the nation's elite. Linking Corn Flakes with the hospital gave the cereal the kind of health food tie it needed to gain acceptance among a wider audience. Though the Kelloggs later broke with the mercurial White, the result of their experimentation turned the Michigan city into the world's breakfast cereal capital.[29]

The Kellogg sanatorium transformed into a hodge-podge of eccentrics, each pushing some wildly fantastic cure for a variety of ailments. The site was overrun with phrenologists, mesmerists, and spiritual healers of varying ideological bents. Despite the circus-like atmosphere at the Kellogg retreat and the rich patrons flocking through its gates, Corn Flakes found success among middle-class consumers who linked the product with good health. Dr. Kellogg managed to stay above the fray despite the presence of the lesser healers and spiritualists. Kellogg won an international reputation as a surgeon and medical guru.

One of Kellogg's ex-patients, Saint Louis real estate magnate and food inventor Charles W. Post, began his own company and sold Grape-Nuts, clearly modeled after Kellogg's Corn Flakes. By establishing the Post Company near Kellogg's, Post gained from the connection to the sanatorium. The success of the two companies led to more firms establishing operations in Battle Creek. At one point there were 44 breakfast food companies and 6 companies making health drinks.[30]

The packaged breakfast foods, artfully advertised by Kellogg, Post, and the others, gained wide acceptance because of middle America's concern about bacteria. Since the food came in a sealed container, the public assumed it was safe. Post, to the dismay of health food activists, also inferred that eating his products made people healthier. He marketed Postum cereal as "brain food" and claimed it cured malaria and loose teeth, among other things. Other cereals claimed to make red blood, cure blindness, and alleviate an inflamed appendix.[31] Even though breakfast food manufacturers came under fire for spouting such nonsense, as a whole they completely altered Americans' breakfast food. "Their clever use of the new promotional techniques had created a mass market for a food product that had not even existed before, one which replaced, not supplemented, competing foodstuffs," said one historian.[32]

William K. Kellogg, who took over the business aspects of the company, realized that by using repetitive advertising and targeting children, he would be able to revolutionize the breakfast table. He pictured children on packaging, especially the instantly recognizable "Sweetheart of the Corn," a young girl who beamed up at the consumer with a bright smile while clutching a corn stock. Kellogg promoted the product by offering children prizes for collecting box tops, gave away free samples, and sponsored corn shows in counties around the nation. Children, Kellogg rightly deduced, held the key to their parents' wallets.[33]

FOOD INNOVATIONS

Many of the foods people take for granted today came to prominence in the 1900s. With the rise of advertising and marketing to promote products and the public's increasing level of disposable income, food companies responded by introducing innovative products which soon became staples in the national diet. In the years just prior to 1900, Campbell's began producing canned soup after figuring out how to condense the contents, thus making storage and shipping practical. The company claimed to have sold 16 million cans in 1904. The next year, Campbell's first magazine ad appeared in *Good Housekeeping*. On the product side, it introduced Campbell's Pork and Beans.[34]

The decade was a rousing success for Jell-O. By 1906 sales flirted with the $1 million mark. The company introduced its first trademark in 1903, the Jell-O Girl, who starred in all advertising promotions. Modeled after the daughter (Elizabeth King) of an artist at Jell-O's advertising agency, she was shown playing in her nursery with Jell-O packages, rather than toys. Over the next four years, the original Jell-O Girl graced magazine ads, store displays, and many items used as sales premiums, including spoons, molds, and china dessert dishes. In 1908 artist Rose O'Neill, the creator of Kewpie dolls, modernized the Jell-O Girl and gave her a more grownup look. Jell-O jumped on the pure food bandwagon in 1904 by producing its first recipe book and stating its approval by food commissioners. Chocolate, cherry, and peach had all joined the family of flavors by 1907.[35]

Although Heinz introduced ketchup in 1876, the product did not find its true calling until 1900 when New Haven, Connecticut, diner owner Louis Lassen placed a beef patty between two pieces of toast and the hamburger was born. Naturally, in hindsight, the very next year the first hotdogs were sold at the Polo Grounds in New York, although they were not called "hotdogs" until 1906, when an artist drew a dachshund inside a bun for the *New York Journal*. Continuing with the fast-food theme, the Pepsi-Cola Company was founded in North Carolina in 1902, and the first soda fountain was set up at Philadelphia's Broad Street Pharmacy. In 1904 the banana split came into being when David Strickler of Strickler's Drug Store in Latrobe, Pennsylvania created the gooey delight. Two years later, the hot fudge sundae was invented at C.C. Brown's ice cream parlor in Hollywood, California.[36]

The 1900s also witnessed the rise of the chocolate empire of Milton S. Hershey. A native Pennsylvanian, Hershey began his career as an apprentice to a candy maker in Lancaster. After moving out on his own, he tried opening shops in Philadelphia, Denver, Chicago, and New York, but they all failed. Hershey finally found success when an importer wanted to introduce his caramels to England. By 1894 Hershey had built a thriving candy business.[37]

Hershey's big breakthrough occurred at the World's Columbian Exposition when he saw a German chocolate-making machine and decided he would make his own. In 1900 he sold off all his other interests, including the caramel factory and his general candy division, and put all his effort into making chocolate. In 1903 Hershey bought a large tract of land in Derry Township, which had been a cornfield, and then built a town around the central factory, later renamed Hershey, Pennsylvania. The candy maker experimented with a variety of ingredients until he devised his own secret concoction. He then turned his attention to the planned community around the factory, which would house his workers and their families. He learned from the mistakes made by George Pullman in establishing a similar planned community in Illinois, and he built different styles of affordable housing for the workers. Hershey took great care in establishing churches, schools, and other institutions.[38]

CONCLUSION

Food production, distribution, and consumption all changed during the 1900s. Technology caught up and surpassed pure physical manpower, allowing farmers to produce more than the nation's food needs.

In turn, these influences modified the way in which people viewed food—never again would products be consumed without concern over contents and additives. People worried about the health consequences of tainted products. Discussion of issues related to food became political fodder and were elevated to the national stage. The president himself wielded his great power to ensure the passage of a pure food and drug act.

The amount of food people ate in the 1900s was in direct relation to their position on the social ladder. Under normal conditions, steelworkers and their families in Homestead could afford a varied menu including fresh fruits and vegetables. However, when the mill cut back operations and workers brought home half as much pay, acquiring food became a critical part of the overall budget, which included paying rent or mortgage and utilities. Those on the other end of the economic spectrum had little or no concern regarding food consumption. They hosted lavish parties with meals that lasted several hours as dish upon dish greeted the guests. With the money to hire professional cooks and servants, food was a means to an end, not something to worry about—unless the neighbor in the next mansion over could outdo your meal or performance. As in today's society, the gap between subsistence and decadence went on for miles.

In the 1900s, like today, food meant many things to different people. Some worked in the food industry, from farmers in the dusty fields to waitresses at lunch counters in downtown department stores; while others toiled in the slaughterhouses of Chicago or St. Louis. For most working-class people, food was simply food, unlike today, with television stations and magazines constantly making preparation and the subsequent meals a grandiose affair. Although women at the turn of the last century looked to magazines for recipes and tips, there weren't any Martha Stewarts or Julia Childs—and certainly nothing like the Food Network—pumping out food-related shows 24 hours a day. Women delighted in cooking well and the housewives in Byington's study were proud of their ability to stretch their food dollar, but in the end, food served as fuel. Technology and big business changed the way people viewed food in the 1900s, but its importance on a daily basis remains constant throughout time.

The 1900s

7

Leisure Activities

We cannot afford to turn out college men who shrink from physical
effort or from a little physical pain. In any republic courage is a prime
necessity for the average citizen if he is to be a good citizen, and he
needs physical courage no less than moral courage; the courage that
dares as well as the courage that endures, the courage that will fight
valiantly alike against the foes of the soul and the foes of the body.
—Theodore Roosevelt (1907)

In the 1900s, one man symbolized the athletic spirit of the nation—President Theodore Roosevelt. Roosevelt embodied what was then known as the "strenuous life," a phrase closely associated with him and also the title of a book of essays he published in 1900. For Roosevelt and, in turn, the nation, the strenuous life meant more than actively participating in sporting events. The kind of life the president exemplified incorporated a dedication to outdoor activities and athletic endeavors on one hand, but also to hard work and strife. In 1899 Roosevelt outlined his thoughts at a speech given in Chicago:

the life of toil and effort; of labor and strife; to preach that highest form of success which comes, not to the man who desires more easy peace, but to the man who does not shrink from danger, from hardship or from bitter toil, and who out of these wins the splendid ultimate triumph.[1]

The president's outdoor exploits and active lifestyle were chronicled on the front pages of newspapers across the country, whether it was hunting in the West or spirited cross-country jaunts through Rock Creek

Park in the nation's capital. Perhaps most important for the psyche of the people, Roosevelt's feats did not seem contrived or have overtly political implications. In other words, unlike modern presidents who "announce" their athletic schedules so the media are on hand with their cameras rolling, Roosevelt's activities were manifestations of his true personality and the way in which he reared his own children. In his autobiography, Roosevelt discussed climbing steep cliffs with army officers and swimming in both Rock Creek and the Potomac River in early spring, with ice floating alongside.[2]

The nation eagerly bought into Roosevelt's call for a strenuous life. People had nostalgic feelings about rural life. It had been only a short time since America was much more rural and focused on small towns. The emphasis on outdoor living put them in touch with these seemingly gentler days. As a result, efforts were made in many cities to build parks and permanent green spaces for people to escape the density of their neighborhoods. As the automobile became more popular, people took day trips into the country, although this involved riding over rough country roads, leading to flat tires and other mechanical calamities.

The transformation of the nation's economy into a culture based on consumerism and leisure solidified the position of sports as a central focus for vast numbers of people. The growth of the middle class in the 1900s led to greater wealth and an increase in leisure time for many. People had the time to attend football and baseball games, amusement parks, and horse races. They also had the money to buy tickets, pay for transportation to and from the games, and indulge in snacks as they cheered on their favorite team. Sports became another part of the business machine at the turn of the century. In 1904 more than 22,000 spectators watched the annual Stanford–University of California at Berkeley football game on Thanksgiving Day. In 1910 attendance at major league baseball games reached 7.2 million, doubling the gate from 1901. Newspapers also played an important role in turning fans into paying spectators. As the decade wore on, newspaper owners realized that they could significantly increase readership if they covered amateur and professional sporting events. The birth of the modern sportswriter can be seen in the 1900s, although a dedicated sports page would not become standard nationwide until the 1920s.

The rise of spectator sports had interesting consequences on the social order in the United States. Sporting events were a venue where rich and poor met and mingled, drawn by the common desire to see a favorite team or player. Saloons provided a space for upper and lower classes to interact, serving as both a male-dominated refuge and a place to wager on different contests. In the first two decades of the new century, saloons reached the height of popularity. For example, in Chicago, more than half the city's population frequented one of the city's 7,600 saloons every

The circus comes to town, enticing the citizens of Oakland, California, with a parade downtown (ca. 1900s). Courtesy of the Oakland History Room of the Oakland Public Library, Oakland, California.

day on the average. Another rift in the social scene occurred when various professional athletes attained great wealth and were propelled into the upper classes. Athletes in the 1900s, like today, were able to shoot up the social ladder through their achievements on the playing fields.[3]

Most sporting activities at the turn of the century were geared toward men, although the two sexes looked to find entertainment venues in which they could interact without strict societal formalities. Dance halls, amusement parks, vaudeville houses, and movie houses gave young people (especially urbanites) a place to relax and spend time together, away from the watchful eyes of parents and elders. Amusement parks, such as New York's Coney Island or Pittsburgh's Kennywood Park, gained in popularity and catered to crowds across social classes. Soon, most cities had one or two amusement parks, which included dance halls, exhibits, band pavilions, mechanical thrill rides, swimming and bathing areas, and even circuses—anything to draw large crowds and keep them there. Folks in small towns and rural areas found the same joy at traveling carnivals and circuses.[4] Commenting on Coney Island's impact on working-class women, one historian explained, "Coney took young women out of the daily round of tenement life and work, but at the same time, it allowed them to extend their culture to the resort, whose beaches, boardwalk, and dancing pavilions were arenas for diversion, flirtation, and displays of style."[5]

Family-oriented entertainment also gained in popularity, since many critics felt amusement parks went too far in allowing young people to cavort. As cities took it upon themselves to set aside park areas, families gathered for picnics and community socials. Traditional places of formal social interaction, including churches, the YMCA, and municipal buildings also remained popular. Church members gathered in the evening for "ten cent socials," a time for frolicking and fun, but also for a good cause. The proceeds were donated to charity or used to aid the poor.

Lodges and union-sponsored social gatherings served as the primary form of entertainment for many families in the laboring classes. In 1908 Margaret Byington found more than 50 fraternal meetings listed in the paper on one day in Homestead, Pennsylvania. Men constituted the overwhelming majority of these groups, but women actively participated in some and benefited from the social aspects granted by their husbands' membership. "To the women especially, whose duties keep them at home," Byington declared, "the lodge offers almost their only chance to meet other people and get for a few minutes into a different atmosphere from that of household tasks."[6]

People in the 1900s accepted the ideal of the strenuous life, even if that meant simply becoming avid spectators at sporting events. However, big business also became both a promoter and sponsor of sports and impacted people's social lives by building grand amusement parks, dance halls, saloons, and other places for enjoyment. While Americans took Roosevelt's call for a life of physical fitness to heart, the message was diluted to a degree by the manner in which it was implemented by business. As with other aspects of 1900s popular culture, as soon as businesses realized they could make money from a new venture, they plunged ahead relentlessly. Thus, in the 1900s, we see the beginning stages of the transformation of sports into big business and the widespread commercialization of leisure time.

THE NATIONAL PASTIME

Baseball was far and away the most popular sport in the 1900s and continued to hold that position without a significant challenge at least into the 1950s. Unlike today's juiced up balls, tiny ballparks, and focus on hitting homeruns, pitchers dominated the game at the turn of the century, leading the period to be called the "dead ball" era. After both the American and National leagues began counting foul balls as strikes, the pitchers really took over the game. The ball itself favored pitchers, since it had a rubber center and did not carry as far as the cork-centered

The 1904 Concord High School baseball team. Courtesy of
the Contra Costa County Historical Society.

balls used today. Despite the prowess of great pitchers, such as Cy
Young, Christy Mathewson, Walter Johnson, and Grover Cleveland Alexander, many gifted hitters emerged. Perhaps the greatest hitter of all
time, Tyrus Raymond "Ty" Cobb, set the record for highest career batting average (.367) from 1905 to 1928. Other feared hitters included Napoleon Lajoie and Honus Wagner, but it was not until one of the league's
best pitchers, Boston Red Sox George Herman "Babe" Ruth, gave up
pitching in 1919, was sold to the New York Yankees, and became the
"Sultan of Swat" that people cheered long ball hitters.

Baseball clubs had formed in New York City as early as the 1840s and
1850s, including the New York Knickerbockers, under Alexander Cart-
wright. He established many of the rules of the game, many of which
are still used today. The Civil War spread baseball's popularity nationwide as soldiers on both sides played baseball in their leisure time. The
Cincinnati Red Stockings became the nation's first professional team in
1869, and seven years later the National League (NL) formed with eight
teams. Baseball players were treated more like factory workers than su-
perstars; team owners placed rigid restrictions on the players and limited
their movement between teams.

The National League dominated baseball before 1900 but faced financial challenges and had trouble finding enough qualified players and

umpires. In an attempt to cut costs and deliver a better brand of baseball, the NL dropped six franchises and settled into an eight-team division in the first year of the decade. Cincinnati native and former sportswriter Byron Bancroft "Ban" Johnson, the president of the Western League, a secondary circuit operating primarily in midsized Midwestern cities, decided to challenge the NL. He adopted the name American League (AL) and moved quickly to scoop up the franchises dropped by the NL.[7]

Johnson and several big-name stars, including legendary managers John McGraw and Connie Mack, barnstormed the country raising awareness of the new league and recruited players. In all, the AL signed more than 100 former NL players and two of the sport's biggest heroes and future Hall of Famers. First, pitcher Cy Young signed with the Boston club, then Napoleon Lajoie, a gifted hitter and infielder, joined Connie Mack's Philadelphia Athletics. The NL had a tight cap on salaries, which played into the hands of the AL owners. Both Young and Lajoie signed for $3,500, a princely sum in 1900. Young, in particular, felt outraged by the salary limit of the NL. When he left Saint Louis, he told owner Frank Robison, "Your treatment of your players has been so inconsiderate that no self-respecting man would want to work for you if he could do anything else in the world."[8]

The AL's first season in 1900 was a success, drawing nearly 1.7 million fans, just 236,000 less than the senior circuit. Chicago won the championship behind player-manager Clark Griffith, an outstanding pitcher who won 24 games. Young won 33 games for Boston, and the amazing Lajoie batted a phenomenal .422 and scored 145 runs. In the NL, the Pittsburgh Pirates won the championship behind the hitting prowess of John "Honus" Wagner, one of the greatest players in baseball history.[9]

The rise of Johnson's AL infuriated NL owners, who questioned the audacity of the new league in challenging the supremacy of the senior circuit. More important, NL owners resented the AL's poaching of their best players. Several court battles raged over players signing for more money to play in the AL, including a high-profile lawsuit involving Lajoie. A judge barred the star from the roster of the Philadelphia Athletics, but the crafty Johnson masterminded a trade to the Cleveland club, where Lajoie played for the rest of the decade. It did not take long for either league to figure out that, if they continued stealing away each other's star players, it would hurt baseball as a whole.

A peace settlement was reached, called the National Agreement of 1903. The pact forced each side to accept the contracts of the other and formed a three-man National Commission to govern baseball as a whole. The 1903 agreement also set up the territorial boundaries of the minor league teams. In effect, the National Agreement of 1903 took away the little bit of power players had over their own career moves. Players who were upset with their contracts had few options since other teams could not sign them away. Baseball players in the 1900s could not have even imagined today's high sweepstakes days of free agency. From 1903 to World War I, players attempted to exert some power by forming unions, but the efforts failed. Early baseball men, some scholars suggest, felt loyalty to their owners and thought jumping from team to team would adversely disturb fans. In addition, the owners obviously had a stake in keeping the players unorganized—they could control wages under the reserve clause agreement.[10]

Arguably the best player of the 1900s was a young firebrand from Georgia, Ty Cobb. Throughout his career, players both despised and feared him for his roughhousing style and his willingness to settle disputes with violence. In 1905 Cobb was a minor league outfielder for Augusta in the Class C South Atlantic League, but by 1907, he led the AL in batting average (.350), runs batted in, total bases, and stolen bases. For 12 years, from 1907 to 1919, Cobb averaged .378, and eclipsed the magical .400 mark in 1911 and 1912. By the end of his career, Cobb held 43 offensive records and set a career average record that probably will never be broken. However, for all his greatness, Cobb may have been the loneliest man in baseball.[11]

Cobb's intensity and fierceness on the field earned him few friends. He was sensitive about his Southern roots and the mysterious death of his father, who was killed by his mother when she thought he was an intruder in their home and shot him twice with a shotgun. Cobb also endured a great deal of hazing in his rookie season with the Detroit Tigers, a common practice in the big leagues, but difficult for the future star. Perhaps the greatest difference between Cobb and his fellow players was his intensity and will to power. Just over six feet tall and weighing approximately 175 pounds, he played far beyond his natural abilities on the basis of his competitiveness and internal fire. "Baseball is not unlike a war," Cobb explained, "a struggle for supremacy, a survival of the fittest." His objective was "the general demoralization of the opposition."[12]

Despite his brilliance on the baseball diamond, Cobb also embodied the 1900s in negative ways. He captured Roosevelt's ideal of the strenuous life, playing the game with vigor and excelling beyond his natural abilities, but Cobb was also a racist and bully. If fans were relentless, he would climb into the stands and challenge them physically. He carried a revolver off the field and used the gun to intimidate anyone who questioned his authority. His treatment of blacks unfortunately typified the abject racism of the day. On at least two separate occasions he hit black women, once kicking a hotel maid in the stomach. Although Ban Johnson fined him and attempted to discipline him, no one could control Cobb. Cobb was his own worst enemy. One of the most famous men in America, he ate alone, traveled alone, and was despised by teammates and foes alike. According to one sports historian, "Fans everywhere came out to see the rampaging Cobb partly in awe of his ability, but also in hopes of seeing him stymied by the local club or of witnessing a brawl in which Cobb would be the principal victim."[13]

Ty Cobb and his fellow baseball players were among the nation's first celebrities, an entertainment class judged by how it amused or astonished the general public. The feeling people developed about sports figures and their place in society helped define American popular culture in the 1900s. Although players did not enjoy the massive salaries they have in today's market, "they were, by virtue of such unremitting scrutiny, beginning to be set apart from, and above, other men."[14] Stadiums were built with dugouts to separate players from the fans. The press focused on the players and their exploits in an attempt to satiate the public's longing for the latest score or feature story about their favorite player.

Perhaps baseball captured the imagination of the country because it had such an easily determined cast of heroes and villains. The clean-cut college graduate, fireballing lefty pitcher Christy Mathewson clearly personified the All-American boy next door; the fiery Cobb was the thug people loved to hate. The spectacle of baseball as the national pastime came together most strikingly in the World Series championships held between the AL and NL pennant winners. As a matter of fact, the first World Series in 1903 between the Pittsburgh Pirates and Boston Beaneaters (changed to the Red Sox the next year) was not officially sanctioned by either league. The animosity between the two leagues ran too deep at the time, resulting in no World Series the next year in 1904.

Led by the mighty Cy Young, the Boston team won the best of nine series in eight games. Young won two games for Boston, and Bill Dineen won three. Honus Wagner played poorly for Pittsburgh, batting a measly .222 and committing six errors. The first World Series vaulted the young American League and validated its place with the National League. Being the first championship of its kind in baseball, the game was followed primarily by the fans of the two cities, but it did draw over 100,000 spectators and brought in receipts exceeding $50,000.[15]

Recognizing the moneymaking potential of the season-ending championship, the league presidents sanctioned the 1905 World Series, which pitted John McGraw's New York Giants against Connie Mack's Philadelphia Athletics. A pitching duel from the start, the series lasted five games with each team winning by shutout. Mathewson and Joe McGinnity blanked the Athletics to post four wins and clinch the series for New York. More important than the winning scores or the individual exploits of the players, the 1905 championship caught the imagination of the public. Fever for the annual World Series swept the nation. "Fans congregated in the city streets to watch the play-by-play progress of the series as reported on the boards posted in front of newspaper offices."[16] Even today, with the overwhelming amount of information flooding people's limited free time, the World Series still captures America's attention each fall. Something magical is in the air during World Series time—something other professional sports cannot capture.

REBIRTH OF THE OLYMPIC GAMES

The father of the modern Olympics, Pierre de Coubertin, a French native from the aristocracy, virtually embodied the spirit of the games and served as the first secretary general and later president (1896–1925) of the International Olympic Committee (IOC). He viewed the Olympics as both a political and athletic event, bringing together conflicting nations and establishing a "quadrennial festival of universal youth." Coubertin designed the Olympic symbol of the five interlocking rings to represent the five continents and the colors of their national flags. He viewed the Olympics as games that exalted both the athlete's individualism and the patriotism felt for one's homeland. Coubertin spent his life studying and promoting athletic endeavors around the world. On a visit to the United States in 1889 he met U.S. Civil Service Commissioner Theodore Roosevelt. Recognizing in each other a focus on the strenuous life, the men quickly became friends and remained so for the rest of their lives.[17]

Coubertin organized numerous sports associations and then set his sights on reviving the Olympic Games. Several attempts had been made to revive the games, the most recent in Sweden in 1834. Coubertin, however, was a master at drawing attention and as the leader of the French sports establishment, people listened when he declared in 1892, "It is necessary to internationalize sports. It is necessary to organize anew the Olympic Games."[18] Even Coubertin faced skepticism. People regarded the idea of the Olympics as sacred, and when he lobbied in the United States to gain the support of the nation's sports leaders, including James E. Sullivan, the secretary of the Amateur Athletic Union (AAU), he was told the idea was impossible. With the backing of England, Coubertin organized an international conference in France, which eventually led to the formation of the IOC. Its organizer decided that Athens should host the first modern Olympic Games in 1896.

The first modern games looked more like a state track-and-field championship than what we would consider an Olympic celebration. Some ceremony and ritual (King George I of Greece opened the event, cannons fired, and doves were released over the spectators) were included, but there was little of the frenzy one associates with today's Olympics. All told, approximately 300 athletes and 40,000 spectators attended the games—most from the host country. Many of the American fans there were young sailors on shore leave from the cruiser *San Francisco*. Just like today's rabid American sports nuts, the sailors offended spectators from European nations for cheering too loudly and acting, in the words of French writer Charles Maurras, "like overgrown children."[19]

Olympic winners received an olive branch, a certificate, and a silver medal; second-place finishers got a laurel sprig and a copper medal. An American, James Connolly, was the first athlete to win an Olympic event, in the triple jump, leaping just under 45 feet. The games were marked by indifference across most of the world and caused little stir outside Greece. Coubertin still had a great deal of work ahead of him to formalize the Olympics and enable the games to achieve worldwide acceptance.

Under Coubertin's guidance the second Olympic Games were held in Paris, coinciding with the World's Fair in 1900, despite the protests of the Greek government, which wanted to host the games every four years. Rather than sparking the interest of fair attendees, the Olympic Games were hardly noticed. Organizers staged the events over the five-month duration of the fair, which diluted any interest in the outcome—the track events took place in July, while the swimming meet occurred in August. In addition, the facilities were so poor that the German delegation thought their French hosts provided them on purpose, adding fuel to the flame of their centuries-old rivalry.[20]

The second Olympics established the dominance of the American and English teams in the track-and-field competitions. In Paris all 24 gold medals in the events were won by athletes from one of the two nations. Alvin Kraenzlein, a German American, won four gold medals at the 1900 games, and John Tewksbury won two gold and two silver medals. The Paris Olympics also marked the first time women were allowed to participate. Margaret Abbott of Chicago had been studying art and music in Paris, but she dusted off her golf clubs and entered the women's tournament. Wearing a long black skirt and oversized hat, fashionable at the time, she won the event and became the first American female gold medalist. Her prize was an antique Saxon porcelain bowl mounted in chiseled gold. The lack of enthusiasm for the Paris games led Coubertin to realize that linking the Olympics to a World's Fair was detrimental to establishing the importance of the events, but it would take eight more years before they became independent.[21]

Although the cry throughout the land in 1904 was "Meet Me in St. Louis" for the World's Fair, relatively few European athletes were willing to travel to the American hinterland for the third Olympic Games. For the most part, they had never even heard of Saint Louis and thought they might suffer from Indian attacks if they were to attend. Of the 554 athletes, 432 were Americans—not a single French or English athlete competed. Small, unrepresentative teams from Austria, Canada, Cuba,

Germany, Greece, and several other nations made the transatlantic trip and trek halfway across the country. Notwithstanding the lack of significant foreign competition, the American sports establishment and press used the 1904 Olympics to trumpet American superiority.[22]

The track-and-field events began on August 29, 1904, and ran until September 3. Opening day brought 5,000 spectators to the new Olympic stadium. The U.S. team completely dominated the events from start to finish, accumulating 80 points on the first day; Ireland claimed second place with 4 points, followed by Germany with 3 points and Hungary with 2 points. At Saint Louis, American organizers originated the custom of awarding gold, silver, and bronze medals. In the end, the United States won 70 gold, 75 silver, and 64 bronze medals. The next closest competitor was Cuba with 5 gold, 2 silver, and 3 bronze. The host nation won 21 of 22 track events, which the press attributed to American dominance in athletics and its physical superiority in comparison with the rest of the world. The 1904 Saint Louis Olympics, like the World's Fair itself, was an exercise in blatant nationalism in which the United States publicly thumped its chest and proclaimed itself the world's strongest nation.

The IOC designated Rome as the host of the 1908 Olympic Games, but the eruption of Mount Vesuvius in 1906, which claimed 2,000 lives, forced the event to be moved to London. London built a new 70,000-seat stadium for the Olympics and adopted strict guidelines regarding what constituted amateur status for the athletes. The 1908 games, however, were marked by protest, particularly regarding the way in which English officials treated Irish athletes, who wanted to compete under their own flag as a separate nation. Much of the protest came from American participants of Irish descent. Shot-put champion Ralph Rose refused to dip the flag to the English king as flag bearer for the United States, sending a shock through the Olympic community.

The United States again dominated the track-and-field events, winning 15 of 27 contests, despite shoddy officiating on the part of English officials. J.C. Carpenter, an American runner in the 400-meter race, was disqualified, and his teammates refused to participate in the final heat, so English runner Wyndham Halswelle won the gold in a one-man race. The marathon also caused great consternation. An Italian runner, Dorando Pietri, staggered, dazed, into the Olympic stadium and fell to the ground four times on the final lap. As American Johnny Hayes closed in on him, British officials grabbed the Italian and dragged him across the finish line. American officials protested when Pietri was awarded the gold medal, which launched accusations of poor sportsmanship in the British press. The IOC overturned the decision and awarded the victory to Hayes. Pietri, however, a kind of folk hero, even won the praises of writer Arthur Conan Doyle, an international celebrity in an age when people cared what was on the minds of its leading thinkers.[23]

FOOTBALL

From its inception, football has been a violent sport. Even with modern padding and protection, more than a handful of players have been paralyzed on the field in recent years. In the 1900s, football was even more brutal—in 1905 alone, the *Chicago Tribune* reported the deaths of 18 football players and serious injuries to 159. Many colleges took measures to deal with the brutality. Columbia abolished football in 1905; Stanford and California suspended play. Charles Eliot, president of Harvard, wanted to eliminate football altogether. The situation grew so dire that President Roosevelt, a football supporter and proponent of the game, stepped into the situation to find a remedy. He put together a committee in October 1905 (including members from Harvard, Princeton, and Yale) to find a way to abolish the violence taking young lives.[24]

Roosevelt acted to save football, which he felt built manly character, but he wanted it to be played cleanly. He attributed the deaths and serious injuries that occurred on the field to dirty tactics and players who disregarded the rules. Roosevelt's football commission reaffirmed a need for "honorable obligation" to stop foul play. The group formed the American Football Rules Committee, which designed plays to open up the game and move away from the power plays and wedges that brought together unprotected players in bone-crushing collisions. Two important rules were developed: moving the first-down markers from 5 to 10 yards and the forward pass.[25]

Despite the injuries, college football dominated the sport in the 1900s and increasingly became a focal point of collegiate life. In the early part of the decade, the teams of the University of Michigan outclassed the rest of the nation. In 1901 Michigan dismantled the University of Buffalo, 128–0, so thoroughly outmatching them that reports from the game state that a Buffalo player was laid out after almost every play in the second half. Over the season, the Michigan team totaled 501 points without giving up a single score. In an attempt to determine who was the best team in the nation, a group of sports organizers put together the first Rose Bowl in 1902, pitting Stanford against the blue-and-maize horde from the Midwest. Once again, Michigan destroyed the competition, winning 49–0, discouraging the Westerners to the point that they did not hold another Rose Bowl contest until 1916.[26]

BOXING

The Baltimore *Sun* ran a peculiar story on April 2, 1901. The newspaper dutifully reported that Elizabeth Moore, a 24-year-old woman, de-

The final punch in the 1910 Nelson-Wolgast
boxing match in Point Richmond, California.
Courtesy of the Contra Costa County Historical
Society.

scribed in the report as "pretty and rather modest-looking," had been
arrested the night before. Her crime had been attending the lightweight
boxing match between the great Joe Gans (the first African American to
hold a championship title) and Martin Flaherty. Moore caused quite a
stir when she took her seat in the third row—dressed as a man, complete
with a curly wig and men's clothing. According to the report, she "had
by her trim figure and girlish face attracted general notice from those
near her." A police captain in the audience was "attracted by the curly
wig." The official charge against Moore was "masquerading in male attire," but her real crime was invading the male-dominated bastion represented by professional boxing matches. Later, her husband picked her
up at the station after posting a $105 bond. Boxing, barely legal itself at
the turn of the century, was no place for women according to societal
norms.[27]
    Despite its viciousness, seedy elements, and illegality in many states,
boxing gained immense popularity in the 1900s. Many prizefights could
barely be considered boxing by modern standards. They were basically
bare-knuckle brawls held secretly in saloons, gyms, or backwoods areas.
Fans followed the sport closely and, like today, took great interest in the

professional heavyweight division. Opponents of boxing, on the other hand, railed against the sport's gambling influences and outright brutality. Roosevelt criticized boxing in January 1901, charging that club owners "made a mistake by not stopping contests when they became brutal, or when it was manifest to all that one of the contestants had no possible chance of winning." One might wonder why a sports enthusiast like Roosevelt would speak out against boxing, but people were dying in the ring at an alarming rate. At least four men died in 1901, although one can speculate that countless more died in illegal fights that were never reported. Even sanctioned boxing matches were vicious and often lasted 25 rounds or more.[28]

James J. Jeffries, a young pugilist from San Francisco, held the world heavyweight title at the start of the decade. He beat New Zealander Bob Fitzsimmons at the Coney Island Athletic Club in 1899 with an eleventh-round knockout. Jeffries, six feet, 1 inch in height and weighing 210 pounds, ruled the heavyweight division for the next four years. Jeffries, who defended his belt at every turn, was a true fighting champion. He defeated his primary challengers, James J. Corbett and Fitzsimmons, on separate occasions before voluntarily retiring in 1905, at 30 years of age. Jeffries gained a great deal of respect when he defeated Corbett, since Jeffries was a former sparring partner of Corbett when he was champion. Corbett dominated the fight for the first 22 rounds, but Jeffries bided his time and caught Corbett coming off the ropes the next round and knocked him out. Jeffries beat Corbett a second time in 1903.[29]

White boxers in the 1900s seemed to take a two-pronged approach to competing with black contenders. On one hand, fight promoters and officials worked with the white champions and tried to deny blacks the chance to go for the title. At the same time whites seemed to believe blacks were cowards and held the general belief that blacks were socially, physically, and mentally inferior. Interracial boxing matches took place in the first decade of the twentieth century and drew huge crowds because of the novelty. African-American fighters, however, were discriminated against at nearly every turn.

The man who would change White America's perception of black athletes in the 1900s was Jack Johnson, a native of Galveston, Texas. Johnson, who left school after the fifth grade, bounced from one menial job to another and traveled around the country, visiting New York and Boston, among other cities. Settling in Dallas at the age of 16, Johnson worked at a carriage shop building horse-drawn buggies. His boss, Walter Lewis, was an ex-boxer and offered to teach the hulking Johnson to box. From 1895 to 1897, Johnson boxed in one dump after another, struggling to make a living, but learning his new trade. His first important fight was against noted heavyweight Joe Choynsky, in Galveston, on February 26, 1901. Johnson was knocked out in the third round, and after the fight, both men were carted off to jail—boxing was still illegal in Texas at the time. For the next three weeks, Choynsky gave Johnson boxing lessons, allowing him to learn from the more experienced veteran.[30]

In 1903 Johnson beat "Denver" Ed Martin to win the Negro heavyweight championship. In 1903 and 1904, all Johnson's opponents were black, since the sport remained segregated. Although little known before beating Martin, Johnson quickly got the attention of the boxing world. In 1903, Jeffries declared, "I will not fight a negro! If Johnson wants to fight for the championship he will have to fight somebody besides me. If I am defeated, the championship will go to a white man, for I will not fight a colored man."[31] Since Jeffries would not fight him, Johnson began to question the champion's character publicly. Jeffries did not change his stance and chose to retire in 1905, claiming there was a lack of competition.

Johnson continued boxing and amassing impressive victories. He did not lose a fight in 1906 or 1907. He set his sights on the heavyweight championship, but the white titleholders continued holding to the color barrier. Johnson's most impressive victory during this time was a win over former champion Bob Fitzsimmons, the first time a black man beat a former titleholder. Johnson started chasing the new champion, Canadian Tommy Burns, all over the globe demanding a title shot. Newspapers jumped into the fray as well. The Saint Louis *Post-Dispatch* and the New York *Sun* demanded that Burns give Johnson a title match. The verbal sparring intensified between the two, and Johnson followed the champ to England, France, and Australia. By the time the two men reached Australia, Burns had literally run out of running room. He finally had to consent to a fight with Johnson. The fight date was set for the day after Christmas in 1908. The total purse for the fight was $40,000, with Burns scheduled to receive $35,000 and Johnson, only $5,000.[32]

Approximately 26,000 fans (including two women) watched Johnson—nearly six feet, two inches and 195 pounds—batter the heavyweight champion, who was six inches shorter and 15 pounds lighter. But it was not size that led to the pounding Burns took, it was Johnson's superior training and his desire to disprove the coward label that some white fighters had been pinning on blacks. Johnson knocked Burns down in the first round with a right uppercut, and by the eighth round Burns's eyes were swollen shut and he was bleeding from the mouth. Johnson taunted and berated Burns throughout the fight, questioning the yellow label. Burns took more punishment through 14 rounds before the police intervened and called an end to the battle. Jack Johnson assumed the heavyweight championship of the world. Serving as ringside reporters were former champion John L. Sullivan and author Jack London. Immediately after the fight, London called out for Jim Jeffries to come out of retirement and defend the honor of whites. Soon, the cry for Jeffries as the "Great White Hope" took hold around the world. Although retired for four and a half years, the pressure and money were too much—Jeffries agreed to fight Johnson.[33]

While Jeffries struggled to lose the weight he had gained in retirement, fight promoters lined up to manage the event. The winning promoter was George Lewis "Tex" Rickard, who bid $101,000. "This proposal constituted the largest legitimate business deal ever consummated by an African-American to that time."[34]

On the sunny, clear morning of July 4, 1910, in Reno, Nevada, the two men came to the center of the ring to fight the battle of the ages. They did not like one another and agreed on one thing—no traditional pre-fight handshake was in order. Jeffries wore purple trunks and came to the ring in street clothes. Johnson made a grand entrance in a floor-length robe with an American flag as a belt. Soon after the fight began, spectators realized that Jeffries was in for a long day. His punches were weak and off-center, and Johnson deliberately punished the ex-champion. He chattered throughout the fight, making fun of Corbett and Sullivan, who predicted that Jeffries would emerge victorious. By the thirteenth round, Johnson openly taunted Jeffries and laughed as he lunged after him around the ring. Two rounds later, Jeffries could not stand any more abuse. Johnson repeatedly set Jeffries down to the canvas and then through the ropes. Jeffries's camp threw in the towel, probably fearing for his life if he continued. After the fight, Johnson lashed out at Jeffries verbally, saying, "I won from Mr. Jeffries because I outclassed him in every department. I was certain I would be the victor. I never changed my mind at any time."[35]

Johnson's victory over the Great White Hope set off a terrifying reaction against blacks across the nation. There were riots and fights in cities as diverse as Omaha, Philadelphia, Houston, New Orleans, and Macon, Georgia. In total, the carnage left 13 blacks dead and hundreds more injured (probably countless more went unreported). The public outcry against Johnson included banning films of the match and making it illegal to transport them across state lines.

The victory over Jeffries may have been the highpoint of Johnson's boxing career. Over the next several decades, he faced prosecution by authorities, not only in America, but also in Europe and Mexico. After trial for trumped-up charges for violating the Mann Act (transporting a person across state lines for immoral purposes) in 1912, Johnson was convicted on 11 counts, ranging from crimes against nature to prostitution and debauchery. He was sentenced to a year and a day in jail and fined $1,000. The case and trial caused another uproar, and white America even called eminent black statesman Booker T. Washington to comment. Washington urged caution and suggested that Johnson act in nonthreatening ways. Black leaders feared violence and threats against the black middle class.

Washington and W.E.B. Du Bois both felt that Johnson hindered race progress, but African Americans used every Johnson victory in the ring as a reason to rejoice. He gave them a sense of pride few blacks had experienced before. According to scholar Joseph Dorinson, "Belittling successful blacks and seeking the company of white prostitutes, Johnson manifested a deep ambivalence, indeed rage." However, Dorinson explained, "He also accomplished much. He overcame hate, oppression, and out casting." Johnson even had an impact on politics. First he campaigned for Democrat Al Smith in 1928 and later he supported Franklin D. Roosevelt.[36]

GOLF AND TENNIS

Other individual sports, such as golf and lawn tennis, gained in popularity in the 1900s. In 1894 the Amateur Golf Association was formed to standardize the game, and changed its name to the United States Golf Association (USGA) a year later. The first U.S. Open golf tournament was held in 1895, and 75 golf clubs sprang up to cater to the wealthy. By 1900, more than 1,000 golf clubs dotted the countryside. The game received a shot in the arm when three-time British Open champion Harry Vardon toured America in 1900, sponsored by the A.G. Spalding sporting goods store.

As the decade wore on, middle-class enthusiasts began to play golf. Soon, every good-sized town could boast of a local golf course, especially in the suburban areas lining the great cities on the Eastern seaboard. By 1914 observers estimated that more adults played golf than any other outdoor sport. Amateur champion Walter J. Travis helped popularize the game by winning the national championship in 1900, 1901, and 1903. The following year, Travis became the first foreign player to capture the British amateur title. A wiry, small man, born in Australia, but making his home in Texas, Travis did not even begin playing golf until he was 35 years old. Not the longest hitter off the tee, Travis excelled at putting and hit precise shots onto the greens. His play could have been the model for the old adage, "Drive for show, but putt for dough." By 1905 he had his own magazine, *American Golfer*, and published *Practical Golf*, a guide to the sport. Jerome D. Travers, one of the first great American players, won amateur titles in 1907 and 1908, then again in 1912 and 1913. He also wrote numerous articles and several books on the sport.[37]

In 1874 New York socialite Mary Ewing Outerbridge, who saw British officers play the game while she was on winter vacation in Bermuda, introduced lawn tennis to the United States. She purchased a tennis set abroad but had to surrender the equipment to customs officials who did not know what it was. She used her family's ties in the shipping industry to get the items into the country. She had a tennis court set up at the Staten Island Cricket and Baseball Club, which her brother ran.

Unlike golf, players from both sexes competed with and against one another. Tennis was a rich person's game, but it did not carry the gender bias of golf. The United States Lawn Tennis Association (USLTA) organized in 1881 and by 1900, the sport had its first great superstar, William A. Larned, who won seven national singles titles (1901, 1902, 1907–1911). More important for popularizing tennis, however, was the International Lawn Tennis Challenge Cup tournament, better known as the Davis Cup, after Dwight F. Davis, who donated the silver cup given to the winning team. Tennis's top players, including Davis, the national college singles champion, decided that an international competition would bolster the game's acceptance. First held between the United States and Britain, and then including Australia, the Davis Cup is still tennis' supreme team competition. The U.S. squad won in 1900 and 1902, but the British held the cup until 1906 when the Australians took over through 1912.

Women were not only accepted in tennis, but also given a chance to compete on the national and international stage. Many strong American players competed with one another throughout the decade, including Myrtle McAteer, Elisabeth H. Moore, and Marion Jones, who earned a bronze medal at the 1900 Olympic Games. May Sutton became the first American woman to win Wimbledon, in 1905, and reclaimed the title in 1907. Decked out in all white, long sleeves, and a knotted tie, Sutton may have caused the biggest stir by wearing a dress that rose two inches above her ankles at the 1905 Wimbledon matches. The dress in these days was a far cry from the flimsy spandex outfits women on today's tennis circuit wear. Imagine Venus Williams in a dress that brushed against her shoe tops and long sleeves rolled up to her elbows.

FAIRS, EXPOSITIONS, AND CARNIVALS

Since the 1890s ("the Gay Nineties"), many people had more free time to spend in leisure, despite long workweeks and low wages. The most popular forms of entertainment were often the simplest—family picnics and community socials. However, as adherence to the consumer culture took hold, families turned to commercial recreation, often sponsored by one's employer or a large corporation. Time for recreational pursuits became yet another commodity and working- and middle-class participants provided the economic grease for the machine. However, if big business capitalized on this new mind-set, the move toward commercial amusement did give people freedoms they had rarely experienced in earlier times. At places like Coney Island or Sandusky, Ohio's Cedar

William "Buffalo Bill" Cody and his Wild West Show at the *Oakland
Tribune* office (1910). Courtesy of the Oakland History Room of the
Oakland Public Library, Oakland, California.

Point, young people were able to mingle without heavy parental super-
vision. Even if some company or groups of companies packaged entertainment into nice little bite sizes for the middle class, at least they could
gain some measure of freedom as their money slipped away.

Since Roosevelt epitomized the strenuous sporting life, many Americans worked to live up to the president's example in their leisure time.
Often this translated into a stay at a spa or resort. Sporting events themselves also took on a kind of religious experience at the turn of the century. Millions of people turned out to cheer their favorite boxer, baseball
team, or college gridiron squad.[38]

County or state fairs, usually held annually, began as celebrations of
the year's agricultural harvest and livestock production, but later became
showcases for American technological might, highlighting consumer
products and innovations. In 1910 the Great Granger's Annual Picnic
Exhibition at Williams Grove, Pennsylvania, showcased 37 different
types of washing machines. By 1912 the exhibition included an auto
show in which rural consumers could test-drive cars. Proving to be moneymaking ventures and extremely popular, state and county fairs took

on the characteristics of cities. Organizers replaced the flimsy, hastily constructed wooden buildings and tents with permanent structures made from brick and steel. They built machinery halls, auditoriums, concession stands, and retail stores.[39]

Popular entertainment became a fixture at fairs. Horse racing developed into a fair mainstay, but music bands, circuses, vaudeville shows, and amusement rides gained in popularity as rural folks strolled down the fair's midway. With the success of fixed location amusement parks, most notably Coney Island, mechanical thrill rides were set up at rural fairs, including Ferris wheels, hot-air balloon rides, and, later, airplane rides. After dark, fairs took on a different role, enabling rural men and women to experience nightlife, as electricity lit up the night sky.[40]

The most popular diversion in America in the 1900s, in terms of attendance and grandeur, was the World's Fair. The United States caught World's Fair fever during the spectacle of the World's Columbian Exposition held in Chicago in 1893. These expositions gave Americans an opportunity to showcase the nation's technological innovations, as well as feature a specific region of the country. Aided by state and federal governments, Buffalo organized a Pan-American Exposition in 1901. The theme of the Buffalo fair was to demonstrate the progress of civilization on both American continents. Unfortunately, the exhibits and innovations at Buffalo are forever overshadowed by the assassination of President McKinley at the event.

Other individual states and cities rushed to hold their own expositions, including the Lewis and Clark Exposition in Portland in 1905, Jamestown in 1907, the Alaska-Yukon-Pacific Expo in Seattle in 1909, and two shows held in San Francisco and San Diego in 1915. Other cities holding expositions between the Chicago and Saint Louis expositions were Atlanta, Nashville, Omaha, New Orleans, and Charleston—in all eight fairs in the 10 years between the two great expositions.[41]

The granddaddy of all expositions in the 1900s was the 1904 Louisiana Purchase Exposition held in Saint Louis. *New York Times* reporter William Martin Aixen called the Saint Louis World's Fair "the biggest show on earth" and reported that many observers thought it was better than the Chicago fair. Aixen encouraged readers to go to Saint Louis: "there is so much that is worthy of careful observation that a trip to St. Louis from any part of the Union will repay the earnest visitor many times over for the time, expense, and incidental discomfort incurred."[42] The Saint Louis Fair featured miles of electric light and countless acres of art and culture, as well as a kind of human zoo portraying real-life Indians (American and Eastern), Africans, Filipinos, Syrians, and other tribes. On the surface, planners designed the anthropological exhibits to show fairgoers how other people lived in their native habitats. However, there was also a great deal of jingoism in the display. In many respects, these people were shipped to Saint Louis to prove American superiority and technological achievement.[43]

Sports in the 1900s increased in popularity as more people had some measure of leisure time. Even the most aggressively professional sports, such as baseball, were a far cry from what we see today. Innocence still surrounded sports in the 1900s, even if money interests soon took total control over the games. Boxing may have been the first to fall victim to rampant professionalism, but the others were not far behind. As soon as businesses realized that sports could become a major part of the blossoming consumer culture, they swooped in to maximize its potential.

On a lighter note, we are accustomed to the Olympics being a grand display of nationalism, pageantry, and commercialism, but it was not always like that. At the 1904 Olympics, held in conjunction with the Saint Louis World's Fair, the planners decided that they would actively perform "scientific" tests on the runners in the toughest test of human endurance—the 26.3-mile marathon. Given the heavy overtones of science during the Progressive Era, it only seemed proper that the organizers would try to learn more about how the body responds to certain situations. Before the race, each runner was measured, weighed, and his heart was tested in an attempt to determine the strain of the race.

As the runners took their places at the starting line, officials pulled up in 20 automobiles, each with a doctor aboard to monitor the conditions of the athletes. Among them were 17 Americans, 11 Greeks, 1 Cuban, 1 South African, and 2 Kaffirs on loan from the fair's Department of Anthropology. The weather was hot and humid and the runners looped out over dusty dirt roads. As the race began, the automobiles sped off to stay just slightly ahead of the runners. The cars sputtered and jerked, kicking up massive amounts of dirt and giving off fumes. Periodically, the athletes had to stop running to choke the dust out of their throats. As a matter of fact, William Garcia of San Francisco swallowed so much dirt that he almost died from hemorrhaging his stomach lining. Two other cars were involved in an automobile accident that nearly turned fatal as they rolled down an embankment.[44]

After these instances of bad luck, the rest of the race turned into a comedy of errors. The two Africans on loan were chased off the path by dogs. One of them ran for his life, but eventually made it back to the race and finished ninth. The Cuban, Felix Carvajal, a mail carrier, ran in heavy street shoes. He cut off his slacks to look more like a runner. Throughout the race, Carvajal stopped to talk with spectators. At one point, he stopped in an orchard and picked some green peaches, which he ate. A little later, the Cuban doubled over in pain from eating the fruit. He recovered to place fourth. One race observer said, "Had Carvajal had anyone with him—he was totally unattended—he would not only have won the race, but would have lowered the Olympic record."[45]

As spectators anxiously awaited the finish of the marathon, hoping for an American victory that had eluded them in the first two modern games, Fred Lorz of New York entered the stadium. The crowd erupted in near pandemonium. Soon, however, it was discovered that Lorz rode some unknown part of the race in a car, anywhere from 1 to 12 miles. Later, the real race winner, Thomas J. Hicks of Cambridge, Massachusetts, entered the track staggering and looking delirious. The scientific examiners had been keeping a close watch over Hicks. Twice in the race they gave him a potion of sulfate of strychnine and egg whites to bolster his strength. When Hicks asked for water, the doctors sponged his mouth out and refused him water. At the 20-mile mark they nearly killed him by soaking him in hot water and giving him a concoction of strychnine and brandy.[46]

Despite Lorz's deception and the insane potions fed to Hicks by race officials, Hicks was declared the winner of the marathon and became a national hero. Hicks was so sick after the race he was unable to lift the winner's trophy. For his trick, Lorz was banned from Olympic competition for the rest of his life. Hicks's victory marked a wacky ending to a crazy marathon that encapsulated everything from wild dogs and hopping a ride to drinking strychnine and literally eating dust. It is hard to imagine that upon these humble beginnings we now have the international extravaganza that takes place today. The 1904 Olympic marathon symbolized many aspects of life in the decade: the emergence of the automobile, racism, concepts of progress through science, and American victory.

The 1900s

8

Literature

I simply want to tell about life as it is. Every human life is intensely interesting . . . [these] are the things I want to write about—life as it is, the facts as they exist, the game as it is played!
                                        —Theodore Dreiser (1901)

At a speech given in Berkeley, shortly after the first decade of the twentieth century ended, philosopher and poet George Santayana derogatorily labeled post-1900 literature as part of a "genteel tradition" and described the era's writing as dull and colorless.[1] Unfortunately, many analysts and scholars since then have been quick to accept his characterization. A deeper look into the decade, however, reveals that a revolutionary transformation took place among America's up-and-coming writers. For the first time, a truly unique style emerged which loosened the nation's long-standing cultural ties to Britain and Europe. Writers in the United States asserted their "Americanness" and began examining life as it was lived by common people on a daily basis.

Interestingly, much of the newfound strength and passion displayed by American writers had its birth far from the center of arts and culture. To a large degree, writers in the period were fueled by the nation's ascendancy in global economic and military affairs and the repercussions of the United States emerging as the world's most powerful nation. Just as the young country thumped its chest around the globe, its writers began the new century with a heightened sense of authority. Naturally, the changes affected the growing community of writers, artists, and intellectuals, who were not only interpreters of events, but also people caught up in the whirlwind of modernization.

All across the United States, people entered the new millennium with high spirits and a renewed sense of optimism. The country basked in unprecedented wealth stimulated by industry and commerce, cities became the center of culture and influence, and the nation entered a phase of amazing scientific and technological innovation. Machinery altered daily life and replaced chores that people had done by hand less than a generation earlier.

The United States stood at the dawn of a remarkable era filled with wealth, political reform, innovations in science, technology, and medicine, and military and diplomatic might. Senator Albert J. Beveridge of Indiana claimed American prosperity as a divine right. "God has marked the American people as His chosen nation to finally lead in the regeneration of the world," Beveridge explained. "This is the divine mission of America, and it holds for us all the profit, all the glory, all the happiness possible to man. We are trustees of the world's progress, guardians of its righteous peace."[2]

While these positives all gave people a reason for excitement, there was a downside as well. For all the improvements, the United States still suffered from horrible race relations, including riots and lynchings, overcrowded cities, labor struggles, and industrial fatalities. In particular, the plight of immigrants plagued the cities. In 1907 alone, 1.25 million immigrants entered the United States. Most of them clustered in ethnic enclaves and ghettos without proper sanitation, waste removal, or ventilation. Adding to the situation, migrants from rural areas, including African Americans fleeing the Reconstruction South, also crowded into Northern cities. Taken together, the conflicting experiences and widening gap between the upper and lower classes offered the day's writers a broad canvas for probing the American experience.

Perhaps more than in any other decade in the nation's history, American writers were charged with interpreting the upheaval occurring all around them. Some reacted bitterly, like the two famous Henrys of the period—Henry James and Henry Brook Adams. The two old friends felt out of place in the new nation at the turn of the century. Henry James, from his perch in London, called the period from the Civil War to World War I "the Age of the Mistake." Flustered with the speed of change in the industrialized nation, Adams declared himself obsolete. In his masterpiece, *The Education of Henry Adams*, privately published in 1907, the descendent of presidents John and John Quincy Adams, portrayed himself as bumbling, searching for meaning in the new century, but ultimately finding only doubt and confusion.[3]

Others relished the opportunity to contribute to the intellectual conversations gripping the nation. Taking their cue from the political leaders of the Progressive movement, African Americans, women, and immigrants lent their voices to a literary movement that included them more than it had in the past. W.E.B. Du Bois and Booker T. Washington made significant inroads for black authors, and a number of women writers impacted the regional and national literary scene, including New England authors Sarah Orne Jewett and Mary E. Wilkins Freeman.

Mixing investigative reporting and literary nonfiction, a group of enterprising writers, angrily denounced as "Muckrakers" by none other than President Theodore Roosevelt, exploited middle-class anxiety by exposing society's ills in newspapers and magazines. Middle-class readers reacted forcefully to stories illustrating the evils of big city life or the growing power of corporations. During the reform era, the nation's politicians listened as well. Upton Sinclair's masterful novel *The Jungle* (1906), depicting the gruesome conditions in Chicago's meatpacking plants, spurred Congress to pass the Pure Food and Drug Act of 1906.

Throughout the Progressive Era, the muckrakers played a crucial role in bringing to light the dark underbelly of capitalism. "They hoped," explained one historian, "that people would not read their sordid stories just for their shock value but that they would be filled with the desire to do something about corrupt bosses, seated labor, civic decay, monopolistic extortion."[4]

As in other periods of the nation's history, sensationalism sold. Newspaper and magazine owners and editors quickly exploited this fact. Throughout the early twentieth century, newspapers and magazines seemed to multiply exponentially. Obviously, since the public could not turn to television or radio, newspapers and magazines wielded a great deal of influence. The sheer number of magazines one could buy attests to their power and the public's voluminous demand. As a matter of fact, as early as 1900, more than 5,500 periodicals were published in the United States. They ranged from literary journals, such as the *Atlantic Monthly, Harper's Magazine*, and the *Century* to general interest or political weeklies and monthlies, including *Cosmopolitan*, the *Saturday Evening Post*, and *Independent*. The circulation figures are impressive, even by modern standards. The literary magazines boasted sales in excess of 100,000 copies a month; others climbed as high as 1 million. In 1900 there were 2,226 dailies with a combined circulation of more than 15 million.[5]

Technological advances in print production, which permitted color to be used more frequently, enabled publishing companies to sell a new style of magazine at 10–15 cents a copy and direct them to specific segments of the reading population. Women, in particular, were targeted in numerous publications. Among the most successful was *Ladies' Home Journal*, founded in 1883 and edited by Edward W. Bok. The magazine's circulation surpassed 1 million in 1902. Bok and other savvy editors realized they could offset the cover price by accepting advertising from the companies that catered to the middle class's newfound consumer culture.

Jack London with his wife, Charmian (1908). Courtesy of the Oakland History Room of the Oakland Public Library, Oakland, California.

Cheap binding, faster print production, and a better understanding of mass marketing all encouraged book sales during the era, leading to the birth of the best-seller. Our predecessors in the 1900s bought sentimental, romance, and historical romance novels approximately ten times as often as the works critics considered "literature." Readers gobbled up the tales of Mary Johnston, *To Have and to Hold* (1900), and Alice Hegen Rice, *Mrs. Wiggs of the Cabbage Patch* (1901).

Although his stature has risen dramatically in the many decades since his death, Jack London actually became America's first millionaire author by capitalizing on the public's insatiable appetite for adventure stories. London failed as a gold prospector in Alaska as a young man, but his tales of the Klondike, such as *The Call of the Wild* (1903) and *White Fang* (1906), made him rich and famous. Undoubtedly, London would have been successful in any era. His work habits were legendary—he worked all day and night, barely breaking to eat or drink, and slept less than five hours a night. Given his determination, reportedly writing 1,000 words a day for 17 years, it is easy to imagine London on today's best-seller lists, competing with Tom Clancy, John Grisham, and Michael Crichton.

Dime novels (so called because of their cheap price and appeal to young readers with action-packed stories), first published in the 1850s and with more than 100 different series in the 1880s, were still extremely popular in the 1900s. Most were published weekly, with lurid covers enticing their mostly male readership. Over the years, dime novels moved beyond Westerns, and readers increasingly picked from stories about detectives, life on the railroads, sports, and the city. The new century did not hurt the popularity of the Horatio Alger stories, which sold in department stores for 19 cents. These rags-to-riches sagas featured city boys preoccupied with making good and ultimately succeeding despite problems along the way.

Rather than envisioning the 1900s as the embodiment of the genteel tradition, it should be appreciated as the foundation upon which subsequent writers erected the great works of the twentieth century. In fact, most, if not all, of the important literary movements occurring later in the century can be traced back to the years between 1900 and 1910. Many of America's most prominent authors recognize the debt of gratitude they owe to Edith Wharton, Frank Norris, Jack London, and Henry James. The works of writers from John Steinbeck and Ernest Hemingway to Norman Mailer and Tom Wolfe all draw from the roots established in the 1900s.

Perhaps the most public homage to the writers of this period occurred in 1930 when Sinclair Lewis won America's first Nobel Prize for Literature. In his touching acceptance speech, he paid tribute to the many authors who could have won the award before him. The first person Lewis mentioned was a poor, college dropout whose brilliant first novel was suppressed for nearly a decade after its initial printing for its gripping portrayal of the seedy aspects of American life. The author's name was Theodore Dreiser.

REALISM AND NATURALISM

The United States entered the new century needing a fresh coat of paint. On one hand, the nation was riding a wave of industrial and military might that solidified its status as one of the world's great powers. But, with the newfound strength, came an ever-growing list of domestic evils, including racism, sexism, and poverty, which mocked America's pledge of allegiance to equality, opportunity, and progress. These disparities made the 1900s much more than an "Age of Innocence" as novelist Edith Wharton labeled the decade.

A more fitting categorization of the 1900s would be the "Age of Contrasts." The decade witnessed a widening gap between urban and rural, black and white, and, perhaps most severe, rich and poor. In the end, a battle raged between the overt optimism brought on by technology, industry, and power and the realities of everyday life for the majority of Americans.

For those willing to open their eyes to the misery, it stood before them like a raging wildfire. The carnage and agony of the Civil War still haunted people's minds, and racial brutality existed as a daily reminder of the conflict. Immigrants poured into the country by the millions, and people content to stay on the family farm a generation earlier flocked to the cities in search of a steady income and better quality of life. City leaders were unprepared for the strain on infrastructure networks. As a result, the worst sections in many cities became ghettos, human cesspools of filth and despair.

Swarming with overcrowded streets, factories, and tenements, American cities in the 1900s turned gritty. Diligent efforts made by local officials could not stem the influx of people nor keep up with the infrastructure demands placed on the swelling cities. For example, New York City grew 500 percent between 1860 and 1900, from a population of 750,000 to more than 3.5 million. On the banks of Lake Michigan, Chicago topped the 2 million mark.

In these frenzied and chaotic times, American writers asserted themselves as interpreters of the change taking place before their eyes. Because large segments of the public yearned for literary work in magazines, journals, and newspapers, they had no shortage of outlets to explore new ideas and theories. "It was through American writers that the American consciousness was preserved and slowly began to evolve," explained one literary scholar.[6]

William Dean Howells, largely ignored by today's scholars, was the era's unofficial dean of letters and led the "realist" school. This loose association of writers explored life and morality in a culture driven by big business and corporations. Realist authors focused on concrete facts and turned away from portraying genteel society, romantic excess, and utopian idealism—notions that dominated the literary scene prior to 1900. Howells and Henry James actively campaigned for the realist cause and their works were widely read by the general public and studied by scholars. Mark Twain, arguably America's greatest author, once told Howells, "Only you see people & their ways & their insides & outsides as they are, & make them talk as they do talk. I think you are the greatest artist in these tremendous matters that ever lived."[7]

Realism in America first took shape in the years following the Civil War but picked up steam at the turn of the century when society seemed threatened to some degree by the changes taking place—incredible technological advances, never-ending streams of immigrants, and a growing reliance on urban life at the expense of the nation's farmers. The attempt to understand the rapidly changing nation proved to be a fertile ground for writers like Mark Twain, Henry James, and William Dean Howells. Realism, however, meant different things to each author. For Henry James, realist fiction explored the inside of characters' minds, a stream of consciousness effect that attempted to reconcile a person's interaction with the outside world and one's inner sensibilities. Twain, on the other hand, displayed his version of realism by concentrating on the use of authentic dialect and shunning the genteel.[8]

Howells, James, and the others brought realistic elements into their fiction, but they did not try to match the realism of photography and journalism. They tried to probe beneath the surface, essentially starting with facts, then using literary imagination and creativity. The ironic aspect of the realism practiced by James and Howells is that they did not want their work to venture into violence, death, or extreme situations. Sarah Orne Jewett, for instance, cautioned American writers to toe "the middle ground."[9]

Closely related to realism was naturalism—so closely, as a matter of fact, that many scholars do not make a clear distinction between the two. If there is a difference, it is that naturalist writers, such as Frank Norris, Theodore Dreiser, and Jack London, took realism a step further into the extreme. In their works, they burrowed down deep into the lives of everyday people by examining characters as victims of society's unchallengeable forces, such as capitalism, poverty, and violence. These authors viewed the transformation of society with a skeptical eye. For London, Norris, and Dreiser, the world was filled with immorality that distorted everyday life and destroyed republican idealism. They disregarded the prevailing sentimentalities of the day and revealed a world that was cruel and indifferent to the plight of the downtrodden.[10]

The biggest difference between the realists and the naturalists, according to one literary historian, is that the naturalists recognized "the overwhelming power of economic forces and nonrational impulses." They were eagerly willing to expose the terrible things that happen in society when people are confronted with forces beyond their control.

Realism, which took hold gradually after the horrors of the Civil War, served as a backlash against the Victorian romanticism popular throughout the nineteenth century. Writers using realism in their work ranged from Mark Twain to investigative reporter Jacob Riis, who photographed the hidden poor for his collection in book form, *How the Other Half Lives* (1890). Because many of the prominent realist authors were associated with regional writing, they do not receive much attention from today's literary establishment: Edward Eggleston (southern Indiana), George Washington Cable (New Orleans), Egbert Craddock (eastern Tennessee), James Lane Allen (Kentucky), and Jewett and Freeman (New England).

However, all these writers helped realism become more accepted by searching for an exact portrayal of character and setting in their works.

Earlier in his career, Howells established his reputation as an influential editor of the *Atlantic Monthly*. In the 1900s, he served as editor of *Harper's Monthly*, where he wrote a column called "The Editor's Easy Chair." From this pulpit, Howells championed realism and earned the title of "Father of American Realism." He advocated fiction that incorporated psychology, sociology, and accurate depictions of everyday life. In his own career, Howells authored more than 100 books, concentrating on the lives of characters from the upper middle class. In his post-1900 work, Howells implemented the psychological theories he studied in the day's medical books and journals. Even his titles point to this interest: *Questionable Shapes* (1903) and *Between Dark and Daylight* (1907), the latter a book of short stories exploring the ghostly images between dawn and dusk. Some critics have chastised Howells because he focused on the lives of the upper middle class instead of the masses, which may account for the lack of interest in his career by today's scholars. However, literary historian Vernon Louis Parrington said of Howells, "it is certain that for twenty years he was a prophet of realism to his generation."[11] Without a doubt, Howells influenced his contemporaries and had a profound impact on the literature of the era.

Although in his sixties during the 1900s, Howells's changing idealism acted as a philosophical bridge between the post–Civil War generation and those who came of age in the early twentieth century. Whereas his contemporaries grew more conservative with age, and turned their backs to social causes, Howells wove questions of social justice, psychology, and sociology into his fiction. Howells also marched in support of women's rights and took part in the creation of the National Association for the Advancement of Colored People (NAACP). At the same time Howells served as a pillar of the literary establishment and urbane society, he championed socialism, the labor movement, and women's rights.

Howells was one of three reigning literary giants in the 1900s. The other two, familiar names still commonly read in high school and college classes, are Mark Twain and Henry James. Both authors adopted realism and actively served as mentors, critics, and friends to the next wave of writers following in their wake.

Although Twain is best known for his works published in the decades prior to 1900, he still cast a wide shadow over the new century, although, by most accounts, Twain had grown increasingly bitter with old age. He spent the 1900s as an "international social lion ... less a man of letters than a whole corporation."[12] In his last decade (Twain died in Redding, Connecticut, in 1910), he moved almost completely into promoting and selling himself and capitalizing on his reputation. He was, in Henry James's words, "incomparable, the Lincoln of our literature."[13]

Henry James occupied a strange space in the first decade of the twentieth century. Some of his novels were considered among his greatest works—*The Wings of the Dove* (1902), *The Ambassadors* (1903), and *The Golden Bowl* (1904)—but he felt alienated from society and his audience. An expatriate living in London, James set foot in America only once during the decade, on a book tour in 1904 and 1905. He later published his diary from the trip as *The American Scene* in 1907. The book stands as a vivid portrait of a writer who no longer understands the changes taking place around him—either the money culture enveloping the nation or the mass immigration propelling city growth. James railed against "a Jewry that had burst all bounds" in New York's Lower East Side and "the New Bostonians" who had taken over his beloved city. Describing the city's Common in late winter, James commented, "The people before me were gross aliens to a man, and they were in serene and triumphant possession." In his many years away from the United States, James had not witnessed the transformations taking place, and his shocked indignation runs rampant throughout his diary entries. Twentieth-century America, in James's mind, was overrun with immigrants and controlled by monopolistic corporations pushing consumption onto "the wage-earners."[14]

The young lions who took up French novelist Emile Zola's call for literature based on truth and grounded in the deterministic forces that shaped life seemed like revolutionaries in the 1900s. The "naturalists" stormed onto the literary scene in the years preceding 1900, led by the frail, intense genius Stephen Crane who some say that along with Zola, was the inspiration for all the best writing from this decade. His *Maggie, a Girl of the Streets*, self-published in 1893, was a grim look at Irish immigrant life in lower Manhattan based on his firsthand experiences. The book did not sell well, but Howells gave it a stunning review in the *New York Press*, comparing Crane to Russian novelist Leo Tolstoy. The praise lifted Crane's spirits, and he pushed on after nearly giving up writing for good.

Crane's prevailing aim was to express the "truth of life" and "get down the real thing."[15] To achieve his goal, Crane waited in a bread line during a blizzard with unemployed workers, slept in a Bowery flophouse, and lived with tramps in immigrant neighborhoods. He approached the lower working class with actual knowledge, not the sentimentality of others. However, it was when Crane turned away from the slums and trained his eye on the Civil War with *The Red Badge of Courage* (1895) that he struck critical and commercial success. The tri-

Frank Norris (ca. 1900). Courtesy of the Oakland History
Room of the Oakland Public Library, Oakland, California.

umph of that work etched Crane permanently into the fabric of the nation. Unfortunately, Crane died at the age of 29 on June 5, 1900.

Frank Norris

American realism found its champion in Frank Norris, who grew up
in the upper middle class in San Francisco. Norris wished to portray life
as it actually was, without the literary pretensions employed by the ro-
mantics. His portrait of daily life played up the tragic or terrible events
that befell mankind.

After enrolling at the University of California at Berkeley and attending writing classes at Harvard, Norris joined the staff of *McClure's Magazine* in New York City. He arranged a meeting with Howells, who
became a mentor to the young man. In an essay, "A Plea for Romantic
Fiction," Norris exhorted writers to show "life uncloaked and bare of
conventions—the raw, naked thing, that perplexes and fascinates—life

that involves death of the sudden and swift variety, the jar and shock of unleashed passions."[16]

Over the next several years, Norris wrote overtly masculine novels filled with brutish characters, including *Moran of the Lady Letty* (1898), *McTeague* (1899), *Blix* (1899), and *A Man's Woman* (1900). With the publication of *McTeague*, the story of a brutal, self-taught San Francisco dentist, Norris became a full-time author and was regarded as one of the top writers of his generation. Thinking the book's portrayal of murder unfit for decent readers, one reviewer said Norris "riots in odors and stenches" and could have called the book, "McTeague: A Study in Stinks." Howells, however, wrote a lengthy review praising the book, pointing to the "little miracles of observation" and "vivid insight."[17]

Norris planned a trilogy, called the "Trilogy of Wheat," which he hoped would be the great American novel. The books followed the life cycle of wheat: growth in California, sale in Chicago markets, and distribution worldwide via railroad and steamship. Norris believed a novel should have a purpose, which he equated with telling the truth. With moral support from Howells and bolstered by the sales of *McTeague* and his other early books, Norris planned a modern epic which would encompass contemporary issues. In preparation, Norris spent four months in San Francisco and the San Joaquin Valley conducting field research and collecting interviews. He decided to base the novel on the bloody battle between wheat ranchers in San Joaquin and a sheriff's posse representing the Southern Pacific Railroad. The bloody encounter at Mussel Slough left eight men dead and forced other ranchers off their land.

After returning to New York, Norris worked at a feverish pace. By some accounts, he wrote the book in one long burst in December 1900, and the publisher worked from the first draft. *The Octopus*, published in 1901, tells the story of Magnus Derrick, a wealthy rancher who tries to stand up to the power of the railroad. He tries to save the valley, but he is predestined to fail—a great man felled by the forces of evil represented by the steel tentacles of the railroad spreading across the land. While the story is dramatic, Norris introduced many of the problems plaguing farmers: foreign competition, high freight rates, railroad regulation, and worker unrest. *The Octopus*, in the spirit of the great muckraking books of the period, examines the dark side of capitalism.

The book cemented Norris's reputation. Howells applauded its Homeric breadth and passion: "a great book, simple, somber, large, and of a final authority as the record of a tragical passage of American, of human events."[18] Praise came too from Jack London, who longed for someone to write an epic of his beloved West, saying Norris "produced results, Titanic results."[19] Unfortunately, Norris died before completing his trilogy of wheat. He finished the next book in the series, *The Pit*, but died in San Francisco of a perforated appendix on October 25, 1902. In spite of his short life, Norris impacted literature through the early 1900s and the decades beyond. His work expanded the definition of American realism and served as a model for a generation of writers who followed in his footsteps.

In an ironic twist of fate, Norris discovered his heir two years before his death while working as a reader for publishing company Doubleday, Page and Company in the summer of 1900. He received an unsolicited manuscript from Theodore Dreiser, a journalist and budding novelist. Norris claimed *Sister Carrie* (1900) was the best novel he had ever read and urged its publication, which led to a contract being offered. Norris even told a friend, "Mark my words, the name of Frank Norris isn't going to stand in American literature anything like as high as Dreiser's."[20]

Theodore Dreiser

Born into a large, poor Catholic family in Terre Haute, Indiana, in 1871, Dreiser experienced poverty on a daily basis. Prior to Theodore's birth, his father had built a thriving business around a wool factory, but he had no insurance and lost everything when a fire destroyed the shop. As a result, the family bounced around various Midwestern cities searching for work. Tired of constantly moving, Dreiser left home at 16. He lived in Chicago for a time and spent a year at Indiana University. After leaving school, Dreiser held a series of menial jobs but later returned to the bright lights of Chicago. He fell in love with the glamour and excitement of the city.

Dreiser caught a break in 1892 when Chicago's smallest paper, the *Daily Globe*, hired him as a reporter. In Chicago, then later at papers in Pittsburgh, Cleveland, Saint Louis, Toledo, and New York City, Dreiser received his real education among the dregs he covered. He witnessed firsthand the brutalities that befell beggars, alcoholics, prostitutes, and the lowest members of the working poor.

Dreiser's transformation into a novelist happened slowly. He first tried writing short stories and published the first four he completed. A friend urged him to write a study of the hard, harsh realities that made up life in the city. Fulfilling that challenge with *Sister Carrie*, Dreiser became the first American writer fully to explore in fiction the landscape of city life.

Sister Carrie chronicles urban struggle in the early twentieth century and the Darwinian ascent of Carrie Meeber, an ordinary girl who leaves Middle America to seek fame and fortune in Chicago. Her fascination with the city mirrored Dreiser's own, and he pulled pieces of the story from the experiences of his own sister, Emma, who had run away with a bartender years earlier. Tiring of factory life, where she first works,

Carrie becomes the mistress of two men and manipulates each of them to her advantage. Instead of being punished for her decadence, Carrie eventually finds stardom as an actress on the Broadway stage. The tragic figure is the saloonkeeper, George Hurstwood, who becomes a shell of his former self and finally committs suicide in a cheap hotel. Dreiser's message is clear: the relentless pursuit of money is a fool's quest and leads to tragedy.

The real-life tragedy of *Sister Carrie* was the way publisher Frank Doubleday treated the manuscript when he returned from a vacation in Europe. Even with Norris's approval, Doubleday requested major revisions, deeming the book too scandalous for the reading public. Unwilling to change the book, Dreiser forced Doubleday to honor its contract by threatening a lawsuit for breach of contract. In response, the publisher printed 1,000 copies but did not promote or advertise *Sister Carrie*. Without the backing of his publishing house, Dreiser's book sold less than 500 copies.

The initial failure of *Sister Carrie*, coupled with several harsh reviews, including disparaging comments made by Howells, drove Dreiser to a nervous breakdown. In 1903 he suffered from depression, insomnia, constipation, and headaches and was unable to write. Doctors diagnosed Dreiser as a "neurasthenic," a debilitating nervous disorder thought to disturb the affluent, who could not cope with the cultural, social, and economic changes characterizing the age. In an attempt to cure Dreiser, doctors submitted him to a rigorous set of exercises, followed by various drugs, diets, and homeopathy.[21]

On the verge of suicide, he was rescued by his brother Paul, a successful songwriter and composer, who sent him to a sanitarium in White Plains, New York. Dreiser rebounded and accepted a position as an editor at Butterick's, a company which published magazines to promote dress patterns. Life as an editor afforded Dreiser the wealth and affluence he craved. In 1907 Dreiser bought one-third of a new publishing company, B.W. Dodge, and reissued *Sister Carrie* himself. The second release proved a success for Dreiser. The book sold more than 4,500 copies in 1907 and more than 10,000 the following year. The book received rave reviews (although some critics still found its contents too wicked) and vaulted the author to the top of the literary mountain.

The power of *Sister Carrie* lies in Dreiser's portrait of urban life filled with wonderful sketches of the Chicago shoe factory, various saloons and hotels, and other streetscapes sprinkled throughout its pages. Dreiser also picked up on the consumer culture gripping the nation and made it a focal point of the book. He also recognized the influence of popular culture on the working class and how entertainment influenced their lives. Carrie Meeber is driven by the quest for money and upon her arrival in Chicago is bedazzled by the jewels she sees hanging around the necks of wealthy women and the trinkets for sale in the city's massive department stores, such as The Fair. "On her first visit," Dreiser wrote, "not only did Carrie feel the drag of desire for all which was new and pleasing in apparel for women, but she noticed too, with a touch at the heart, the fine ladies who elbowed and ignored her, brushing past in utter disregard of her presence, themselves eagerly enlisted in the materials which the store contained."[22]

In delivering a novel with the power of *Sister Carrie*, Dreiser expanded the notion of what literature could be. His bottom-up look at contemporary society shocked upper- and middle-class readers, but at the same time alerted them to another world running in parallel to their own. Perhaps Carrie's sexuality and her clawing her way to fame and fortune scared readers at the turn of the century, but this kind of battle has served both movies and television well. Carrie's story and variations on its theme have been used as the cornerstone of everything from daytime soap operas to primetime dramas such as *Dynasty* and *Melrose Place*. And, Dreiser's influence on the writers that followed him, from Steinbeck to Fitzgerald and Hemingway, simply heightens his place in the literary canon. Dreiser's work broke new ground in the early 1900s, and his legacy is formidable.

THE READING PUBLIC

Although the decade's revered authors and rising stars moved toward realistic portrayals of everyday life, other writers fed the public's appetite for nostalgia, romance, and adventure. In fact, the backlash against realism began almost immediately, if it can even be termed a counterattack. Maybe a better explanation is that the romantic novel never went out of style. It remained the most popular form of fiction after the Civil War and continued to hold the title, weathering the blip of realism and continuing to dominate the best-seller lists.

Although history, biography, and poetry all sold well during the 1900s, fiction was the cornerstone of the industry. However one interprets the era, it is impossible to mistake the fact that readers liked their fiction both romantic and sentimental. Eager to capitalize on the market, publishing houses pumped romances out in massive quantities using the distribution systems built in the last years of the previous century. Improvements in print technology and paper production also aided the publishers. As the decade progressed, many serious authors found their way onto the best-seller lists, including Jack London and Edith Wharton. The mainstays, however, were writers who wrote about love, heroism, and the nostalgic past. As early as 1900, critic Maurice Thompson summed up the feeling in the *Independent*: "Great commercial interest seems to be turned or turning from the world of commonplace life and the story of the analysis of crime and filth to the historical romance, the story of heroism, and the tale of adventure."[23]

There is no doubt regarding the public's desire for romance and historical romance. In the summer of 1901, Paul Leicester Ford sold 275,000 copies of *Janice Meredith* (1899), while Johnston's *To Have and to Hold* numbered 285,000. Even more impressive, Winston Churchill (not related to the British statesman) concentrated on historical fiction and sold more than 700,000 copies of *Richard Carvel* (1899) and *The Crisis* (1901), the romantic story of a fiery Southern heroine and a solemn Yankee hero. Other authors produced works so popular that they sold well for years. Rice's *Mrs. Wiggs of the Cabbage Patch* and John Fox Jr.'s *The Little Shepherd of Kingdom Come* (1903) both remained popular. Edward Westcott's *David Harum*, published posthumously in 1898, a tale of a shrewd, heroic country banker, had sold an amazing 1.2 million copies by 1909 and was made into a movie in both 1915 and 1934, the latter starring Will Rogers.

One of the most prolific novelists of the period was Francis Marion Crawford, who produced more than 45 novels between 1882 and 1909. He wrote formulaic, though historically accurate, historical dramas, which gave readers a glimpse of life in India, Germany, Turkey, and other exotic locales. The public gobbled up his tales which ranged from New York debutantes to middle-class Romans. Of his own work, Crawford said, "We are nothing more than public amusers." He felt novelists should concentrate on producing fiction that made people laugh or occasionally bring them to tears, but mostly deal with love. A novel, for Crawford, was nothing more than giving humanity a way of "carrying a theater in its pocket."[24]

Book publishing itself turned from a genteel profession prior to 1900 to one driven by profits, despite the outcry from many honorable older publishers who equated their professions with teaching and the ministry. Publishers feared meeting the fate of Harper's and Appleton, two of the country's oldest and most respected houses, which had to be saved from bankruptcy in 1900 by Wall Street financiers. The Wall Street influence led to a wave of business managers entering the publishing profession, who were more concerned with money than art. The infusion of business-minded professionals changed the industry, enabling it to adopt new ideas, including marketing, globalization, and the widespread use of innovative technologies. In 1900 more than 600 publishers combined to produce in excess of 7,000 new books; the number reached a record in 1907 of 9,620.

The importance of marketing and sales increased dramatically. Publishers battled to entice the insatiable reading public. With more and more companies vying for advertising space in magazines, ad rates shot up, and estimates revealed that even small publishers spent upward of $50,000 a year on advertising. The 1900s began a trend in the book industry that continues to this day—high advertising and marketing costs cut deeply into the profits, even on a best-seller.[25]

At the end of the nineteenth century, technological improvements had lowered the prices of magazines and newspapers, making them afford-able to a wider audience. The introduction of paper made from wood pulp, rather than rags, dropped costs dramatically, as did the use of photoengraving. A related factor was the general expansion of the na-tion's school system, which fed new readers into the circulation cycle. School enrollment more than doubled from 7 million in 1860 to 15.5 million in 1900. Illiteracy dropped from 17 percent in 1880 to 11 percent at the beginning of the new century.

At the same time reading became more commonplace, American busi-nesses produced an array of consumer goods that needed publicity. A new style of magazine emerged which served as a vehicle for gaudy advertisements; half the space was devoted to ads. The combination of technological advances and money acquired through ad sales dropped the price of the general circulation magazines, in turn upping circulation. A magazine like *McClure's* sold for 15 cents a copy in 1893, while *Collier's* cost only 5 cents. In contrast, older weeklies, such as *Harper's* or the *Century*, were still selling for 25 cents an issue.

Women's magazines served an important role in the 1900s. They in-troduced American households to the growing consumer culture, while delivering domestic advice. The *Ladies' Home Journal*, under editor Ed-ward Bok, advised women on everything from marriage and hygiene to architecture and interior decorating. The magazine also introduced read-ers to fiction written by Twain, Howells, and Jewett. *Good Housekeeping* set up a research institute in 1900 to test every product mentioned in its pages. The magazine introduced the Good Housekeeping Seal of Ap-proval in 1909. Other magazines, imitating the pioneering work of *Good Housekeeping*, spread awareness of food quality nationwide.

In *Selling Culture*, Richard Ohmann explained the influence of maga-zines at the turn of the century, "Magazines that came into homes helped establish and announce the social level of those homes. They also pro-vided their readers with a range of information and interests that linked them conversationally to other readers in the same circle of acquaintance, and culturally to like-minded readers across the nation."[26] In helping readers orient themselves to the transformation taking place around them, the magazines played a role in defining the professional-managerial class and culture established during the period, providing a cultural middle ground.

As circulation figures rose at the *Journal*, so did Bok's influence. He banned suggestive advertising copy and all references to alcohol and tobacco. Although a conservative, Bok took a progressive stand on sex education. In a public battle, Bok joined with the Woman's Christian

Temperance Union to oppose patent medicines, which contained high doses of alcohol and narcotic drugs. In 1904 Bok began printing the contents of the most popular patent medicines. He urged the estimated 80 million users to boycott the dangerous drugs. The $59 million dollar industry fought back when Bok printed incorrect information about Doctor Pierce's Favorite Prescription and forced him to print a retraction and pay damages. Bok's advocacy helped popularize the legislation that eventually passed through Congress as the Pure Food and Drug Act of 1906.[27]

Publishers found an eager audience among children as well. Two publications stand out: the monthly *St. Nicholas* (founded in 1873) and the weekly *Youth's Companion* (founded in 1827). *St. Nicholas* featured the work of Twain and L. Frank Baum, author of *The Wizard of Oz*. *Youth's Companion* had a circulation above 500,000 until 1907, when numerous changes were made and the magazine went into decline. Youth readers, especially boys, gravitated toward another type of magazine, called the dime novel, which were really long short stories bound into five- or ten-cent magazines.

The titles of these magazines were written to attract young male readers, but the subtitles tell the real story. They ranged from *Pluck and Luck: Stories of Adventure* to *Might and Main: Stories of Boys Who Succeed*. The greatest hero of the age was Frank Merriwell, created by George Patten (alias Burt L. Standish) for *Tip Top Weekly*. A star athlete and student at Fardale Academy and Yale University, Merriwell embodied the ideal traits in a young man. Along the way he outwitted urban bullies, Texas bandits, and even Chinese hooligans. For 20 years, Patten churned out story after story. Even though he had an estimated 125 million readers a week, Patten received only $150 per issue and died in poverty.

As innovations in the color press improved in the 1890s, newspaper publishers added color supplements to their Sunday editions. Often, they reprinted color illustrations and art from various humor magazines. Comic strip artists realized the potential of the medium and were supported by publishers hungry for an edge on the competition. The early comic artists mixed humor with social satire. Richard Felton Outcault, at one time a technical artist for Thomas Edison, began publishing a one-frame comic titled "Hogan's Alley." In the mode of the realist authors of the day, the comic featured a poor urban neighborhood and centered on a jug-eared toddler, dubbed the Yellow Kid, who captured the public's heart. Outcault's Yellow Kid fed a merchandising bonanza for Joseph Pulitzer's *New York World*, everything from Yellow Kid cigarettes to a Broadway musical.

Outcault eventually tired of the strip and grew frustrated at critics who declared comic strips were crude. In response, he created Buster Brown, an upper-class boy who terrorized everyone around him and created a constant wave of chaos. Each "Buster Brown" strip ended with a homily inspired by Ralph Waldo Emerson or Henry David Thoreau (transcendental writers and philosophers of the time), explaining what Buster had learned in the course of his adventures. The success of his strips made Outcault wealthy, and he became caught in the battle between Pulitzer and his archenemy William Randolph Hearst, the owner of the *New York Journal*.

MUCKRAKERS

At the turn of the century, America entered a reform-minded period with politicians, reporters, and civic activists spearheading the charge. Driven by society's ills and a desire to expose the seedy underbelly of the new age, a group of enterprising writers began to poke into government and corporate corruption. President Roosevelt derisively labeled them "Muckrakers," after a character in John Bunyan's *Pilgrim's Progress* who slandered those engaged in public work. While the president thought they went overboard and focused on the sensational, middle-class readers clamored for more. In fact, the muckrakers directly influenced the work of politicians and subsequent legislative efforts.

Like the realist fiction writers of the era, the muckrakers reacted to the changes sweeping the nation, focusing primarily on injustices in the corporate world and government. Investigative journalism came of age in the early 1900s, but it had its roots in the work done after the Civil War. Even the yellow journalism promoted during the Spanish-American War contributed to the muckraker movement by expanding the public's craving for news and sensationalism. The muckrakers grabbed the spotlight when technology made magazines less expensive to publish and national illiteracy rates dropped. These influences, combined with the progressive political and social movement, made the first decade of the new century ripe for the muckrakers.

Magazines and investigative journalists fed off one another in the Progressive Era. The muckrakers fueled the growth of magazines and at the same time were given a platform on which to present their work. Prices gradually dropped to ten cents a month and a dollar for a year's subscription, which allowed the pioneering *McClure's* to jump from just over 100,000 in circulation in early 1895 to 370,000 in 1900 and half a million in 1907.[28] Other magazines that grew through the publication of muckraking articles included *Collier's, Cosmopolitan, Everybody's*, the *Independent, Success*, and the *American Magazine*. The January 1903 issue of *McClure's* ushered in the muckraking movement when it published an article on municipal graft written by Lincoln Steffens, a chapter from Ida Tarbell's history of Standard Oil, and an essay written by Ray Stannard Baker. The magazines found a ready audience in middle-class readers.

"The portrayal of urban poverty, corruption, and business rapacity alternately delighted and disgusted, but always compelled and fascinated middle-class readers."[29]

The muckraking movement ran virtually in parallel with Roosevelt's presidency. Although he disliked the sensationalistic tactics employed by some writers, he respected their work. The president knew the writers and editors at the journals and sometimes invited them to White House luncheons. Many of the muckrakers, from Tarbell and Steffens to Baker and Upton Sinclair became quite famous in their own rights. Baker and Steffens actually fought over the title of the first muckraker later in life, while most historians give the nod to Steffens.

Upton Sinclair's *The Jungle*

The most famous muckraking work was Upton Sinclair's *The Jungle* (1906). The book tells the fictionalized story of Jurgis Rudkus, an immigrant who works in Chicago's meatpacking industry. Sinclair wrote the book after accepting $500 from the Socialist weekly, the *Appeal to Reason*, in 1904 to write a novel exposing the appalling practices in the city's packinghouse industry. Amazingly, after the novel was serialized in the magazine, four book publishers rejected the manuscript before Doubleday, Page and Company accepted it in 1906. An immediate bestseller, it sold steadily for a year and was then translated into 17 languages.

Sinclair discussed the intensive research he conducted prior to writing the book: "I went out there and lived among the people for seven weeks. . . . I would sit in their homes at night, and talk with them, and then in the daytime they would lay off their work, and take me around, and show me whatever I wished to see. . . . I studied every detail of their lives." Sinclair noted, "*The Jungle* is as authoritative as if it were a statistical compilation."[30]

Sinclair intended *The Jungle* to be a Socialist propaganda piece, but its gruesome scenes of the meatpacking industry appalled all readers. The vivid descriptions of the way diseased meat (and, in some cases, the workers themselves) made its way into sausage and onto the nation's dinner tables sickened people. Sinclair spared no detail in bringing these practices to light. In one scene, Antanas Rudkus is hired as a "Squeedgie" man, who works in the pickle room, "slopping the 'pickle' into a hole that connected with a sink, where it was caught and used over again forever . . . where all the scraps of meat and odds and ends of refuse were caught." Every few days, Rudkus had the "task to clean these out, and shovel their contents into one of the trucks with the rest of the meat!"[31]

Although Sinclair's book is still widely read and considered a classic piece of American literature, its socialistic aspects have been downplayed, such as Sinclair's scathing attack on the viciousness of capitalism and the corrupt nature of organized labor. The author realized how *The Jungle* affected readers. The book missed his intended mark: he had aimed for the public's head, but instead hit the public in the stomach. The subsequent furor, reaching all the way to Roosevelt, forced the government to intervene. After the meatpacking industry refused to permit federal inspection, the president released a government report critical of the industry. Almost overnight, meat sales plummeted by more than 50 percent. The only way the meatpackers could restore the public's confidence was to beg for intervention. Congress passed both the Meat Inspection Act and the Pure Food and Drug Act on June 30, 1906.

VOICES OF WOMEN AND BLACKS

While the years following 1900 were filled with optimism and hope for many individuals and groups, these years offered little optimism for blacks in the United States. Racial divisions that plagued the nation since its founding continued unabated at the turn of the century. According to one historian, "The dominant national view in America at the turn of the century was that all other peoples were inferior to the white race and indeed to persons of western European descent."[32]

Blacks and other non-Anglo citizens were denied their basic freedoms through violent intimidation, legal wrangling, and segregation. This volatile environment led to 214 blacks being lynched in 1900 and 1901 and an average of 100 a year through World War I.[33] The *Plessy v. Ferguson* (1896) case before the Supreme Court made segregation constitutionally legal and solidified the second-class status of African-Americans. The court case upheld the idea of "separate but equal," which made discrimination legal if facilities and accommodations for whites and blacks were equal. Racism was institutionalized in the Southern states with *Plessy v. Ferguson*, but blacks did not fare much better in the North. Factories and shop floors were more open to immigrants than they were to blacks in search of better lives in Northern cities.

In this environment of fear, intimidation, and legal manipulation to keep blacks disenfranchised, African-American writers fought to have their voices heard, but few were given the opportunity. Even in the South, where local authors explored the distinct flavor of the region, black authors had little impact in comparison with their white counterparts. The reading public looked to white writers, such as Joel Chandler Harris, to interpret the rural South and the black culture. Harris published the bestselling Uncle Remus stories, written in African-American dialect and based on folk characters, which remained popular, even after his death on July 3, 1908.

For the most part, women authors found it difficult to publish, especially writers who crafted serious literature. Publishers and critics, who were mostly males, marginalized many top female writers or ignored them altogether. Immigrant and black female writers found it even tougher. Few found a wide audience for their work. Publishing houses also played a role in marginalizing women and blacks. They were concerned with profitability and loathed putting out books that would not garner a large audience. Often, as in the case of critically-acclaimed African American author Charles Waddell Chesnutt, the few blacks and women who did get published only had a couple of chances to prove they could sell, or they would get dropped.

Some women writers, however, were able to find an outlet by producing popular fiction, mainly romance or historical romance works. A quick glance at the best-seller lists from the period shows more than a smattering of female representation. Their success may be linked to the political attention women gained from the suffragette Susan B. Anthony, before her death in 1906, and social worker Jane Addams. In addition, the seemingly more open-minded stance of the Progressives might have also helped women writers gain some measure of acceptance.

Despite the rampant racism and sexism of the publishing industry in the 1900s, several outstanding female and African American writers were able to emerge, most notably Edith Wharton, Booker T. Washington, and W.E.B. Du Bois. Unfortunately, the works of countless other female and black writers were suppressed in the first decade of the twentieth century and have faded into oblivion, neither read today or studied by modern scholars.

Edith Wharton

Edith Wharton (1862–1937) emerged from an affluent family that tried to squelch her literary aspirations. Despite their lack of support, she persevered and became the period's most noted woman writer. Because of her status in the leisure class, Wharton received no encouragement regarding her writing career from those in her social circle. In fact, most observers believed education to be a burden for upper-class women, ultimately weakening their constitution. After her marriage to Teddy Wharton, a wealthy Bostonian 13 years her senior, Wharton suffered from severe neurasthenia and did not recover until 1900. She later told a friend that for 12 years she experienced intense nausea and constant fatigue. Her case could be seen replicated in many female intellectuals of the day. The utter lack of mental stimulation caused acute depression and angst.

Wharton's first book, *The Decoration of Houses* (1897), written with architect Ogden Codman, examined household design. The empowerment she felt after the first book propelled Wharton toward her first book of fiction, published two years later, a collection of short stories, *The Greater Inclination*. Although well into her thirties, when most women of her class were tending to children and running the day-to-day affairs at estates, Wharton embarked on a career as a novelist and writer. After her mother's death in 1901, the Whartons moved to Lenox, Massachusetts, where she built a mansion called "the Mount." Wharton designed the house to allow her the privacy to write without interruption and as a sanctuary from her loveless marriage.

Wharton then undertook a blistering publishing schedule, producing nearly a book a year throughout the 1900s. In addition, she wrote short stories, travel accounts, and poems. Wharton set her first novel, a historical romance, *The Valley of Decision* (1902), in eighteenth-century Italy. Though the book showed talent and earned praise from noted novelist Henry James, he urged her to write about the world around her, especially the high society of old New York. She followed his advice and wrote *The House of Mirth* (1905), which established her as a best-selling author and a respected member of the literary class.

The House of Mirth tells the story of Lily Bart, a woman of New York high society at the turn of the century. Trapped by her class, and expected to marry a man of status, she longs for escape. The satirical elements of the novel are scathing, fully illuminating what Wharton regarded as a vacuous world occupied by the rich. Longing to be free, Lily is pulled back by the trappings of her social class. Ultimately, she overdoses on sleeping medication—the only freedom she had power to grasp. "As perhaps the best social historian of her day," states literary scholar Katherine Joslin, "Wharton studies the phenomenon of marriage in turn-of-the-century capitalist America, where the male barters to own a female and the female negotiates to secure a male." *The House of Mirth*, Joslin explained, portrays the "dilemma of the single woman, a capitalist commodity, who must earn her social place by enticing a wealthy male into marriage."[34]

The House of Mirth established Wharton as a literary celebrity and the book broke sales records at the time, staying at the top of the best seller list for several months. It was released in October 1905 and by Christmas, 140,000 copies were in print.[35] Her editor said the book had "the most rapid sale of any book ever published by Scribner."[36] In 1906, Wharton earned $27,000 from the royalties of *The House of Mirth* (more than $250,000 in today's dollars). Fellow authors applauded Wharton, including Henry James, Hamlin Garland, and William Dean Howells. Reviewers and critics also universally praised the work, ranging from labeling her a "genius" to saying that the book was "an absolutely flawless and satisfying piece of workmanship."[37] Wharton remained a critic's favorite throughout her career, only drawing disapproval for the pessimistic outlook portrayed in her novels. Wharton, however, was perfectly aware of this criticism, rebutting that American readers want a tragedy, only with a happy ending. Toward the end of her life, Wharton's critics charged her with being out of touch with contemporary America and not understanding the working class.

In her own life Wharton defied the picture she painted of New York society. After years of a loveless marriage, she moved to Paris in 1911, divorced in 1913, and lived out a rich intellectual life. Wharton continued to publish and two of her later books are considered classics: *Ethan Frome* (1911) and *The Age of Innocence* (1920).

Amazingly, *Ethan Frome*, a stark look at the differences between the present and recent past through the eyes of a young narrator who rec-ollects back over 25 years, became Wharton's most popular book in her lifetime, and some insisted it was her best, although she actively resisted that notion.[38] Wharton wrote the bleak tale to counter the rosy picture of New England spun by fellow authors Sarah Orne Jewett and Mary E. Wilkins Freeman. *The Age of Innocence* returns to the New York high society scene. The novel won the Pulitzer Prize in 1921, which cemented Wharton's friendship with Sinclair Lewis, since the book edged out his *Main Street* for the prize. Two years later, Yale awarded Wharton an honorary doctorate, making her the first woman to receive such an honor from any American university.

Wharton's rise to fame—conquering both the best seller lists and those who follow serious literature—is astonishing, given that female writers were simply not given the same opportunities men were in the 1900s. She had to overcome publishers, critics, and others who actively worked to keep female writers in their place. Wharton also had to fight members of her own social class, who pressured her to give up her silly hobby and were convinced that writing was a waste of time.

Collectively, her short stories, novellas, and novels from the decade paint a vivid picture of life in turn of the century America. One scholar contends that "Wharton's achievement is as varied and extensive as that of any American woman writer to the present time, and the critical work done on her in the last twenty years has irrefutably established her com-manding position in American letters."[39]

Booker T. Washington

One of the first widely accepted black writers to take the national stage in the new century was Booker T. Washington (1856–1915). His autobi-ography, *Up from Slavery* (1901), shows a life of overcoming enormous odds to achieve a semblance of the American Dream. As a child, Wash-ington lived in a one-room shack with a dirt floor, and his stepfather forbade him to learn to read or write. Instead of retreating to a life of abject poverty, his early experiences pushed Washington to emphasize education and learning. Washington rose to become president of Tuskegee Institute and advised presidents and other leaders regarding race relations.

Washington served as such an agent of polarization when he joined President Roosevelt for lunch at the White House in October 1901. The event erupted into a firestorm of protest against both men. In describing the reaction, journalist Arthur Wallace Dunn proclaimed, "For days it was one of the most widely discussed subjects in the country. In the southern states the President was universally condemned by public men and in the press."[40] Ironically, neither Roosevelt nor Washington planned the meeting to make a point about racism. The intellectual Roosevelt simply wanted to meet with the black leader to discuss a wide-ranging set of issues. However, the public outcry over a simple lunch date showed how far the nation had to go to make any kind of progress in regard to race issues.

W.E.B. Du Bois

Washington's approach to improving the lives of blacks through vocational training drew criticism from other black leaders, most prominently W.E.B. Du Bois (1868–1963). Du Bois believed it was the wrong tactic to follow. In Du Bois's mind, Washington supported a system which fundamentally denied African Americans their basic rights. Instead Du Bois favored blacks organizing their own businesses to achieve economic independence. He criticized Washington in an essay in his book *The Souls of Black Folk* (1903). Both men believed they should serve as the ultimate role model for blacks.

In contrast to Washington, Du Bois grew up in a middle-class family in Massachusetts and became the first black to earn a Ph.D. from Harvard University. Du Bois did not believe in civil rights as defined by other leaders. He urged Southern blacks to move north. After a bloody race riot in Springfield, Illinois, Du Bois and his followers held conferences at Harpers Ferry and Niagara Falls, which eventually led to the creation of the NAACP. Du Bois served as the first editor of the NAACP journal, the *Crisis*.

Comments from Du Bois's "Resolution at Harper's Ferry" speech made clear his anger: "In the past year the work of the Negro hater has flourished in the land. . . . We claim for ourselves every single right that belongs to a freeborn American, political, civil and social; and until we get these rights we will never cease to protest and assail the ears of America." On the site of executed abolitionist, John Brown's raid, Du Bois outlined the demands of black Americans and called for the nation to overturn its "cowardly creed," which had led to a "fear to let black men even try to rise lest they become the equals of the white."[41]

Other Black Writers

Black writers asserted themselves as far as possible in a white-dominated publishing system. Poet Paul Laurence Dunbar (1872–1906) and novelist Charles W. Chesnutt (1858–1932) both gained fame during the 1900s. Booker T. Washington dubbed Dunbar, a native of Dayton, Ohio, as the "Poet Laureate of the Negro Race." Although talented writers, neither Dunbar nor Chesnutt enjoyed the fame or attention heaped upon their white contemporaries. Even the most talented black writers struggled to make a living as artists. Dunbar faced financial difficulties his entire life and eventually found meaningful work in the Reading Room of the Library of Congress. Chesnutt settled down in Cleveland, Ohio, and found success as a lawyer and legal stenographer.

While financial success eluded Dunbar most of his life, he became one of America's most popular poets during the 1900s and achieved international fame. Dunbar used black dialect and standard English in his poetry. He began began publishing his verse in 1895, with *Majors and Minors*. With his first book, Dunbar grabbed the attention of William Dean Howells, who wrote a favorable review. The glowing review Howells gave regarding Dunbar's dialectic poems, however, hindered the young man as he tried to break away from the genre. American literary critics accepted black poets only when they employed the dialectic of ex-slaves. To gain acceptance, Dunbar portrayed them as contented and free of the ills associated with racism, at least in part to ease white America's guilty conscience.

A victim of tuberculosis, Dunbar died in 1906, cutting short a promising career. In addition to his volumes of poetry, he published four novels and four collections of short stories. Although today's scholars rarely study Dunbar, his career demonstrated the struggles blacks endured to be heard, even if being heard meant stifling one's heartfelt feelings. In "The Party," Dunbar employed dialectic in describing an evening of fun: "Dey had a gread big pahty down to Tom's de othah night/Was I dah?/You bet! I nevah in my life see sich a sight/All de folks f'om fou' plantations was invited, an' dey come/Dey come troopin' thick ez chillun when dy hyeahs a fife an' drum." In contrast is "Sympathy," a standard English poem which carries none of the joy contained in his dialectic work: "I know why the caged bird sings, ah me/When his wing is bruised and his bosom sore/When he beats his bars and would be free/it is not a carol of joy or glee; But a prayer that he sends from his heart's deep core/But a plea, that upwards to Heaven, he flings/I know why the caged bird sings!"[42] Contemporary African American author and poet Maya Angelou titled her autobiography, *I Know Why the Caged Bird Sings* as a parody on the Dunbar poem, which laments physical human bondage and the mental bondage that accompanies it.

Born in Cleveland, Ohio, Chesnutt spent most of his life until age 25 in Fayetteville, North Carolina. Self-taught through rigorous studies, he served as a teacher and administrator in schools in North and South Carolina until moving north in the 1880s. Eventually, he moved to Cleveland. Chesnutt began writing short stories, many of which were published in newspapers. In 1887 one was published in the *Atlantic Monthly*, the first time a black writer's work was published in the magazine. His first two short story collections, both published in 1899, *The Conjure Woman* and *The Wife of His Youth*, explore the grim world of slavery. Chesnutt confronted issues of racial prejudice, including the actions of middle-class blacks in Cleveland, which he renamed "Groveland." As an African American writer in the 1900s, Chesnutt used irony to make points about racial stereotypes, and the short story served as his primary weapon.

Chesnutt also published three novels during the 1900s: *The House Behind the Cedars* (1900), *The Marrow of Tradition* (1901), and *The Colonel's Dream* (1905). Collectively, these works examined interracial love, cooperation, and harmony. In Chesnutt's last novel, a Southern aristocrat tries to overcome the slave culture, but despite his efforts, he is driven out of the region. Once again, Chesnutt's talent could not overcome the racial imbalance. "For the last thirty years of his life, he remained active in civil rights work, but he wrote almost no fiction," said one scholar. "His blighted career and enforced silence remain an eloquent indictment of America's racial beliefs."[43]

Racist Writers

Despite the efforts of Washington and Du Bois, blacks continued to fight against stereotypes and racism daily. The new century brought hope and optimism, but it did not deliver tolerance or harmony. White supremacists attacked blacks and used "pseudo-scientific" methodologies, such as skull measurement, terminology, and supposed expert opinion, to support their position that blacks were physically and mentally inferior. William P. Calhoun's *The Caucasian and the Negro* (1902) and William Pickett's *Negro Problem* (1909), both racist works, attempted to justify the position of white supremacy. Whites, when they included black characters in fiction, most often portrayed blacks as savages or simpletons. And, these kinds of books flourished in the North and South.

Thomas Dixon Jr., a former Baptist minister, promulgated racial division. He wrote three racist books that were commercially successful: *The Leopard's Spots* (1902), *The Clansman* (1905), and *The Traitor* (1907). Dixon celebrated the racial violence of the Ku Klux Klan, lamented that the

South had lost the Civil War, and criticized Reconstruction. Despite the nation's progressive political attitude, Dixon's works sold well, even prompting filmmaker D.W. Griffith to use *The Clansman* as the outline for his legendary film *The Birth of a Nation* in 1915.

The 1900s

9

Music

What we must arrive at is the youthful optimistic vitality and the
undaunted tenacity of spirit that characterizes the American man.
That is what I hope to see echoed in American music.
—Edward MacDowell

In the early years of the twentieth century, music ranked just slightly
behind literature as the most popular art form in the United States. By
1900 most major cities had orchestras or would establish them in the
next decade. American classical musicians were steeped in the musical
traditions of Europe and, most classical composers trained on the Continent. Although serious music in the country had strong European (primarily Germanic) influences, some innovative renegades hungered for a
truly "American" sound. In the attempt to define a national music, these
composers searched for the country's roots and unique folklore or looked
to the alternative forms blossoming in Russia and France. In deciding
what American folklore actually meant, these artists turned to the types
of music deemed most primitive: the music of American Indians and
blacks. According to one music history scholar, "Through the first three
decades of the twentieth, folklorism exerted a strong pull on many composers, who yearned to free themselves from a European musical yoke,
hoping to be somehow recognizably 'American.' "[1] Native American
songs and black spirituals inspired a number of symphonic works.

During the decade, cities and towns built concert halls, opera houses,
and theaters. Middle- and working-class tastes ran toward the music
found in outdoor concerts, saloons, dance halls, and vaudeville houses.
Churches also served as an important source of music. Church-related

social gatherings, such as choir practice, provided congregation members with a way to express themselves musically and spread song into the community.

Music filled many American homes as members of the family participated in various forms of musical expression. Family members played the piano, banjo, guitar, and harmonica and sang together. The availability of sheet music (containing both classical and popular compositions) spurred on these spontaneous performances. Throughout the 1900s, publishing companies specializing in sheet music, concentrated in New York City on Tin Pan Alley, catered to the constant demand for new popular pieces people could play in their homes. Long before radio or television invaded American households, families provided their own forms of musical entertainment.[2]

ORCHESTRAL MUSIC

Serious music in the 1900s was dominated by foreign influences, particularly those of Germany. Many of the most popular and renowned native-born composers trained in either Germany or Austria, then returned to the United States after receiving classical instruction. The roots of the Germanic influence stretched back to the mid-1850s when prominent Continental musicians performed with the New York Philharmonic, Chicago Symphony, and Boston Symphony.

Native composers and musicians took cautious steps toward discovering a truly American sound in the 1900s, by writing music that could be identified as American.

They found inspiration in American folklore directly related to life in the young nation. The ability of these musical vanguards to break the ties to Europe allowed an iconoclast like Charles Ives to explore a variety of unique musical styles in the decades after the 1900s.

A small group of influential American composers formed a tight-knit group. Many of them studied together at various times in their careers. The group included John Knowles Paine, Frederick S. Converse, Horatio W. Parker, Henry K. Hadley, and Arthur Farwell. The most famous and popular composer of the period, however, was Edward MacDowell. As the decade passed, most of the important composers linked themselves to large universities and budding music departments.

Paine (1839–1906) held the first chair of music at an American university when he won an appointment to Harvard in 1873. He also served as the college organist. Parker became a professor of music at Yale in 1894, while working as the director of music at Boston's Trinity Church. An opera Paine composed, *The Pipe of Desire*, became the first American opera performed at the Metropolitian Opera House (1910). Converse

(1871–1940) joined Paine at Harvard and also taught at the New England Conservatory.

Edward MacDowell (1861–1908) was born in New York City and studied piano and composition in Paris and Frankfurt. After more than a decade in Germany, teaching, composing, and playing concerts, MacDowell returned home, then later lived in Boston. In 1895 Columbia University invited MacDowell to become its first professor of music. At his appointment, university officials hailed MacDowell as "the greatest musical genius America has produced."[3] He taught at Columbia for the next nine years, until 1904, when he became embroiled in a public dispute with university officials and retired. MacDowell's composing also came to an end that year as a result of declining health, aggravated by a horse-cab accident, a growing problem confronting urban residents in the 1900s.

MacDowell composed works that expressed his vision of an idealistic life that could be inspirational. He thought that music was meant to do more than just please the ear. The notes, MacDowell believed, should bring out the spiritual aspect of life, make people want to aspire to achieve great things, and bring hope and faith. When composing, MacDowell worked tirelessly, both day and night, revising what he had previously written and waiting for the touches of inspiration that he felt were almost supernatural.[4]

MacDowell's reputation, in part, rested on his prolific publishing output. He wrote symphonies, piano concertos, sonatas, and many other pieces, primarily for the piano. An avowed romanticist, MacDowell explored landscapes, seascapes, and medieval romance in his compositions. Among his works were a symphonic poem (*Lancelot and Elaine*), a suite for orchestra (*Les Orientales*), and childhood memories ("From Uncle Remus," *Woodland Sketches*), all in the romantic vein.[5]

Arthur Farwell (1872–1952), a student of MacDowell, served as an early pioneer in establishing an American sound. He looked to Native American music, primarily based on Omaha tribal dances and songs. In 1901 Farwell established the Wa-Wan Press to encourage others to explore nontraditional forms of expression and give them a forum for publication.

Farwell demanded that music education break free from German domination and that common people be given educational opportunities. The Wa-Wan Press, headquartered in Newton Centre, Massachusetts, scraped by on minimal funding and few profits, but gave younger artists a place to publish, mostly short piano pieces. In 1903, Farwell went on a combined concert/lecture tour to keep Wa-Wan afloat. Two years later, Farwell established the American Music Society in Boston and opened centers in other cities across the nation. At the end of the decade, Farwell moved to New York City. He worked as a music critic, supervisor of the city's park concerts, and was director of a music school settlement.[6]

Farwell concentrated on Native American music because he thought that they were connected to a universal creative spirit. The simplicity and spontaneity of Native American song, in Farwell's eyes, was a soothing contrast to the chaotic, money-driven music he thought was taking over the nation. Farwell did not limit his work to Native American influences. He also produced songs that contained African-American spirituals and songs that combined the two, such as *Folk Songs of the West and South* (1905).[7]

Eleven years after founding the press, Farwell sold the business to G. Schirmer. At that time, Wa-Wan published works by 37 composers, many specializing in Native American and black music. Henry F.B. Gilbert (1868–1928) also championed the use of black music. He composed the operas *Comedy Overtures on Negro Themes* (1905) and *The Dance in Place Congo* (1906).

Gilbert never undertook the formal musical training of his contemporaries, although he was a skilled violinist, but did study composition with several outstanding teachers, including MacDowell. His single goal was to make music that was strictly American and un-European. Gilbert wrote pieces that would "smack of our home-soil, even though it may be crude."[8]

Poor health forced Gilbert to work part-time on his musical career, but he did find the strength to help Farwell run the Wa-Wan Press, which published six of his piano pieces and more than a dozen of his songs. Gilbert drew inspiration from popular authors, such as Mark Twain, Walt Whitman, Henry Thoreau, and Edgar Allen Poe. He also favored the use of humor in music.[9]

Gilbert's importance was in forcefully advocating a different point of view as a pioneer of American music. He was not a stylist, but his music came alive with optimism and buoyancy. Gilbert's music did not pander to the high society, but reveled in the minutia of everyday life. This ideal led his critics to label Gilbert vulgar and simplistic. His supporters, however, applauded the music's freshness, vigor, and individuality.

ORCHESTRAS

The first important orchestra founded in the new century was the Philadelphia Orchestra. It was formed from two competing musical groups in the city—the Philadelphia Symphony Society and a smaller ensemble of professional musicians, the Thunder Orchestra. Fritz Scheel, a German active in New York, Chicago, and San Francisco since his arrival in the United States in 1893, served as the conductor. The group's first concert took place on November 16, 1900.

Backers found Scheel and the musicians so impressive that they set up a fund of $15,000 to fund the group. After a successful first season, the Philadelphia Orchestra Association formed, and the orchestra began touring nearby Pennsylvania towns. By the third season, the company had gained a great reputation, which led to performing concerts in Baltimore, Washington, D.C., and New York City.

Just over 300 miles north, the Boston Symphony opened a new concert hall in October 1900. From 1898 to 1906, Wilhelm Gericke conducted. After Gericke, the orchestra acquired Karl Muck, an outstanding musician and conducting genius. Under his direction, the Boston Symphony climbed to its greatest peak and reputation to date. Muck's first tour of duty with the symphony lasted only two years. In 1908 the German Kaiser Wilhelm demanded Muck return to Berlin's Royal Opera. In 1912 Muck returned to Boston where he continued his fine work with the symphony.

Given its current place atop the cultural world, one would assume that New York always had the finest musical groups. However, Boston operated as the ideological center of the musical world in the 1900s. Paine led a group of composers and musicians collectively known as the Second New England School. There were no formal ties among members of the group; most were colleagues or students of Paine.

Collectively, the Second New England School, or the Boston Six, as they were also known, wished to produce indigenous American music, distinct from European composers. Members of the group, including John Knowles Paine, Horatio Parker, George Chadwick, Edward MacDowell, Amy Beach, and Arthur Foote, wrote the first substantial body of classical music in the United States. For example, Foote, who studied under Paine at Harvard, became widely known for chamber music, art songs, and music for choirs. His early prowess led many critics to consider him the "Dean of American Composers" in the 1900s and 1910s. He influenced subsequent generations of musicians through his writings.

SINGERS HIT THE HIGH NOTE

Concerts most often featured famous singers rather than instrumentalists. Even the early phonograph companies, including Columbia Phonograph Company (1887) and Victor Talking Machine Company (1901), specialized in recording opera stars.

The proving ground for many singers was Maurice Grau's Academy of Music in New York City. Grau gave his operatic stars free rein to pick their own music, their own roles, and even allowed them to tinker with the score. As long as crowds packed the hall, Grau kept them happy. He paid Polish tenor Jean de Reszke the princely sum of $2,500 a performance during the 1900–1901 season, even though the accompanying musicians barely made a living wage.

The most famous opera singers in the 1900s were Italian tenor Enrico Caruso and American soprano Geraldine Farrar. Caruso made his first appearance at the Metropolitan Opera on November 23, 1903. It was the first of his more than 600 performances with the Met. The Italian star paved the way for the Italian repertoire. Later, during the 1905–1906 season, Caruso sang *Faust*, his first French opera in New York.

Interestingly, the New York opera season of 1905–1906, ended more than $100,000 in the black. In an ironic twist of fate, the San Francisco earthquake erased the profit. The Metropolitian Opera was playing there and the resulting fire razed the company's scenery and costumes. Replacing them ate up the budget. Most detrimental to the fortunes of the company, all the advance ticket sales had to be refunded.

On November 26, the opening night of the New York 1906–1907 season, the Metropolitan welcomed a 24-year-old singer named Geraldine Farrar, making her American debut after five successful years in Europe, wowing crowds from Berlin to Monte Carlo. In short notice, the Melrose, Massachusetts, singer became the only opera star who could equal Caruso as a box-office draw.

Admirers described Farrar as dark, vivacious, and girlish. Known for her beautiful and pure voice, Farrar also had a reputation for hard work and intense loyalty. "Intensely independent, she was also reasonable, fair, and generous," said author and historian Edward Wagenknecht. "Above all else, she had a brain, and she applied it to everything she did."[10]

TIN PAN ALLEY

The focal point of popular music in the 1900s surfaced on a single block in New York City at 28th Street between Fifth Avenue and Broadway. In 1903 Monroe Rosenfeld, a songwriter and journalist, researching an article on popular music for the New York *Herald*, dubbed the area "Tin Pan Alley." According to legend, Rosenfeld visited the famous songwriter Harry von Tilzer in his office and heard the distinctive von Tilzer sound, a tinny piano with paper wrapped around the strings to produce the effect. Soon, the term represented not only that area, but the entire music industry in the United States. Von Tilzer, ever the showman, insisted years later that he came up with the designation.[11]

On that single block, the nation's most powerful music publishers set up shop to be close to the stars and stages of Broadway. The first firm on Tin Pan Alley was M. Witmark and Sons, which opened offices at 49 West 28th Street in 1893. Shortly thereafter, the street was lined with music publishing firms trying to cash in on the demand for sheet music

"I Won't Be Home Until Late, Dear! (I've Some Real
'Pressing Business' On Hand)," words and music
by W.P. Chase (1909). Courtesy of the Oakland
Public Library, Oakland, California.

nationwide. Next, Tin Pan Alley swelled with an influx of pianists, ar-
rangers, composers, conductors, and lyricists—the grease that oiled the
publishing machine.

As the demand for new songs increased, the quality of the work suffered, even though young writers such as George Gershwin and Irving
Berlin got their starts in the firms along Tin Pan Alley. The publishing
companies were highly competitive and blatantly copied words or
themes. The music houses played a cutthroat game, since the possible
payout for a hit song could be very high.

Tin Pan Alley has been described as a musical assembly line, so it is
appropriate that many songs were written specifically to exploit the latest American technological achievements, such as airplanes, automobiles,
and telephones. If a particular word or name gained popularity, dozens
of writers grabbed the idea and many competing versions sprang into

"Take Me Up With You Dearie," words by Junie
McCree, music by Albert Von Tilzer (1909).
Courtesy of the Oakland Public Library, Oakland,
California.

existence. "The sole yardstick by which Tin Pan Alley measured its success was the number of copies sold of the sheet music," explained one
music historian, "since the sheet music sale represented the only source
of income for both publisher and writers."[12]

Although it had no altruistic ideas at heart, Tin Pan Alley did cut a
wide swath through American life. In 1903 native American songs were
the most popular. Songs devoted to airplanes, such as "Come, Josephine,
in My Flying Machine," and automobiles, like "In My Merry Oldsmobile," celebrated the innovations of the United States, newly minted as
a world power. "Meet Me in St. Louis, Louis," directed the nation's attention to the 1904 Saint Louis World's Fair, another spectacular display
of American might and ingenuity. Music served an important role

throughout the period, bonding people together (often immigrants from vastly different cultures) and playing upon their patriotic heartstrings.[13]

Vast fortunes were the name of the game on Tin Pan Alley as million dollar sales grew increasingly more frequent. Von Tilzer (1872–1946), perhaps the most famous musician, composer, and publisher on Tin Pan Alley, had great success with "A Bird in a Gilded Cage" (1900), which sold over 2 million copies. Von Tilzer later claimed to have published more than 2,000 songs in his career. By the end of the decade, "In the Shade of the Old Apple Tree" by Beth Whitson and Leo Friedman sold an astronomical 8 million copies. In all, nearly 100 songs sold more than a million copies of sheet music in the 1900s. If a song sold a million copies, the publisher might make $100,000 in profit, which doubled if he also wrote the song. Composers and lyricists who were not publishers earned about $50,000 each. In the 1900s, most writers charged a royalty of five percent.[14]

The publishing companies used both common tactics and unusual strategies to get people to hear their songs. One avenue was to sell sheet music at department stores and five-and-dime shops. In the 1900s department stores grew into a major source of sales. The publishing houses employed "pluggers" to go to the stores to perform the songs as an enticement. In essence, the pluggers were the 1900s version of MTV. They gave mini-performances, playing to the crowds who yearned to hear the latest music. The role of the plugger expanded beyond the department stores to encompass duties similar to today's publicists and public relations specialists.

In addition to singing songs for any audience that would listen, pluggers exerted pressure on major stage stars to sing their songs. If a big name singer decided to use a song, it could mean the difference between success and failure. The ingenuity of a plugger pushed some songs to best-seller status. Mose Gumble, a bald singing plugger, prowled Coney Island, New York City amusement park and boardwalk, dance halls, ice cream parlors, and restaurants singing to the crowds. Some nights he even slept on the beach to be there in the morning in an effort to persuade Coney Island singers to use his songs during that day's performances. In 1905 Gumble's efforts lifted Egbert Van Alstyne's "In the Shade of the Old Apple Tree" to one of the year's most popular songs.

When nickelodeons, a new kind of storefront theater showing films all day long, came into vogue, pluggers were there to capitalize on the captive audiences. Pluggers cajoled house pianists to play their songs, which served as the background for silent movies. Nickelodeons were a perfect venue for debuting songs since they featured fictional films, so the Tin Pan Alley hits became almost like soundtrack pieces. It was common to find pluggers singing songs prior to the beginning of the movie or during intermission. It was not unusual to find a plugger working up to eight

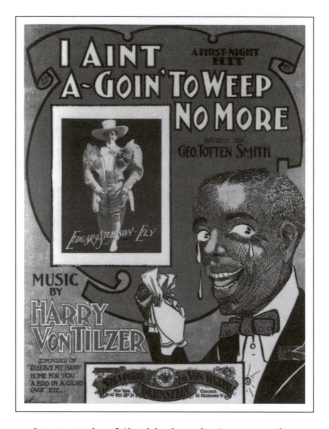

An example of the black caricatures used as covers for Tin Pan Alley sheet music: "I Aint a-Goin' to Weep No More," words by George Totten Smith, music by Harry Von Tilzer (1900). Courtesy of the Oakland Public Library, Oakland, California.

theaters an evening and countless more on the weekend. Former baseball player turned plugger, Sammy Smither, claimed that he could plug a song 50 times in one evening.[15]

THE KING OF RAGTIME

No craze swept the public's imagination in the 1900s more than ragtime, which first appeared on sheet music in 1893 in Fred S. Stone's "My Ragtime Baby." The term was used on and off over the years, but is most closely associated with Scott Joplin, who was known as the "King of Ragtime." In 1899 his piano piece "Maple Leaf Rag" became the first

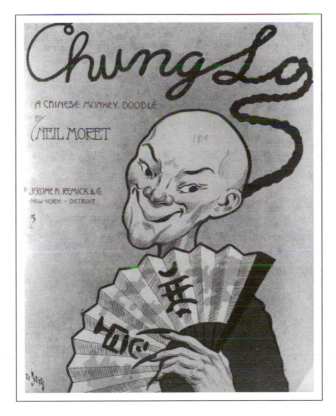

An example of the racism rampant in Tin Pan Alley songs: "Chung Lo: A Chinese Monkey Doodle," by Neil Moret (1910). Courtesy of the Oakland Public Library, Oakland, California.

ragtime composition to hit best-seller status. Joplin's success started a rage that swept the nation. Before long, ragtime tunes were played by piano bands and dance bands around the country and on player pianos, and enjoyed substantial sheet music sales. In the same year as Joplin's first hit, novelist Rupert Hughes described ragtime as "a mood that is having a strange renascence and is sweeping the country like a plague of clog-hopping locusts."[16]

Scholars have not been able to pin down the definitive origin of ragtime, but do know that it blossomed in the late 1890s. Ragtime developed in the Mississippi Valley, the creation of mostly black pianists that lived and traveled through the region. Some scholars trace its origins to minstrel shows, while others believe that it developed from dance music and the Cakewalk, a burlesque dance performed primarily in Southern minstrel shows.

In its simplest form, ragtime is syncopated music that is often either high-spirited and danceable or slow and romantic. Ragtime's popularity in the seedy dance houses and saloons at the turn of the century fueled a national dance craze. While ragtime began as racy dance music, it slowly gained a measure of dignity. African American artists and composers used ragtime as a means of pushing into the music business.

Joplin (1868–1917) was born in Texarkana, Texas, on the dusty, dry border of Texas and Arkansas. As did most blacks in the Reconstruction era, Joplin had a difficult childhood. His father, Jiles, was an ex-slave who worked on the railroad and later deserted the family. Raising Scott and his brothers fell on his mother, Florence, who worked as a domestic servant to white families.

Music played an important role in Joplin's early life. Reportedly, his father played the fiddle and his mother played the banjo, and he and his brothers were taught to sing along. The northeastern section of Texas called home by the Joplins was filled with people from the South who had brought their regional songs with them. It is likely that Joplin experienced different varieties of music from all the Gulf Coast states and especially from New Orleans. Growing up in a biracial community also exposed Joplin to music from the white community, such as waltzes and polkas.[17]

Florence Joplin worked for a wealthy attorney in Texarkana who allowed Scott to play the piano while his mother cleaned. The boy displayed an innate natural ability. Word spread quickly, and by the age of 11, he was receiving free lessons from a German teacher in sight reading and classical composition. His father even managed to save enough money to buy a piano for the boy. Although Joplin's total immersion in music grew into a sore spot for Jiles, the youngster played at church gatherings and community events. He also played professionally, by himself and later with a local band, the Texas Medley Quartette.[18]

Joplin left Texas and toured the country as a professional musician. At the age of 24, he found himself in Chicago at the World's Columbian Exposition in 1893. The world of the exposition was a far cry from the small towns Joplin had lived in since leaving Texarkana. Jackson Park exploded with light from the glittery electric lights, and the midway pulsed with thousands of visitors from all over the world. The Columbian Exposition was the first time the young performer heard ragtime, with its roots in slave songs and complicated African cadences.

Joplin later moved to Sedalia, Missouri, where he took classes at the George R. Smith College for Negroes. While there he taught piano and composition at the school. At night, Joplin played piano at the Maple Leaf Club, which he later immortalized in his most famous rag composition. In Sedalia, Joplin met John Stark, a music store owner, who served as his publisher. In 1900 the musician moved to Saint Louis in an attempt to capitalize on his growing fame. The city was a mecca for black musicians, especially ragtime pianists.

Joplin's success in 1899 with "Maple Leaf Rag," which sold well for the next decade, had cultural ramifications that become clearer in hindsight. Many observers considered ragtime the "first genuine American musical expression." Joplin's work also helped, to some extent, to bridge the color barrier between the races. One Joplin biographer points out that "African American ragtime musicians created the music, but white businessmen, musicians, and writers mediated the presentation of African American ragtime to its audience and market."[19]

In fact, throughout the rest of the twentieth century, whites often co-opted black music and presented it in a watered down version to appeal to white audiences, especially during the first two decades of rock and roll. The most notable example of this is Elvis Presley, whose early hits were often remakes of songs originally done by black artists. Elvis, however, wasn't alone. Many white performers gained popularity with black songs, including the Beatles and the Rolling Stones. On today's music scene, one sees white rap performers building on the groundwork laid by black artists to make the music more palatable for white middle class suburbanites.

Although Joplin wrote hit after hit in the 1900s, he still faced the limitations placed on black musicians. Although Joplin wrote ballets, operas, and musicals during this period, his publishers only wanted to see short, popular piano pieces. Though Joplin and Stark described his work as "classical ragtime" to separate it from other versions, in the end, even someone of Joplin's stature could not move beyond ragtime. Joplin spent the last decade of his life in New York City, trying desperately to leave a lasting impression on American music.[20]

Joplin's life and work reveal both the advantages and limitations of living in America in the 1900s. As a black man, Joplin achieved great wealth and fame. However, his color kept him from enjoying the kind of success he desired as a serious composer. Although ragtime is acknowledged as one of the first truly American forms of music and was all the rage in the 1900s, it also evoked images of slavery. The cover for Joplin's song "Original Rags" depicts an old hunched-over black man, smoking a corncob pipe in front of a ramshackle house with a mangy dog in the front yard. The cover of his song "The Easy Winner," however, portrays a vastly different world. This cover shows sailboats, horse racing, and young whites playing football. The dichotomy Joplin represented is one that still afflicts America today. "Scott Joplin was intimately involved in the making of American music," notes biographer Susan Curtis, "the distinctive American sound depended on the artistry of African Americans."[21]

JAZZ

The nation's preoccupation with ragtime, based on African American music, gave rise to another uniquely American music—jazz. Born in a section of New Orleans where blacks gathered on Sundays, jazz sprang to life from the horn of Charles "Buddy" Bolden (1871–1931), who played dance music for the crowds. Bolden and other Louisiana musicians heard the syncopated melodies of ragtime and gave them an uptempo beat. The earliest jazz blended dance music, the blues, and ragtime into one musical whole.

Bolden grew up in a social setting that set the stage for jazz to come alive. As a boy, he undoubtedly heard the brass bands that played in clubs around the black neighborhoods and heard the same groups at social gatherings, including the elaborate funeral marches played in the South. He would have also heard the field songs sung by plantation workers and the classical works played by educated Creoles. Bolden got his start playing in small string bands, which allowed him to experiment with bolder styles.[22]

By 1905 Bolden was famous around New Orleans for his swinging beat. Pianist Ferdinand "Jelly Roll" Morton, a young Creole who became an important figure on the jazz scene, remembered hearing the wail of Bolden's horn from all over the city, calling out the start of a dance in Lincoln Park. Bolden also had an impact on Louis Armstrong, who, as a young boy, listened to Bolden perform around New Orleans. As Bolden's fame grew, he appeared regularly at the Union Sons Hall, renamed "Funky Butt" by the dance crowd. "Funky Butt" also served as the title of Bolden's theme song. Soon people were singing the song up and down the mighty Mississippi River.[23]

Bolden's success was short-lived. Even as his popularity peaked, he began experiencing severe mood swings and depression, which he tried to cure by drinking. In 1907, after experiencing fits of violence, Bolden was sent to a state mental institution, where he remained for the next 24 years. It is unlikely Bolden ever heard the way his music flowered into the jazz explosion that swept the country in subsequent years.

Luckily, jazz survived Bolden's decline and did not go out of style. Other black horn players, notably Buddy Petit and Bunk Johnson, took up where Bolden left off. Bands around New Orleans set up shop on the back of horse-drawn wagons and played as they were pulled through the streets. Freddie Keppard, who formed the Olympia Orchestra in 1905, rose to prominence, playing both classical shows for high society gatherings and jazz at area dance clubs. Keppard later joined the Original Creole Orchestra, the first jazz band to play outside New Orleans, which traveled to San Francisco in 1913 and to Chicago a year later.[24]

From its humble origins in New Orleans, jazz crept across the nation,

"The 'Jelly Roll' Blues (Fox-Trot)," by Ferd "Jelly
Roll" Morton (1915). Courtesy of the Oakland
Public Library, Oakland, California.

slowly picking up pace. A number of factors helped spread the music,
including early records (after 1917), World War 1 (which spread black
performers around the United States and Europe), and the radio (after
1920). In the second decade of the twentieth century, jazz became so
enveloping that the era was renamed the Jazz Age.

In the first decade of the twentieth century, while classical and symphonic music labored under the spell of European influences, popular
music arrived to define what it meant to be an American. In the 1900s,
one sees the beginning of pop music and the powerful way it seized the
public's imagination. American musicians worked in the popular vein to
develop a truly national music, although classicists thumbed their noses
at music that grew from slave songs and African beats. Pop tunes,
whether played at home from sheet bought at the nearby department
store or heard at an outdoor concert on the town square, enabled the
definition of Americanism to be widely dispersed, then solidified.

10

Performing Arts

Gentlemen will please refrain from Smoking, Spitting or using Pro-
fane Language During the Performance.
                    —Notice to the audience on a nickelodeon screen (1900s)

It is not a stretch to claim that Americans craved entertainment in the
1900s more than in any previous decade. For the first time, many families
had excess leisure time and spending money. The billions of pages of
Tin Pan Alley sheet music sold, and the plays, musicals, and concerts
performed nationwide reflected an increasing demand for amusement.
Later in the decade a new form of entertainment gained an overwhelming following—motion pictures, or "flickering flicks," as they
were also known.

The cult of celebrity propelled the public's desire to see theater—musicals, dramas, and comedies—in the early years of the new century. In
New York City alone in 1900 there were 40 theaters, six vaudeville
houses, and several stages specializing in entertainment for specific ethnic groups, such as the Yiddish theater. But it was the players, much
more than the plays, people turned out to see. The emerging middle
class put on their Sunday best and paid for the opportunity to cheer
world-famous actor William Gillette as the methodical Sherlock Holmes,
the legendary Sarah Bernhardt in Edmond Rostand's *L'Aiglon*, and perhaps the greatest actor of his day, Richard Mansfield, whose ego and
tantrums matched his ability on stage in *Dr. Jekyll and Mr. Hyde*. Thea-
tergoers were starstruck, and just a glimpse of their favorite actors and
actresses made the evening out all the more enticing.

Working-class individuals often preferred a less sophisticated form of entertainment—vaudeville and burlesque. Whether or not its leaders publicly acknowledged it, nearly every town in America had a vaudeville theater in the 1900s. Musical comedies also thrilled audiences looking for titillation rather than highbrow entertainment. But, like saloons, racetracks, and betting houses, vaudeville performances were a place where rich and poor mixed. People across social classes also flocked (whether openly or secretly) to seedier forms of entertainment, such as "leg shows" and striptease acts. As long as audiences clamored for this kind of entertainment and backers could make money from it, the seedy side would be available for those who wanted it.

Vaudeville houses in the biggest markets performed two shows a day to packed houses in glitzy theaters. In smaller cities and less glamorous locales, there might be as many as six shows a day. Theaters such as the Majestic in Chicago and the 27-house chain Orpheum Theater, headquartered in Chicago with branches in Brooklyn and San Francisco, were first-run palaces in which families held reservations year after year for weekly performances. The popularity of vaudeville shows drew crowds away from more serious theater, but not as dramatically as movies soon would.

Scholars and film historians have not come to a consensus on the importance of film during the 1900s. Certainly Theodore Roosevelt never realized its potential. He did not use the medium to his advantage, although he was filmed on different occasions while he was president. When Henry Cabot Lodge suggested that Roosevelt use film in his upcoming campaign, the president sarcastically asked if he should do a dance for Thomas Edison's motion picture camera.

Notwithstanding Roosevelt's shortsightedness, by the end of the decade there were approximately 10,000 movie theaters in the United States, whether they were converted vaudeville palaces or ramshackle sheds in rural areas. And people were going to movies as often as possible—approximately 10 million people a week were going to motion pictures at the end of the decade. Scholars believe that in 1910 movies did a greater volume of business than all the various forms of theater, dime museums, lectures, concerts, and street carnivals combined. Only vaudeville drew more customers than movies.

Attendance in the 1920s jumped to an average of 40 million per week, which then increased to 90 million by 1930. Dipping slightly during the Great Depression, weekly attendance had returned to 90 million by the late 1940s. In contrast, today's attendance figures now average less than 20 million a week. Most movies today are shown at giant multiplexes, huge subdivided spaces that can hold as many as 20 smaller theaters.

Also similar to our own times, movies came under fire in the 1900s from churches, reform groups, and social workers for loosening standards of morality. The fervor reached a peak in New York City in 1907 when mayor George B. McClellan revoked the licenses of the city's 600 theaters after the clergy banded together to dispute films they deemed immoral and the practice of showing movies on Sundays. In response, production companies banded together to form a self-regulated overseeing body, known as the National Board of Review of Motion Pictures (NBR), which placed restrictions on movies in hopes that it would end censorship at the local level.[1]

The NBR, in cooperation with local municipalities, ushered in an unprecedented period of growth for the movie industry. As a result, former vaudeville theaters were renovated and turned into grand palaces where families could enjoy spending their free time (and money) seeing a movie. Business interests quickly realized the moneymaking potential of the movie industry and set out to legitimize the business. According to one historian, "As reformers successfully pressured movie exhibitors to clean up their theaters, to install paramilitary ushers to protect women and ensure order, and to remove objectionable films, middle-class patrons flocked to films with the same enthusiasm as did immigrants and workers."[2]

Beginning with serious theater and vaudeville and moving quickly to motion pictures, the entertainment industry in the 1900s grew at a phenomenal rate. It was during this period that people (especially the middle and working classes) became comfortable with the idea of spending time and money on leisurely pursuits.

In the mill town of Homestead, Pennsylvania, workers at the Carnegie Steel works found some measure of respite at the nickelodeon, although most mill workers barely scraped by near or at the poverty line. Summing up the appeal of motion pictures, sociologist Margaret F. Byington declared, "What it ordinarily offers does not educate but does give pleasure . . . for five cents the nickelodeon offers fifteen minutes' relaxation, and a glimpse of other sides of life, making the same appeal, after all, that theater and novel do."[3]

BROADWAY—THE GREAT WHITE WAY

In 1900 Broadway was awash in electric light. Broadway, known as the Great White Way, at the turn of the century, was the mecca of the theater world. Though the New York theater district set the standard in the United States, many critics found American musical theater (and other forms of performing arts) parochial and lacking in creativity. Critics cited an interesting contrast—weak plots, uninspiring performances, and manipulated emotion against lavish production elements designed for mass appeal. Basically, Broadway suffered from an abundance of style, but little substance, despite the number of playgoers who turned out for the performances.

For middle-class citizens, going to the theater was a formal affair in the 1900s. Spectators donned their best attire to take in the glitter and pomp of plays, musicals, comedies, and dramas. The conservative middle-class audiences did not want their theater driven by the problems encountered in day-to-day life. They demanded damsels in distress and cookie-cutter heroes and villains. The theater scene degenerated to the point that in 1902 the *New York Times* questioned whether the musical theater would soon be "dead."

When Broadway nearly reached its demise, George Cohan came to its rescue and revived the musical comedy almost single-handedly. Born into a vaudeville family, Cohan had been on the road since the age of eight. The Four Cohans became one of the nation's most popular vaudeville acts. By the time he reached his late teens, Cohan was writing and choreographing most of the act, and he created a buck-and-wing dance that audiences loved. He wrote his first two musicals in 1901, but both met with box-office failure. The ambitious, aggressive young man refused to give up, but he needed a financial backer to move up to bigger theaters in New York.[4]

Cohan found his backer in fellow theater enthusiast Sam H. Harris. Together, the two produced *Little Johnny Jones* (1904), the story of American jockey Tod Sloan, who rode in the previous year's English Derby. Cohan played the part of Sloan (fictionalized as Johnny Jones) emphasizing his patriotism, which appealed greatly to audiences. Cohan sang, "I'm a Yankee Doodle Dandy/ A Yankee Doodle do or die/ A real live nephew of my Uncle Sam/ Born on the Fourth of July." Although the show ran nearly five hours, Cohan introduced speed and fluidity into the musical, so the performance contained action throughout. Cohan also pioneered the use of slang in theater. In his show, women were called "birds," and lines included a waiter asking a customer, "Shall I call you a hansom, sir?" to which the customer replied, "Call me anything you like." Despite its groundbreaking aspects, critics panned the show, and it lasted only 52 performances. Cohan, however, would not be denied. He took the musical on the road, always honing and editing. When he returned to Broadway a year later, the show enjoyed two long runs.[5]

Cohan's next musical, *Forty-five Minutes from Broadway*, opened on New Year's Day, 1906. The successful show included one of the decade's most enduring hits, "Mary's a Grand Old Name." Responding to a critic, the egotistical, brash Cohan said, "I write my own songs because I write better songs than anyone else I know of. I write my own plays because I have not yet read or seen plays from the pens of others that seem as good as the plays I write."[6] In spite of his bombastic nature, one thing cannot be denied—Cohan was the dominant Broadway performer of his time. Audiences loved his musicals and brought millions of fans into the Broadway fold.

A scene from Mrs. Fiske's *Salvation Nell*, produced at the Valencia Theatre, San Francisco (1909). Courtesy of the Oakland History Room of the Oakland Public Library, Oakland, California.

Cohan and others fought to save Broadway, but as late as 1906 Richard Mansfield wrote in the *Atlantic Monthly*, "the ship of the stage is drifting somewhat hither and thither." The answer, according to Mansfield, would be to establish a recognized American school of acting. "America has become too great," he wrote, "and its influence abroad too large, for us not to have a great and recognized theater." He believed the reliance on British and other foreign plays and playwrights was a detriment to the evolution of a truly American theater.[7]

Like so many other business endeavors in the 1900s, a trust, known as the Theatrical Syndicate, controlled financial backing on Broadway. Three men controlled the trust: Charles Frohman, Marc Klaw, and Abraham Erlanger. They reigned over Broadway for 15 years until internal squabbling broke up the group. The syndicate worked because theater owners received star-studded shows and, in return, merely had to book the performances through trust contracts. Any theater owner who chose to work outside the syndicate was forced to book second- and third-rate shows. Anyone who balked at the system got blacklisted, which could cost performers their careers.

The Theatrical Syndicate was at its peak power during the 1900s. It forced playwrights to author plays showcasing a certain actor or actress, virtually stifling creativity. On the financial side, the trust collected 5 to

10 percent of each theater's gross income and set terms for all its members. While some actors, playwrights, and theater owners got rich from the monopoly in the industry, many more were exploited by the system. Some actors, actresses, and producers actively fought the trust, including Eugene O'Neill's father, James O'Neill, and producer-playwright David Belasco, one of the most popular producers in the United States in the period. Because actresses Minnie Fiske and Sarah Bernhardt took active stands against the syndicate, they were forced to play in skating rinks and tent theaters during the height of the trust's power. The power of the syndicate did not waver until a rival group, led by the Shubert brothers, began a monopoly of their own. By 1910 the brothers had 1,200 theaters in their control nationwide against the syndicate.[8]

One of the most popular shows on Broadway during the decade was *The Merry Widow* (1907). While walking down the streets of New York before the musical even opened, one could hear people whistling the music of a Viennese operetta, since the lack of copyright law made it possible to sell the sheet music before the show ever opened. The success of the sheet music "The Merry Widow Waltz," at five cents a copy, propelled a huge advance ticket sale to the show. Soon, 100 companies were performing the show around the world.

When the show opened, theater critic Richard Aldrich reported, "The applause was almost terrifying in its intensity." Little-known comedy soprano Ethel Jackson played the lead, while Donald Brian was the leading man. The musical won widespread acclaim and its popularity led to a fashion craze of *Merry Widow* products—the *Merry Widow* hat, a huge monstrosity topped by a bird of paradise, corsets, shoes, candies, cigars, and gloves. The success of the musical also led to six years of Broadway shows dominated by Viennese operettas, including Oscar Straus's *A Waltz Dream* and *The Chocolate Soldier* and Ivan Caryll's *The Pink Lady*.[9]

Some playwrights shunned musical comedies and produced plays on serious topics based on real-world experiences. These playwrights followed in the path of the Muckrakers and such realist writers as Theodore Dreiser and Frank Norris, who were concerned with the seedier aspects of daily life in the United States (see chapter 8). After reading Ida Tarbell's *History of the Standard Oil Company* (1904), Charles Klein wrote the play *The Lion and the Mouse* (1906). The play, which examines the monopolistic tendencies of big business, centers around a main character who closely resembles oil magnate John D. Rockefeller. It enjoyed a two-year run on Broadway. Rachel Crothers wrote, from a feminist point of view, *The Three of Us* (1906) and *A Man's World* (1909). Other playwrights examined the social issues of labor struggles, poverty, and women's abuse.[10]

No matter what the subject of the play or musical was, audiences went to see their favorite stars. Actresses Lillian Russell and Anna Held, for example, were as famous in their day as the era's sports stars and athletes. Actors and actresses developed loyal audiences who would return to see them season after season regardless of the play itself. Some became famous for one role, such as Maude Adams, whose performance as Peter Pan captivated audiences.

Anna Held, backed by her common-law husband, the irrepressible Florenz Ziegfeld, captured the public's imagination as a Parisian beauty and seductress. Ziegfeld, a master of publicity, used his influence to make Held a huge star. He leaked stories to the press about Held's daily 40-gallon milk bath. As she put it in her silky French accent, "The milk she preserve zee creamy complexion." As a matter of fact, milk sales rose across the United States as the day's fashionable ladies tried to emulate Held. The actress also persuaded Ziegfeld to put together a revue, which later evolved into *Ziegfeld's Follies*. In 1907 the *Follies* had a successful run on Broadway and then toured in Baltimore and Washington. For the year the show made $120,000, which would translate into millions of today's dollars.[11]

Florenz Ziegfeld's success as a producer made him a legendary figure in theater history. The basic inspiration for *Ziegfeld's Follies* came from a long-running Parisian revue that presented political and social commentary through skits, as well as other numbers that featured scantily clad women. When Ziegfeld Americanized the show, he added lavish production numbers, featured songs written by the nation's top composers, and organized a chorus of attractive women. Ziegfeld's show took the idea of minstrel theater, vaudeville, and cabaret and expanded them, while also adding an air of sophistication, ensuring that women would not be offended by the show.

The early success of the Follies in a small theatre in New York led to the review being booked in the New Amsterdam, Broadway's largest and most attractive theater. Part of Ziegfeld's genius was in surrounding himself with the best talent he could find, from set designers and technicians to musicians, writers, and actors. For example, Ziegfeld's chorus girls had glamorous costumes, designed by the era's best fashion mavens. He also made sure that the lighting and stage productions showed the women in the best light possible.

Later editions of the Ziegfeld Follies in the 1910s and 1920s featured talent as diverse as W.C. Fields, Will Rogers, and Eddie Cantor, and had songs composed by Irving Berlin. Ziegfeld himself gained such notoriety and fame that his story was made into a movie, *The Great Ziegfeld* (1936). The movie won an Academy Award for Best Picture and made $3 million at the box office, making it one of the year's highest grossing films.

VAUDEVILLE AND BURLESQUE

Vaudeville in the United States was a mixed bag of ventriloquists, jugglers, animal acts, singers, short one-act plays, and other, more bizarre acts. The level of skill displayed by these early artists varied greatly. Vaudeville performers expected a great degree of crowd interaction— some of which included throwing rotten fruits and vegetables at hapless stage acts. The Cherry Sisters, dubbed "America's Worst Act," actually sang with a net between them and the audience to protect the sisters from projectiles. On the other end of the spectrum stood the Three Keatons, a comedy act in which six-year-old Buster Keaton thrilled the audience as "The Human Mop" and teased his real-life parents, who combined acrobatics and constant banter.

An article published in the *Berkeley Daily Gazette* told the story of the quick rise in vaudeville's popularity. Playing at the local opera house on Thursday and Friday evenings, "The vaudeville stage now predominates over everything else in the theatrical line." Those who once went to dramas or comedies now turned to vaudeville for its variety of features. "Famous actors, operatic stars and other leading lights of the profession have of late been allured to the vaudeville stage by the enormous salaries offered," the paper reported. At the famous Orpheum Theater in San Francisco, a ticket had to be ordered days in advance if one hoped to catch a vaudeville performance. The local Berkeley stage offered a juggler, a ventriloquist, a soprano, a humorist and impersonator, and a slack wire walker.[12]

Some observers hoped that vaudeville would rise above its pedestrian roots. In a 1905 article appearing in *Cosmopolitan*, writer and playwright Israel Zangwill argued that vaudeville should stage the comeback of the one-act play and lamented that audiences were too comfortable with the lighthearted fare. "The artlessness of the public and the artfulness of the manager will long keep the present pabulum unaltered, save in increasing staleness."[13]

Many of vaudeville's top acts were multitalented performers who could sing, act, juggle, tell jokes, and do just about anything else to get a reaction from an audience. One of the early stars was Leo Carrillo, from one of California's richest families, who told Chinese dialect stories. Another big star, Julian Eltinge spoofed the famous Gibson Girl in 1907 with a female impersonation he called the Simpson Girl. Some major theatrical stars, including Sarah Bernhardt and Ethel Barrymore, joined vaudeville troupes between seasons.[14]

Most vaudeville players spent their lives on the road. Most made little money and never hit the big time. Contortionists, animal trainers, weight lifters, and other odd performers struggled on night after night. Anything that could hold the crowds' attention found its way into vaudeville—dogs that howled while their masters sang, transvestites, magicians, dancers, and crude comics. Public relations whiz Willie Hammerstein, cousin of composer Oscar Hammerstein, often used freak or stunt acts in his theater on West 42nd Street in New York City. Freak acts did not mean that the people in the acts were freaks; they were individuals the audience wanted to see because of their fame or notoriety. Often infamous criminals, who lamented their illicit ways, would be part of vaudeville shows. Author and public speaker Helen Keller was a "freak" act, as was Dr. Cook, who took the stage to discuss his adventures in the North Pole controversy.[15]

Vaudeville featured many eccentric acts. Blatz the Human Fish read and played the trombone underwater. Eva Tanguay made the amazing sum of $3,500 a week by prancing around the stage as if she were possessed, screaming out songs, in varying stages of undress. Unfortunately, Tanguay lost all her money in the stock market crash and was hobbled by arthritis. In perhaps the most extreme act of the 1900s, Chung Ling Soo (the alias of William Ellsworth Robinson) caught bullets in his teeth, but in 1918 he died during his act when a bullet pierced his right lung. Robinson, once billed as the "world's greatest magician," carried on the charade of being Chinese for 20 years before the world found out his secret when he met his death on a London stage.[16]

The greatest burlesque star of the 1900s was Millie de Leon, who mimicked Eva Tanguay's trancelike movements but also made physical contact with the audience. Like all great vaudeville and burlesque actors, de Leon used negative publicity to further her career. When she was arrested in Brooklyn in 1903, the charges against her only spread her fame. She also spread rumors of alleged liaisons and affairs to keep the attention of audiences. Spurning the period's morality standards, de Leon often took the stage without wearing tights, long before bare legs were acceptable for women in public.

Burlesque began as musical productions making fun of current events or famous plays, which was said to be "burlesquing." The women who appeared in burlesque wore revealing tights to titillate the male audience. Beautiful scenery, music, and comedy were also used to attract men to the shows. While most people associate burlesque with striptease, that aspect only dominated the shows during its later years, when audiences became more used to seeing scantily clad women. The early years certainly featured sexually aggressive women—spoofing the Victorian image of the dainty, submissive female. These acts were balanced with comedy and musicals, often also spoofing Shakespeare or other cultural icons.

By the mid-1900s, some promoters moved to censor burlesque and make it more respectable. In 1908 the Star and Garter opened in Chicago, offering "Clean Entertainment for Self-Respecting People." However, for most audiences, burlesque remained, in the words of a press agent, "a conglomeration of filthy dialog, libidinous scenes and licentious songs and dances with cheap, tawdry, garish and scant scenery and costumes." Although many observers may have shared this view at the time, burlesque's popularity increased over time.[17]

Burlesque became a kind of minor league for vaudeville and musical comedy. Entertainers such as Sophie Tucker, Red Skelton, and W.C. Fields began their careers in burlesque, only to move up to vaudeville, radio, and movies in later years. In the 1920s, burlesque dropped many of its skits and comedy routines and focused on striptease. The change led to burlesque's becoming more popular than vaudeville in the years leading up to the Great Depression. Burlesque houses dominated Times Square in those days, until law enforcement cracked down on the striptease shows in the 1930s.

MOVIES

As early as 1894 and 1895 crude animated films were shown on screens in the United States. The first picture show in New York City, in fact, took place at Koster and Bial's Theater on April 27, 1896. The early animations were difficult to see, but they fueled a great deal of curiosity. The development of moving pictures was an outgrowth of advances in photography.

By the turn of the century, nearly every household had a stereoscope, a handheld device that made pictures look three dimensional. In 1901 the Underwood Company produced 25,000 stereo views a day and sold a total of 300,000 stereoscopes. Other companies sold stereo views through the mail via catalogs, such as Sears; others sold them door-to-door. The machines brought the events of the world to ordinary Americans. People collected stereo views of events ranging from the World's Fair to the flights of the Wright Brothers, and the building of the Panama Canal.[18]

Meanwhile, George Eastman's handheld Kodak camera made it possible for anyone to take snapshots. Beginning as an amateur photographer, Eastman founded his company to take advantage of the technological innovations that would make photography available to the masses. In 1900 Eastman's chief designer, Frank Brownell, developed a cheap, easy-to-use camera made specifically for children, the "Brownie," which could be bought for just one dollar. Kodak advertised the camera with illustrations of mythical creatures made popular by Canadian writer Palmer Cox in the children's magazine *St. Nicholas*. Kodak also set up camera clubs and sponsored photography contests to keep consumers interested in buying Kodak products.

Throughout the nineteenth century, inventors and artists searched for a way to represent motion, but it was not until Thomas Edison began working on film devices that the Kinetograph and Kinetoscope were born. After displaying his inventions at the Chicago World's Fair, parlors were set up around the country featuring early motion pictures. Penny arcades allowed viewers to see "actualities," or short scenes of everyday life and people—a girl dancing or a man sneezing. The commercial prospects of Kinetoscopes developed as promoters realized they could make money if many people could watch a projected movie simultaneously.

The motion picture industry grew quickly, especially after Edison established the first studio in 1905, "Black Maria," a tarpaper-lined box that swung around to catch the sun for filming. Other groups raced to produce films, including the Vitagraph Company of Brooklyn, the Lubin Company of Philadelphia, and several firms in Chicago.

Early pictures varied from scenes of important cultural or political events, such as William McKinley's inauguration or a simple prizefight or a moving automobile. "In the beginning the miracle of movement in a picture was the essential thing, and the nature of the movement was immaterial," recalls writer Edward Wagenknecht. "Dance acts and prizefights were popular because they accommodated themselves comfortably to the then fixed and narrow camera range."[19] In 1903 Edison may have filmed the first commercial, an advertising piece for the Lackawanna Railroad, showing company mascot Phoebe Snow riding the "Road of Anthracite" in a long, white dress to show how clean railroad travel had become. One of the first films to use narrative was Edwin S. Porter's *The Great Train Robbery* (1903), an 11-minute tale of a train robbery and the capture of the thieves. Porter, an early innovator in camera work, filmed one scene in which a robber fires his gun directly at the camera. The audiences, tricked by the technique, screamed and some spectators passed out in terror.[20]

Porter went on to do even more visually stunning films over the next several years. In 1906 he made *The Dream of a Rarebit Fiend*, which uses the camera to let the audience see the world through the eyes of a drunken man. Other Porter motion pictures included *The Ex-convict* and *The Kleptomaniac*. *The Kleptomaniac* examines the way in which a wealthy woman shoplifter is handled by the authorities versus the brutal way they treated a poor woman who had stolen a loaf of bread.

Most films lasted 15 to 20 minutes, short enough for people to fit them into their daily lives, especially children after school. Some families spent Saturday afternoons traipsing from theater to theater to take in all the different types of pictures. Most early nickelodeons were located close to working-class and immigrant neighborhoods, often close to trolley lines and busy shopping streets. Then, as now, location was everything in the theater industry. To keep up with the demand, theater owners imported nearly half of their films from overseas. Observers generally credited France with having the leading film studios in the world in the 1900s.[21]

Porter was an early innovator, but D.W. Griffith was the master film-maker of the 1900s, despite his racist three-hour epic *The Birth of a Nation* (1915), which showed a Southern family being saved by blacks through the support of the Ku Klux Klan. Griffith's first film, *The Adventures of Dollie*, which opened in 1908, told the story of a child kidnapped by gypsies who is saved after floating down the river in a barrel. During his stint with the production company Biograph, which lasted until 1913, the Kentucky native directed approximately 450 films. A study of Griffith's early work shows that he was the first director to use many of the techniques we take for granted today, including the close-up and distant shots, the pan shot, the fade-out, and sustained suspense, among others.

A 1908 report in *Independent* estimated that within the previous two years a motion picture theater had opened in every town and village in the country, and they were visited by 2 or 3 million patrons a day.[22] By 1910 reports state that there were 10,000 movie theaters servicing an audience of more than 10 million a week.[23]

The film industry was born in the 1900s, but it was not until the 1910s that motion pictures were firmly embedded in American life. Several important factors coalesced in the 1910s that solidified the industry, perhaps most notably the movement of the industry from New York to California. Cecil B. DeMille was the first to make films in California and the newly christened "Hollywood." By 1913 most film companies had moved to the Golden State. Gradually, as more money and influence entered the scene, Hollywood dominated the film industry worldwide.

DANCE

Dancing in the United States prior to the 1900s was regimented and had a sense of restraint, a holdover from the nation's early Puritan settlers. People were not encouraged to express themselves through body movement until the late 1800s. Formal dance, which had come from Europe, was considered high culture. On the other end of the social scale, public dances, held since the 1880s, were considered vulgar and a sign of lower-class standing. Working-class families were not as rigid, and young children often danced in the streets during playtime.

Despite these attitudes, and preconceived notions about the evils of dancing, a dance craze broke out at the turn of the century, fueled by young adults in the working class. After a full day in the factories, these young people flocked to neighborhood halls and saloons or ballrooms and danced the night away in their finest dress clothes. Children in working-class families were more likely to dance at an early age, so by the time they hit their teenage years, dancing was common. A survey conducted in 1910 revealed that nine out of ten girls between the ages of 11 and 14 claimed they knew how to dance, compared with only about one-third of the boys. Dancing offered young adults a chance to mix with the opposite sex without parental interference. Dancing also gave people an avenue for expressing themselves in public.[24]

For blue-collar workers, especially women under 20 years of age, participation in the dance craze was part of the courting ritual. Attendance at the dances increased as a young girl matured, then after finding a boyfriend, dropped off significantly and for most women ceased altogether after marriage. One 16-year-old female dance hall enthusiast said, "When I'm eighteen or nineteen I won't care about it anymore. I'll have a 'friend' then and won't want to go anywheres."[25] In New York City, every ethnic group had their own dance halls, and in one district, there was a dance hall every two and a half blocks. According to historian Kathy Peiss, there is no indication that any one particular ethnic group had a monopoly on dancing.[26]

Dancing encompassed many aspects of life in the working classes. While people attended dances, they engaged in cultural and social dynamics that defined who they were. What dance steps groups favored, where they attended the events, how they interacted with one another, and what clothing styles they wore, were important facets of their day-to-day lives.

The influence of business and the commercialization of dance reveal much about the 1900s. As ragtime and Tin Pan Alley became more pervasive, the wild beat of the music ended much of the formal heritage of dance in America. Tin Pan Alley dictated which dance steps would become most popular, and new dances were invented for particular songs, leading to increased sales. Also, business interests took control of the public dance halls and the liquor being served. For example, 80 percent of the dance halls in the Lower East Side of New York City were adjacent to saloons. Hall owners made their profits from the liquor served, which led to a dance lasting anywhere from three to ten minutes, then an intermission lasting from 15 to 20 minutes, in which drinking was encouraged.

Hall owners also promoted social interaction to drive customers to their clubs. They would give unescorted females discounted admission—charging 10 to 15 cents, rather than the usual 25 to 50 cents per couple—while others let single women in free. As more and more large commercial dance halls opened to meet the demand during the national craze, owners enticed patrons with bright lights, blaring music, and a carnival atmosphere, like circus barkers. Middle-class reformers were outraged over the conduct of young people in the dance halls and warned against bawdy behavior, but while prostitution and other forms of vice existed, the majority of dancers were simply playing out the intricate social rituals to the best of their ability given the staid nature of the day.

DANCE AS ART

Dance as an artistic outlet had been taught in the United States since the 1820s. Artistic dance was called Delsartianism after its creator, François Delsarte (1811–1871). Delsartianism focused on flexibility and natural movement, a graceful expression of the human form. Interestingly, Delsarte was not a dancer, but a student of music, voice coach, and movement theorist. After his own singing voice collapsed because of poor training, Delsarte studied anatomy to learn more about the larynx. His investigations into anatomy led to a preoccupation with motion and emotion. He spent years watching how people reacted under certain stressful situations. Delsarte used his findings to teach actors to use a greater range of dramatic expression. Delsartianism, however, greatly influenced dance and body movements. His ideas set off a dance craze in which young men recited poetry while prancing around gracefully. Females donned white robes and white face paint and held classical poses. Upper and middle-class Americans supported Delsartianism as a form of exercise.[27]

In the 1900s, Isadora Duncan (1878–1927) popularized Delsartianism and branched out to create her own unique, innovative form of dance, which audiences regarded as both scandalous and titillating. She shocked the staid audiences of the era, but at the same time she gave them a sense of liberation.

The San Francisco native enjoyed a classical education and was raised by an independent mother, both unusual during the waning years of the nineteenth century. Duncan's mother also encouraged the young girl to express herself through dance. By her teenage years, Duncan had already focused her dance style on natural movements and graceful expressions of the human body. By the time she was 21 years old, Duncan had scandalized audiences by dancing with an unprecedented degree of nudity— her arms and legs were both bare! Soon, Duncan gained admirers and critics based as much on her attire (or lack thereof) as on her dance moves. Some viewed her with disdain, but others recognized her artistry and embraced her as an avant-garde genius.[28] Her innovations in dance had a profound effect on ballet and the development of modern dance.

Duncan spent most of her life in Europe and Russia, which opened their arms to the young dancer. After touring Russia in the aftermath of the 1905 Russian Revolution, Duncan's views took a radical turn. She applied these thoughts to her dance, essentially liberating her body from the strict movements of traditional ballet. In 1921, while living in the Soviet Union, V.I. Lenin asked Duncan to create a school of dance in

A rare early portrait of Isadora Duncan in San
Francisco (1889). Courtesy of the Oakland History
Room of the Oakland Public Library, Oakland,
California.

Moscow. Duncan used the school to promote art for the masses with
political overtones. Later in life, this episode came back to haunt her. In
1922, on a trip to the United States, immigration officials detained Duncan because of her close ties to the Soviet Union. Newspapers quickly
picked up the story, and headlines declared Duncan a Soviet provocateur. She was stripped of her citizenship and lived the rest of her life in
France.[29]

Show business flourished in the 1900s. The syndicate virtually controlled theater in the United States and money flowed like water from a
spigot. Regardless of a person's place on the social ladder, some form of
entertainment existed to fill the yearning for leisurely pursuits. People
in all income brackets had money for entertainment and industry captains knew it—where there was a dollar to be spent there surely was a
theater owner, vaudeville troupe, or movie production house gladly will-

ing to accept it. Perhaps the plays produced were not necessarily high art in the 1900s, but they were what the public demanded.

One thing is for certain, the widespread appeal of dramatic theater, Broadway, and motion pictures that took hold in the first decade of the twentieth century evolved into major cultural influences and would become barometers for the entire century. These forms of entertainment began to consume more and more time in people's lives, especially movies. For many Americans, a trip to Broadway or certain movies served as important milestones and markers on their way to adulthood or became life-defining events that they would cherish forever. This is the power of entertainment and the influence it has in American culture.

*The 1900s*

11

Travel

Yes, I enjoy my automobile immensely.
But I never see you out.
Oh, I haven't got that far yet. I am just learning to make my own repairs.

—A joke from *Life* magazine (1904)

People were on the go in the 1900s. As the decade wore on, mass transportation and personal means of travel advanced greatly. What had once been far-fetched ideas (like the automobile) or outrageous flights of fancy (such as airplanes) became realities and opened a world of travel to people up and down the economic scale. From the gregarious "cottages" of the ultrarich to the boardwalks of Atlantic City and Coney Island, Americans not only traveled and enjoyed vacations, but found new outlets for social interaction and leisure. The 1900s began a century of travel in which all four corners of the earth would be opened up to average people, whether journeying across the Atlantic or across the globe.

Americans were on the move. Whether emboldened by the westward movement, driven by a higher level of disposable income generated during the era, or in search of work, an unprecedented amount of travel occurred in the first decade of the twentieth century, facilitating a travel explosion that continues to this day. Although in 1900 there were fewer than 200 miles of paved roads in the United States, railways linked the coasts, and thousands of towns sprang to life to service the railroads. Cities across America were lined by growing suburbs, most within walking distance of railroad or trolley lines. Commuters made the daily journey aboard these trains into the city and back again in the evening. Many

The bustling Southern Pacific Railroad depot in Berkeley, California (1908). Courtesy of the Oakland History Room of the Oakland Public Library, Oakland, California.

cities began electrifying their trolley lines to apply the latest technological innovation to city travel. Ferries also transported commuters and goods.

VACATION

Like their counterparts in Europe, affluent Americans traveled in the summer. Most often summer vacations meant residing in a second home—exclusive cottages in Newport and Narragansett, Rhode Island; Palm Beach, Florida; and Santa Barbara, California. The most favored form of transportation was aboard private railroad cars, which offered privacy and luxury, shielding the wealthy from the general population. Countless resorts and spas sprang up in the most popular travel destinations, including Florida, California, Georgia, the Carolinas, and Virginia. Middle- and lower-class travelers were enticed by reduced rate tours to Niagara Falls, Atlantic City, and other points along the seaside or lakeshore and in the mountains.

Vacations became common for middle-class Americans in the 1900s. The New York Department of Labor conducted a study of 1,500 factories and found that 91 percent gave their office staffs paid vacations, although the hourly workers did not receive the same benefits. With their new-found leisure time, many Americans traveled widely. Studies show that in the two decades before the outbreak of World War I more than 200,000 vacationers went to Europe each year. Travel agencies serviced a growing clientele and arranged for passage to Europe aboard passenger ships and tours of the Continent (costs ranged from $400 to $600 per person).[1]

The dizzying pace of life in the 1900s led many people to search out spas and resorts for their vacations. Diagnosed with neurasthenia—a bizarre psychological plight, which caused nervousness, paranoia, fatigue, rashes, and other physical ailments—some of America's most influential artists, politicians, and business leaders sought therapeutic vacations where they could relax and recover their health. People suffering from "American nervousness" ranged from writers Edith Wharton, Theodore Dreiser, and William and Henry James to President Theodore Roosevelt.[2] Under the watchful eye of doctors and therapists, these people were treated with hydropathy, a water therapy that made places like Hot Springs, Arkansas, and French Lick, Indiana, destinations for the mentally and physically exhausted.

Certain resort areas, especially ones on the ocean, became destinations for rich and middle-class alike. Atlantic City, New Jersey, offered activities for every social class, although the resort town teemed with people who tried to mimic the looks and actions of the wealthy. A visitor to Atlantic City found gigantic piers stretching out into the water bustling with music, vaudeville performances, theaters, and movie houses. The resort's seedier side was found near the lion tamers, snake charmers, and cheap trinket shops, as well as the flophouses and saloons. In the mid-1910s, travel writer Harrison Rhodes summed up the duality of Atlantic City, "It was a dreadful place, and yet oddly enough, it is . . . exactly what the majority of us really like."[3]

There were also enclaves where ethnic groups vacationed together. Others went south to Florida, a booming vacation site championed by Henry Morrison Flagler, a former partner of John D. Rockefeller. Flagler established a string of resort hotels on the eastern coast of Florida and linked them via a railroad that stretched nearly the entire length of the state. Flagler's tireless promotion of Florida as a vacation destination led to much of the state's future economic development.[4]

During the presidency of Theodore Roosevelt, the nation took up his call for leading an active life. As a result, many people vacationed in the mountains and open spaces plentiful in America. Roosevelt, perhaps the most conservation-minded president in American history, started a national park movement, which included Yellowstone, Yosemite, Grand Canyon, and Mount Rainier, among others. In 1903 Roosevelt traveled to Yosemite to publicize his vision of a national park and to meet Sierra Club founder and naturalist John Muir, one of his personal heroes. The enthusiastic Roosevelt was so eager to meet Muir that he called it "the bulliest day of my life."[5]

Later, at a speech given to mark a trip to Yellowstone in 1903, Roosevelt outlined his feelings about the positive impact of travel to great national parks. "I have always thought it was a liberal education to any man of the East to come West," the president explained, "and he can combine profit with pleasure if he will incidentally visit this park, the Grand Canyon of the Colorado, and the Yosemite." Roosevelt then went on to point out the "essential democracy" Yellowstone represented for Americans, its "preservation of the scenery, of the forests, of the wilderness life and the wilderness game for the people as a whole."[6]

In his book *Our National Parks* (1902), Muir commented on the nervous workers from the city who visited the nation's parks; he labeled them "nerve-shaken." Muir (and Roosevelt) both held that the national park system could offer city dwellers a way to fight the neurasthenic battle brought on by constant stress and wear from life in bustling cities. Muir, in part, earned his living by acting as a guide for wealthy patrons who wanted to take a "retreat into the wilderness" in search for some mental and physical relief.[7]

In 1908 a group of millionaires ranked the most exclusive resorts in the United States. At the top of the list was Newport, Rhode Island, so exclusive that the report warned those just past the million dollar mark to beware—an entire fortune could be spent keeping up with the likes of Cornelius Vanderbilt, coal baron E.J. Berwind, and John Jacob Astor. The rich in Newport built grand mansions, which they modestly called "cottages," although the most unassuming cottages could have 30 rooms and cost $1 million to build—a fortune in that decade. On the other end of the scale was Vanderbilt's magnificent 70-room Renaissance fortress, named "The Breakers," which cost $5 million to build. William K. Vanderbilt built his "Marble House" for a meager $2 million, but spent more than four times that much decorating it, including marble imported from Africa and a ballroom paneled in gold.[8]

High society in Newport centered on entertaining in a lavish, flamboyant style, mainly dinner parties. One reporter from *Cosmopolitan* noted in 1907 that an upper-class family might spend $1,000 a month just on fresh flowers for small dinner gatherings. Other expenses included at least two chauffeurs and an automobile helper and a minimum of four cars (Astor reportedly had 17 cars at Newport alone); a chef from Paris for $5,000; a private secretary to the lady of the house, which cost $3,000; and other helpers, maids, and nurses which all added up to a typical expense of approximately $24,000 a season.[9] Social satirist Finley Peter Dunne (writing as the commoner "Mr. Dooley") scoffed at the vulgar displays put on by the nation's rich. "I'm glad there is a Newport," he said. "It's the exhaust pipe . . . I wish it was bigger."[10]

The women of Newport prided themselves on entertaining 100 or more guests in an evening at their palatial cottages. Some families built brightly illuminated midways in courtyards surrounding the mansions, containing shooting galleries, dancers and singers, and other forms of entertainment similar to those offered at amusement parks. In 1902 Mrs. Cornelius Vanderbilt hosted a lavish dinner party with the featured entertainment provided by the cast of the Broadway musical comedy *The Wild Rose*. She simply had the cast and scenery shipped to Newport for the performance. For the daughters of the rich, life in Newport was constant leisure. A typical day involved horseback riding before nine, taking in a tennis match at the Newport Casino, a ferry out to a yacht for lunch, and a polo match in the afternoon. The evening consisted of dinner parties and perhaps a late night ball.[11]

TRAVEL IN CONGESTED CITIES

The turn of the century witnessed a huge building spree in many congested cities to alleviate overcrowding. City planners and officials elected to build trolleys and street railway systems. Electric engines were more economical and faster than steam engines and adapted to the crowded terminals much better. From 1902 to 1907, more than 2,000 miles of track a year were laid out in congested cities. Both New York and Chicago built elevated steam-driven lines before 1900; Boston followed with its own in 1901. However, steam engines were not as practical as electric lines. New York adopted electricity for its elevated lines in 1901.[12]

With the crushing influx of people, primarily immigrants, cities like Boston, New York, Chicago, and San Francisco had to introduce innovative means of public transportation. Electric trolley cars, like the ones tourists flock to in San Francisco, first spread from downtown areas into the suburbs, then began linking communities. The remnants of old trolley systems can be seen in many cities across America—some are quite visible, like the skeletal remains of the trolley tracks in Cleveland. Soon, trolleys not only linked cities with outlying suburbs; one could travel halfway across the country on electric lines. In 1906 the New York Central railway began electric operations from Grand Central Station, and two years later, lines ran all the way to Stamford, Connecticut.[13]

Despite the advent of electric trolley lines and the growing influence of the automobile, railroads expanded their mileage in the 1900s. From 1850 to 1900, railroads added an additional 3,800 miles of track on average each year. From 1900 to 1914, the mileage increased to 4,000 miles per year. It would be incorrect, though, to think that the railroad industry was not harmed by other modes of transportation. After 1907 railroad profits slipped markedly and the nation seemed to be approaching a saturation point.[14]

The Jacksonville Metropolis automobile used in a 1909 endurance race from Tampa to Jacksonville and back. The promotional stunt sponsored by the Tampa *Daily Times* was to show Florida citizens the need for a statewide highway system. From the Louise Frisbie collection, courtesy of the Florida State Archives.

THE AUTOMOBILE

In 1900 automobiles (or "horseless carriages" as they were at first known) were frail machines, given to sputtering oil, fire, and smoke on a regular basis, while shaking their occupants silly. Cars were also expensive—play toys of the rich who could afford the exhaustive upkeep and repairs. Repairs were common because automobiles lacked paved roads and were forced to inch along dirt roads, trails, and paths, where both the driver and the automobile were clearly out of their element. Many who favored horse-drawn carriages got a good laugh at the expense of automobile owners, often seen hopelessly stuck in a muddy ditch or nearly overturned by a rut in a dirt road. There were no roadside gas stations or tow trucks to help drivers in such predicaments. They had to rely on their own ingenuity or the help of others in pushing the car to safety.

One-third of the early automobiles were electric, and many more were driven by steam. In 1900, at the first car show held in the United States, in New York City, nearly all the contraptions were electric or steam, despite the limitations of both types. Electric cars had a limited range of motion, since they needed to be renewed at electric charging stations; steam cars required an owner to get a steam engineer's license, since they were perceived as being very dangerous.[15]

Early automobiles often lacked much of a body. Henry Ford's first car, preserved in Dearborn, Michigan, looks like a bicycle with four wheels and a carriage seat. A distinct feature that jumps out at the modern observer is the reed-thin wheels that were used in early cars. It is obvious that early automobile engineers placed much more emphasis on engines than on wheel design or body type. As car design progressed in the 1900s, the outside changed significantly. Later in the decade, passengers sat high above the engine and the wheels. The driver's side was on the right, and the front two seats looked like leather recliners. An ornate carriage seat took up the whole back of the car. Cars at that time looked like giant sofas on wheels.

Despite the crude early looks and design of automobiles, the machines grabbed people's imaginations, either positively or negatively. Soon, autos became an influential part of the American scene. As they crowded the already jam-packed streets in American cities, safety became an issue. An alarming number of pedestrians were injured or killed by auto enthusiasts. The outrage over vehicular deaths caused New York City officials to ban horseless vehicles from Central Park. In 1904 New York State passed a law setting the maximum speed limit at 10 miles per hour in built-up districts, 15 miles per hour in villages or outside congested areas, and 20 miles per hour elsewhere. Newspapers capitalized on anti-automobile public sentiment, but businesses that were affected by this outrage mobilized to resist the legislation.

The New York *Tribune* informed the public of one such accident which occurred on Christmas Day in 1900 when a young nurse was struck and killed.

The vehicle was moving rapidly. . . . The engineer in charge of it saw the young woman crossing the street and rang the gong in warning. Apparently, however, he did not abate the speed of the machine nor attempt to steer it out of the way. He considered his responsibility fully discharged by the ringing of the gong.[16]

The automobile (and the "car culture" that has emerged because of it) not only changed America economically, it had a profound impact on the way in which people lived and interacted. Once automobile pioneers understood the impact the car could have on the world, they moved quickly to make its influence a reality. In 1900, 4,192 automobiles were sold in the United States for a total of $4.89 million. Ten years later, the

A wealthy family in Concord, California, with their first automobile
(1908). Courtesy of the Contra Costa County Historical Society.

number jumped to 181,000 cars for $215.34 million. In pretty short order, by the mid-1920s, automobile manufacturing became the number one industry in America and accounted for 6 percent of the total value of all manufacturing in this country.[17]

Various inventors and engineers had tinkered with producing an automobile in Europe and the United States as far back as 1769, when French artillery officer Nicholas Cugnot made a primitive car, which was built on three wheels and was equipped with a boiler and an engine. However, it took until the years just preceding 1900 for the idea to take shape. Charles E. and J. Frank Duryea built the first gas-powered car, in Springfield, Massachusetts, in 1893; while Ransom Eli Olds was credited with first attempting to build cars under a system of mass production in the late 1890s. The first Oldsmobile was manufactured in Lansing, Michigan, in 1901, and Olds sold a total of 425 cars that year alone. By 1904 Olds had sold 5,000 automobiles, an impressive figure given that 241 auto companies had formed between 1904 and 1908.[18]

Throughout the decade, automobiles were mainly for the wealthy. Henry Ford and others changed this perception. Early manufacturers advertised their cars with posters illustrating upper-class lifestyles.

Cleveland-based Peerless Motor Car Company played on its slogan "All That the Name Implies" and showed rich women in big, feathered hats being carted around a department store by two chauffeur drivers. Another Cleveland auto company, the Baker Motor Vehicle Company, was an early pioneer in getting women interested in buying automobiles. Self-proclaimed "Aristocrats of Motordom," Baker brought out the "Queen Victoria," an electric car that it touted as the "safest to drive" and "easiest to control." Owning an automobile was a symbol of success for Americans. Carmakers capitalized on this feeling with ads highlighting grandeur, speed, and power. Price was rarely mentioned in the classic automobile ads. If a person had to ask the price, he could not afford it.[19]

The importance of the automobile for the American economy stretches far beyond the early car manufacturers into the countless small businesses and parts suppliers that fueled the growth of the industry. Inevitably, entire cities began to cater to the growing auto manufacturers. Akron, Ohio, soon became known as "Rubber City" after a number of successful tire manufacturers settled on the banks of the Cuyahoga River in northeastern Ohio, led by Goodyear and Firestone.[20]

Just after the Civil War, a 29-year-old entrepreneur scoured the country looking for a place to relocate his twice-failed New York rubber company. His financial backers made one stipulation: the new location had to be west of the Allegheny Mountains, where the company would not face competition from its Eastern rivals all clumped around distribution centers in New York and New Jersey. Dr. Benjamin Franklin Goodrich, a surgeon by training and burgeoning real estate developer, visited many cities in his search. While on a trip to Cleveland, Goodrich read an Akron Board of Trade brochure and scouted the city.

Goodrich was attracted to Akron's supply of coal and water, transportation system, and abundance of labor. Although other cities offered Goodrich money, Akron businessmen pledged almost $14,000 in startup funding if the company located there. In 1871, the machinery was shipped from New York to Akron. By 1888, the year B.F. Goodrich died, company sales reached nearly $700,000. Thus began Akron's journey to becoming the rubber capital of the world.

Other entrepreneurs rushed to imitate Goodrich's success and profit from the early development of the automobile industry. By 1909, there were 14 rubber companies in Akron, including future giants Goodyear and Firestone. Five years later, rubber accounted for nearly 20,000 jobs and over 33 percent of the industry's yearly output. As automobile manufacturing centered in Detroit and industrialization increased across the Midwest, tire manufacturers had a constant demand for their products.

The automobile swept across America like a plague in the 1900s. By 1907 a New Yorker could see "throngs of cars of every description upon

Fifth Avenue, the theater buses at night, the endless procession of automobiles faring out in the country of a week-end, the industrious little electrics."[21] However, before the real car culture could grip America, someone had to make an auto the masses could afford to buy and maintain. The man who bridged the gap was Henry Ford, a farmer's son who left the fields of Michigan to make his way in Detroit. Ford was responsible for making the automobile affordable for the average man by perfecting the use of mass production. His contribution to America's car culture was huge.

HENRY FORD: THE FATHER OF THE AUTOMOBILE

Although he did not invent the technology that made him famous, Ford perfected the assembly line, establishing mass production as the mechanism for economic power. Under Ford's tutelage, the automobile moved from a luxury to a necessity and inaugurated the car culture.

Born in Dearborn, Michigan, in 1863, Henry Ford had an early aptitude for machinery. However, it was the sight of a coal-fired steam engine in 1876 that set in motion his later triumphs. By age 16, leaving the family farm against his father's wishes, Ford apprenticed in a machine shop in Detroit. Next he joined the Westinghouse Engine Company, repairing old steam engines and setting up new ones.

Ford soon realized that steam engines were not the wave of the future. German engineer Karl Benz developed a reliable internal combustion engine which ran on gasoline. Ford traveled around Detroit questioning its best engineers and later produced his own two-cylinder, four-cycle engine, which generated four horsepower. Ford mounted the engine on a borrowed chassis, and his "quadricycle" made its maiden run on June 4, 1896. It was a huge success. People clamored around Ford's invention and wanted to try it for themselves. He sold his first for $200, then built a second one, bigger and more powerful. Backed by investors, Ford opened the Detroit Automobile Company (soon reorganized as the Henry Ford Company). He was the first car manufacturer in "Motor City."

Ford entered his cars in races and won a reputation for speed and daring. Soon, he built racers that set speed records, and additional investors pumped money into the company, thus beginning the close union between the auto industry and auto racing. Over the years, the alliance led to overall improvements in car design and technology, benefiting the industry as a whole.

What makes Ford such a revolutionary business thinker is that he realized that everyone should benefit from his innovation. Ford proclaimed, "I will build a motor car for the great multitude," and he decided that the way to make them affordable was "to make them all alike, to make them come through the factory just alike." Ford had to convince his backers that his idea was sound. By 1908 he had bought out many and owned 58 percent of the company. In the fall of 1908, the first Model T rolled out. The car had several new features that made it more negotiable on country roads, and the engine was encased for protection. Ford set the price at $825, which he knew made it too expensive, but he believed the price would fall through improvements in assembly-line technology. With Ford in control, efficiency was the keystone of his operations. For 20 years, Ford produced black Model T's, and only T's (often called the "Tin Lizzie" or "flivver").

Ford sold 11,000 cars in 1908 and 1909, and then outdid himself with the 1910 model, selling 19,000. Soon, sales skyrocketed, reaching 248,000 in 1914, or nearly half the U.S. market. By allowing the masses to purchase cars, Ford set in motion the creation of a car culture in the United States. Ford's influence on popular culture is felt every day. According to historian Harold Faulkner, "It is doubtful if any mechanical invention in the history of the world has influenced in the same length of time the lives of so many people in an important way as the motor car."[22]

TAKING TO THE SKIES

Few events symbolized American power in the 1900s more than the Wright brothers' successful flight in 1903. For centuries, man had yearned to fly and searched for ways to overcome gravity. As early as the 1790s, people got airborne in gas balloons and 100 years later, people flew in crude gliders. Advances were made in the late 1880s when people took to the skies in gas-filled dirigibles, or hot-air balloons, but truly flying, in which a person controlled the movement, seemed a dream of the future.

On December 17, 1903, Orville and Wilbur Wright, both wearing starched collars, ties, and dark suits, emerged from their small cabin at Kill Devil Hills, North Carolina, just four miles from the town of Kitty Hawk, ready to test their machine. For years the brothers, bicycle mechanics from Dayton, Ohio, had dreamed of building an aircraft that would fly. The Wrights tinkered with various designs, including a box kite with wings and gliders, to test their theories, then headed to Kitty Hawk, which offered steady wind, open spaces, and, most important for the two patent-minded brothers, privacy.

In 1903 the Wrights started piecing together their self-nicknamed "whopper flying machine" based on an engine they had designed and built, with a box frame that required the pilot lie in the middle of the ship, using his hips to work the wings. As the world debated man's ability to fly and "experts" sounded out against the feat in *McClure's*, *North American Review*, and the *Independent*, the Wrights put the finishing touches on their airplane. For two months, in October and November, the brothers made adjustments. Finally, on December 17, they set up the plane's launching device, a 60-foot-long monorail that would send the plane skyward. Because it was a windy day, they set the monorail up on the beach, instead of the hillside they had used in earlier efforts.[23]

With Orville lying down at the controls and Wilbur running alongside, balancing the machine as it gained speed, the chain-driven engine roared to life, shaking the entire plane. As it rolled down the monorail, the plane jerked into the wind. Forty feet down the track, Orville inched the plane upward and it slowly climbed up to ten feet off the ground. In the 12 seconds it was airborne, the Wright's ship traveled 120 feet.[24] This moment was caught on film, but the small crowd who had gathered (mostly rescue swimmers from the nearby life-saving station) did not even cheer. The sober Wright brothers simply pushed the plane back to the starting blocks for another run. By the fourth flight, at noon that day, Wilbur used his knowledge, gleaned from years of flying gliders, to keep the plane up for 59 seconds and traveled 852 feet.[25]

Amazingly, the national press reacted with complete indifference to the Wrights' feat. No newspaper reporters were present that day, and most did not run stories about the event. Only Norfolk *Virginian-Pilot* editor Keville Glennan understood the importance of the flight and printed the story on the front page. Ironically, the United States Armed Services did not consider the Wrights' achievement useful. In 1904 a representative of the British government approached the brothers, but U.S. services ignored their achievement until 1907 when they had been successfully flying for more than four years.[26]

It took nearly five more years for the Wrights to get the coverage they deserved after they held a public demonstration of the airplane in 1908 at Fort Myer military base in Virginia, outside the nation's capital. A crowd of 5,000 watched the plane turn in the air, fly over their heads, then land on the grassy field nearby. The demonstration flights in 1908 received a lot of press coverage, but it would be years before people really believed in man's ability to fly. They had to see it with their own eyes to understand what the Wright brothers had accomplished. In 1909 Wilbur put on an exhibition over New York harbor that drew more than 1 million spectators. He delighted the crowd by flying along Manhattan and around the Statue of Liberty.[27]

THE PANAMA CANAL

A passageway through Central America had long been a dream of American industrialists, and it was regarded as an important strategic move by the nation's governmental and military leaders. Connecting the oceans through the seemingly thin slice of land across Panama would cut weeks off the trip between New York City and San Francisco. Roosevelt bought the rights to the Isthmus of Panama from the French for $40 million, over the objections of the Colombian government, who disputed the French claim to the land.[28] The president saw building a canal as an assertion of American will—he would not be denied by lengthy negotiations with Colombia. Roosevelt called the Colombians "contemptible little creatures" and encouraged a revolution led by two French members of the Panama Company.[29]

Roosevelt sent American warships to a station off the coast of Colombia in a display of force. The maneuver sent a message, not only to the leaders of Colombia, but also to European nations: America and America alone would decide what happened in its hemisphere. The United States quickly recognized the rebel leaders and the new nation of Panama. The new canal treaty with Panama gave the United States rights to five miles of land on each side of the site, along with the right to build, operate, maintain, and defend a canal. After the U.S. Senate ratified the treaty on February 23, 1904, Congress set up a seven-member commission to organize the cutting of the "pathway between the seas."[30]

Almost immediately, construction began on the "Big Ditch." The project, which took a decade, cost the nation $367 million, and more than 22,000 workers lost their lives to yellow fever and malaria in the disease-ridden swamps. Despite the lives lost, the site became a thriving vacation spot. In 1913, 20,000 vacationers went to Panama to gaze at the engineering wonders taking place. The Panama Canal, which stood as a symbol of American technological superiority, ranked as one of the nation's most impressive engineering feats.[31]

Medical knowledge played as important a role in the completion of the canal as engineering and technical skill. Colonel William Crawford Gorgas, the man who exterminated yellow fever in Havana, Cuba, was given the task to eradicate disease from the tropical swamps of Panama. Using methods similar to those he used in Havana, Gorgas had eliminated yellow fever by September 1905. Next he turned to malaria and encouraged workers to eliminate stagnant water sources and ordered vegetation cut within a 200-yard perimeter around the construction crews. Gorgas never completely eliminated malaria from Panama, but contraction rates had fallen from 40 percent to 10 percent between 1906 and 1913.[32]

12

Visual Arts

If America is to produce great painters . . . their first desire should be
to remain in America to peer deeper into the heart of American life,
rather than to spend their time abroad obtaining a superficial view
of the art of the Old World.

—Thomas Eakins

The Progressive Era in America carried beyond the world of politics and
social justice into the nation's arts and culture. American artists started
to push beyond the constraints of the established art scene of Europe
and America, and some expressed their social leanings on canvas and in
sculpture. Although they still turned primarily to Europe for guidance
on artistic styles and customs, their work began to encompass all aspects
of society in the United States, from poor tenements and urban decay to
the manicured lawns of the leisure class and the sprawling mountains
of the Western regions.

Art critic Robert Hughes labeled the era stretching from the 1870s
through the early 1900s the "American Renaissance" in visual arts. At
the core of the period, according to Hughes, was a "conflicting idea
which tried to come out as serene idealism. Essentially, it was that nationalism and cosmopolitanism had to be fused. They boasted of their
limitless potential, and in order to make the potential actual they boosted
their artists and architects."[1] Later, American artists, architects, and photographers focused on urban life and realistic scenes of everyday living,
especially among the poor.

In large cities, such as New York and San Francisco, however, support
for the arts came from the wealthy, who filled their homes with works

of art. They spared no expense in finding the next hot artist and buying artworks as fast as they could be commissioned.

On the other hand, the lower classes were restricted by their place in the social strata and comparably meager earnings. With extremely limited disposable income, the poor, in general, flocked to vaudeville houses, dance halls, amusement parks, and nickelodeons. Most entertainment tied directly to a person's ethnic heritage.

The expanding middle class, unable to buy "authentic" paintings, instead bought printed reproductions, which were made available for the first time as a result of technological advances in printing processes. By purchasing reprints, the middle class was exposed to the culture of the wealthy, but within their own social strata. Many members of the middle class also found that they had the leisure time to frequent museums subsidized by the rich.

The middle class decorated their homes and parlors with lithographs, essentially less expensive reproductions of famous works. Lithographs were extremely popular at the end of the nineteenth and the early part of the twentieth century. One firm, owned by Nathaniel Currier (later Currier and Ives) produced reproductions of 4,300 paintings between 1835 and 1907. Lithographs sold for anywhere between 20 cents and $3 apiece. Although some critics belittled lithographs as art by machinery, the lithography firms extended art to the general public.[2]

In the 1880s and 1890s, famed photography inventor George Eastman began the process of photoengraving, which enabled large-scale reproduction of paintings from all around the world. For the first time, average citizens could see the works of European artists. In fact, the artists themselves used the new sources to inspire their own works.[3]

PAINTING

The first wave of painters in the American Renaissance directed their energies toward proving their ability to the European art establishment. Thus, most of the recognized American artists traveled to Europe to take traditional training in Paris and elsewhere. As a result, much of the early work of American painters mimics the work of the Old World. Artists in the United States gradually realized that they needed their own independent art scene, not completely separated from Europe, which would actually grow to rival it.

In the years following the Civil War, painting gained importance in the United States, and a genuine American art establishment flowered. Fueled by the likes of J.P. Morgan and other incredibly wealthy collectors, American museums and private collectors acquired many of Europe's masterpieces. During the era, some American artists gained an international following. Thomas Eakins (1844–1916), John Singer Sargent

(1856–1925), Winslow Homer (1836–1910), and James McNeill Whistler (1834–1903) ranked among the greatest artists of the day, on either side of the Atlantic Ocean. Although these artists were still producing during the 1900s and their reputations carried into the period, for the most part, they achieved their fame at the end of the nineteenth century.

Impressionism dominated the art scene, influenced by the great impressionist painters of Europe—Claude Monet, Camille Pissarro, and others. Homer, Sargent, and Whistler all practiced the art of turning unyielding real images into a series of brushstrokes that came together to form a whole. A close inspection of impressionist art looks like nothing more than smudges and sweeping strokes; however, with distance the picture is revealed—an image softer than reality, but with a beauty that is awe inspiring. The most important American female artist in the 1900s was Mary Cassatt (1845–1926). Her work, especially her paintings of domestic life, popularized Impressionism in the United States, although she chose to work and live in Europe, as did Whistler and Sargent. In fact, all three served as important figures bridging the space between the nineteenth and twentieth centuries.

Born in Lowell, Massachusetts, the son of a railway engineer, Whistler scorned the art world's distinction between European and American painting and the idea that the Americans were naïve students who required Europe's firm guidance. For most of his life, Whistler lived overseas, studying in Paris, then moving to London, but he remained fiercely American in his attitudes. A self-invented man, he paraded around London acting like a Southern gentleman; however, Whistler's reputation helped later American artists become accepted by European critics and audiences.[4] Paris accepted Whistler like it had few American artists before him and won the respect of Édouard Manet and Edgar Degas. In public, Whistler was known for his quick wit and sharp tongue, but in his studio, he worked diligently, with great self-discipline.[5]

Whistler believed in art for art's sake, not as a vehicle for moralizing or imparting romantic ideas. Thus, he called his most famous painting *Arrangement in Grey and Black, No. 1* (though it has been called simply "Whistler's Mother" ever since because she was the sitter). He denied that his critically acclaimed *The White Girl (Symphony in White, No. 1)* had a story behind it. To him any painting was just an experiment with the subtleties of color, in this case white.[6]

Whistler did much to raise the status of American art. Many collectors snatched up his paintings and brought them home for display. Detroit railroad millionaire Charles Freer amassed hundreds of works by Whistler or collected by him, and he later donated the collection and it is housed in the Freer Gallery in Washington, D.C.[7]

The only American painter to rival Whistler's fame in the waning days of the 1800s and early 1900s was another expatriate, John Singer Sargent.

In fact, some observers claim Sargent was the single representative painter of his era. He was born in Florence and grew up in Italy, since his American parents had retired there. Sargent specialized in portraits, particularly of the cultivated set, and soon became the most expensive and sought-after portraitist of his era. Though he made thousands of dollars for each portrait and he was regarded as the modern master of portraits, his critics regarded his work as elitist, since he excelled in capturing the narcissism of his subjects.[8]

Portrait painting made Sargent fantastically wealthy and famous, but his success trapped him to a degree. So many patrons flocked to his studio to have their portraits done that Sargent had little time to explore other avenues. He once called the portrait "a painting with a little something wrong about the mouth" and later said portraiture was "a pimp's profession."[9] Sargent escaped painting portraits by producing amazing watercolors and taking on commissions to paint murals in the United States and throughout Europe. His murals for the Boston Public Library and the Boston Museum of Fine Arts have been called the finest murals painted in the nation during the American Renaissance period.

In the 1900s and then in his later years, Sargent traveled the world, recording his experiences in sketches and producing remarkable watercolors. Although he lived abroad his entire life, the artist remained American in spirit. He even refused a knighthood in Great Britain to retain his American citizenship. Sargent's career provides modern observers with a pictorial history of the upper classes in the late 1800s and early 1900s.

While Sargent and other older painters plied their trade in Europe, a younger group of American artists returned from schools in France to bring Impressionism back to the United States. The primary group called themselves Ten American Painters or, more commonly, "The Ten." They sought to apply the skills they had learned overseas to American scenes and atmosphere.

Founded in Boston by Frank Weston Benson, The Ten included Joseph De Camp, Childe Hassam, Thomas Dewing, Robert Reid, Willard Metcalf, Edmond Tarbell, J. Alden Weir, Edward Simmons, and John Twachtman, although Twachtman's death in 1902 occasioned William Merritt Chase's inclusion as a replacement. As a group, The Ten were tired of the conservative attitude among the established art organizations in America, the large exhibits forced upon painters, and the multitude of styles presented at the exhibits. Worst of all, American collectors bought French Impressionist works and practically ignored American pieces. The Ten signed an agreement in 1897 to exhibit together in New York City in small galleries around the city. Benson's works sold the best among the group and his reported annual income exceeded six figures, although the reputations of Chase and Hassam have carried more weight into modern times. In fact, Hassam is widely regarded as America's premiere turn-of-the-century Impressionist.

Chase's work as a teacher (among his students were Georgia O'Keeffe and Edward Hopper) and his fanciful lifestyle made him immensely popular. Over the course of his career, Chase probably trained more students than any other instructor of the era. With the same energy he brought to teaching, Chase also created a public image of himself and then lived up to it every minute of every day (kind of a 1900s version of Madonna or Andy Warhol). Chase could be seen parading down the streets of Fifth Avenue dressed in a cutaway coat, topper, and a jeweled neck scarf, with Russian wolfhounds on a leash. Chase also had a black servant who he dressed as an African prince. These gimmicks worked wonders for Chase. He became one of New York's most sought after portraitists.[10]

Influenced by the infusion of light made popular by Monet, Hassam did not adopt Impressionism until the late 1880s. His first works in the genre captured his friend, the writer Celia Thaxter, on Appledore Island, off the New Hampshire coast. Hassam's works gained popularity, in part, because of a wave of nostalgia America felt for its colonial past. His Impressionistic paintings recalled a softer, quainter lifestyle.[11]

As the 1900s progressed, the American Impressionists seemed less avant-garde, and new schools of art surfaced. While the American Impressionists had recognized that art could and should be based on scenes from American life, other painters, driven by the excitement and technological innovations of the new century, created new forms of artistic expression.

The Ashcan School

A group of artists came together in New York City to form a group called The Eight, or the Ashcan school (because they could find art in the "ashcans" of dirty cities). Led by Robert Henri, The Eight included George Luks, William Glackens, John Sloan, Everett Shinn, Arthur B. Davies, Maurice Prendergast, and Ernest Lawson. The Eight never formed a society or a school, but they all looked at everyday life through the lens of a journalist. Many had worked as illustrators at magazines or newspapers, which contributed to their journalistic approach. Critics, who did not want to see such vulgarity displayed in art, called the group the "Revolutionary Black Gang." Where the Ashcan artists came together was in their disdain for academic pretensions in the established art world.[12]

The Eight held their first exhibition of their own works in 1908. The event clearly separated them from their contemporaries. In 1910 Henri and his students held another show that was so popular and sensational

that riot police had to be called in to subdue the crowd of 1,500 spectators. However, the true impact of the Ashcan school on the international art scene did not occur until three years later when they put on
the Armory Show, by some accounts the most important art exhibit ever
held in the United States. The Armory Show presented more than 300
artists and approximately 1,300 paintings. About one-third of the artists
were American, and the Ashcan school was well represented. More than
300,000 Americans saw the Armory Show. The term "modern art" had
been invented.[13]

The two most important members of the Ashcan school in the 1900s
were Robert Henri (1865–1929) and his student George Bellows (1882–
1925). Henri was the son of a Mississippi riverboat card shark. After
dabbling in work as an illustrator for a newspaper, the boy entered the
Pennsylvania Academy of Art in Philadelphia where he met many of the
others who eventually formed The Eight. In the late 1880s, Henri studied
in Paris for three years and started down the Impressionist path.[14]

Henri began teaching at the New York School of Art, headed by Chase.
After several years, Chase resigned and left the school in Henri's care,
since the former leader could not compete with Henri's popularity. In
1904 Bellows enrolled at the school and worked directly with Henri. The
teacher believed that an artist must be a realist and that art existed to
advance the progress of mankind. In 1910, Henri explained, "What we
do need is art that expresses the spirit of the people of today. . . . I want
to see progress. It should be impossible to have any feeling of jealousy
towards those who are young and are to accomplish the future."[15]

Henri and the other members of the Ash Can movement took Winslow
Homer as their spiritual guide, always looking for reality. Henri also
looked to the great poet Walt Whitman for inspiration. He thought his
students should "contain multitudes" like Whitman urged in *Leaves of
Grass*, so he read the poem aloud to his classes. Henri insisted on his
pupils finding their own vision—developing the instincts that would
drive them toward truth. Bellows later called Henri the single most important person in his artistic development, because he helped the student
find himself.

Henri's own paintings resembled Impressionism, but darker. He
worked quickly and spontaneously, rarely stopping to retouch his works.
His *Snow in New York* (1902) is a murky view of a snowy street barely
lit by a single lamppost among the skyscrapers lining each side of the
street. The shadowy figures in the painting seem to be in a losing battle
with the wintry New York night. Although Henri had gifts as an artist,
his real importance was as an agitator and rebel. He had the courage to
fight the established art leaders of the 1900s and the leadership ability
to bring the Ashcan school into a loosely knit association which stood
up to its critics.[16]

In the short time between arriving in New York City in 1904 to his untimely death of a ruptured appendix in 1925 at age 42, Bellows became the most famous, most highly regarded American artist of his day. The Columbus, Ohio, native fulfilled his ambition through hard work and continual output. It is estimated that he produced more than 700 works in his career, an average of more than 33 a year from 1904 to 1925. He painted most of his famous works by the age of 31, which makes his production even more astonishing. Bellows yearned for success and was not bashful about telling his fellow students about his ambitions. In fact, he had turned down a chance to play professional baseball to pursue a career as an artist. In his first summer in New York, while his friends returned home or searched for ways to make cash, Bellows played semi-professional baseball with a team in Central Park.[17]

Bellows made friends with another teacher at the school, John Sloan (a member of The Eight), and Henri invited Bellows to his house every Tuesday evening for informal gatherings with the other members of the Ashcan group. Bellows spent the other summer evenings traveling in the slums of New York seeing firsthand how the poor struggled to survive. This prepared him for the intellectual discussions that took place at Henri's meetings. The most important thing in Bellows's life, however, was painting, and as Henri's prized student, his career took off.[18] Bellows's art seemed to embody the spirit of the age—Roosevelt's plea for a strenuous life, combined with a raw, big view of the world around him.[19]

Bellows shocked the Pennsylvania Academy in 1908 with his painting *Forty-Two Kids*, depicting 42 young street urchins swimming naked in the polluted East River. The judges found the subject matter offensive (not the nudity, rather that the subjects were street children). One critic at the time called the painting "a tour de force of absurdity . . . most of the boys look more like maggots than humans."[20] Bellows used dark hues to create a somber scene of boyish frivolity, though the river ominously engulfs them. In other paintings, Bellows continued his portrayal of the underbelly of urban life. Both *River Rats* (1906) and *Cliff Dwellers* (1913) show urban America as swarming with life: chaotic and fast-paced. A common pastime among upper-class Americans in the 1900s was to go "slumming," touring the working-class neighborhoods to glimpse the downtrodden. The way people viewed the poor, with a kind of detached sentimentality, contributed to Bellows's popularity, although he did not hold these convictions. By this time, he had become a Marxist.[21]

Bellows could not get the streets of New York out of his system, and he began painting the excavations under way to build Pennsylvania Station. His first in a series recording the digging was finished in January 1907. Designed by the architectural firm McKim, Mead and White, Penn

Station was one of the city's largest urban projects ever undertaken. The tunnel leading to the terminal required digging under both the Hudson and East Rivers and demolishing four city blocks. The only hole ever dug that size was the recently completed Panama Canal, which epitomized America's technological prowess.

Although Bellows's New York street scenes were critically acclaimed, he gained his fame and lasting reputation on the basis of his boxing paintings, which is remarkable, since he produced only five boxing works out of approximately 700 total. Although boxing was illegal in New York in 1907, Tom Sharkey's saloon, just across the street from Bellows's studio, evaded the law by converting the bar into a club for the evening. The cheap dues allowed "members" into the back room to observe the fight. Bellows's friend, Ed Keefe, invited him to see a match at Sharkey's. From this first visit, Bellows painted *Club Night*, revealing Bellows's ability to portray brutal energy and strength on canvas.[22] From the thick calf muscles and biceps of the combatants to the puffy face and misshapen nose of the fighter on the left, Bellows seems to have caught a punch being thrown in midair. An observer can almost feel the pain of the boxers in *Club Night*. The painting also highlights the dichotomy between the beaten and battered fighters and the ringside spectators, arrayed in formal attire. The faces of the fans are hideous and devilish. *Club Night* led to other boxing paintings (*Stag at Sharkey's*, 1909, and *Both Members of This Club*, 1909), possibly the most powerful paintings done in the 1900s.[23]

PHOTOGRAPHY

In the 1900s, art patron Alfred Stieglitz, who is credited for introducing modern painting to America by debuting shows featuring the works of Henri Matisse, Pablo Picasso, and Paul Gauguin, broke ground in another blossoming art form—photography. However, in this case, Stieglitz himself played the role of artist. It became his mission to have photography accepted as an art form—the equal of painting or literature. In this role, Stieglitz mentored young photographers and founded the photography journal *Camera Work* (1903).

Born in New Jersey to wealthy Jewish parents, Stieglitz (1864–1946) learned photography in Germany in the 1880s. Stieglitz ruled the American art scene with an iron fist, arrogance, and a sharp tongue. He encouraged the development of a uniquely American art and one that characterized the conditions of life. Art critic Robert Hughes explained that Stieglitz believed art was a way to "communicate the purity, freshness, and honesty that lay in the artist's own character. This is why Stieglitz expected so much from 'his' artists, and it explains the some-

George Bellows, American, 1882–1925. *Stag at Sharkey's*, 1909. Oil on canvas, 92 × 122.6 cm. © The Cleveland Museum of Art, 2001, Hinman B. Hurlbut Collection, 1133.1922.

times bruising rejections and quarrels that arose in his various relationships with them."[24]

In the 1890s, Stieglitz began his campaign for photography as a "pictorialist," a person who attempts to make photos look like paintings. He preferred the "hard" school of pictorialism, a realistic look, as opposed to the soft branch that tried to make photos seem like watercolors or oil paintings. The hard pictorialists derisively called the soft photographers "fuzzyographers." Similar to Impressionist painting, in that it emphasized suggestion over detail, Stieglitz's photography helped usher in a wave of modernism to the United States.

In 1902 Stieglitz formed the Photo-Secession group, along with friends and colleagues Edward Steichen, Clarence White, and Gertrude Kasebier. The group rebelled against two things: the stringent academic thinking that dominated the arts in the 1900s and the bad photography they felt soft pictorialism represented. Stieglitz founded *Camera Work* in 1903 to showcase the group's photographs. They held their first exhibit at the National Arts Club Show in New York City, which was a great success and placed them in the forefront of the art photography movement.

From 1902 to 1905, Stieglitz and his cohorts exhibited at galleries around the United States, Canada, and Europe. Next, under Stieglitz's leadership, they set up a permanent gallery at 291 Fifth Avenue in New York, which became known throughout the art world simply as "291." For the next two years, until 1907, 291 showed nothing but photography, following Stieglitz's lead.[25]

A vocal champion of modernism, Stieglitz expanded beyond photography into other art forms. The 291 served as a hub for avant-garde artists and became known as a place for experimentalists who were shunned by the art community. One critic referred to the gallery as a "bedlam of half-baked philosophies and cockeyed visions." In hindsight, however, Stieglitz's passion for modernism is validated by the universal appeal of the European artists he showcased at the studio. From 1908–1911, the list of artists who displayed works at the 291 reads like a who's who of the world's greats, including Picasso, Matisse, Renoir, Cézanne, Rodin, and Toulouse-Lautrec. In his own time, though, Stieglitz pushed too far ahead of the pack to effect great change on the nation as a whole. He did not have the personality or inclination to carry modernism into the heartland.[26]

While Stieglitz carried on his modernist crusade, other photographers used their lenses to capture realistic pictures of everyday life, revealing the real spirit of the age. Frances Benjamin Johnston, from her studio in Washington, D.C., traveled to Hampton, Virginia, to capture stills that represented the progress African Americans had made since the Civil War. Hampton was held up as a model for integration. As one of the most successful photographers of the 1900s, Johnston could have easily turned down such a commission. A member of the well-to-do society in the nation's capital, she photographed diplomats and government officials, including Admiral George Dewey and Secretary of State John Hay.[27]

Johnston, a free spirit, led a group of artists and writers in Washington called The Push, who captured their parties on film. In a revealing self-portrait, Johnston posed as a "new woman," a beer stein in one hand and a cigarette in the other. Her skirt is hiked up above her knees, and a rogue's gallery of jilted suitors stares down from her mantle. Her playful demeanor and ability to catch magical, informal moments made her reputation. This ability led to the commission she received from Thomas J. Calloway, the agent in charge of finding work for the "Negro Exhibit" at the 1900 Paris Exposition.

By the spring of 1900, Johnston had shot more than 150 images for the exhibit. She contrasted the photos of enterprising young Hampton Institute graduates with ones of elderly African Americans struggling to survive. When Calloway saw the photos, he immediately wrote Johnston to tell her that he felt they were the best at the Paris exhibit. By contrasting the young college-educated blacks with their poorer brethren, Johnston constructed a portrait of African American life at the turn of the century that proved how little blacks had advanced as a whole, but still contained some hope for the future.[28]

On the surface, there seems to be a world of difference between the work of Stieglitz and Johnston. However, they both had similar goals, perhaps unspoken, to have photography accepted as an art form and to widen its framework to include images of the everyday world. Although they faced opposition, especially the prickly Stieglitz, 1900s photographers laid the foundation for these objectives to be fulfilled.

SCULPTURE

Augustus Saint-Gaudens

American sculpture in the 1900s revolved around one man: Augustus Saint-Gaudens, not only the greatest sculptor of his age, but possibly in all American history. The Irish-born Saint-Gaudens (1848–1907) came to the United States with his parents during the potato famine while he was still a baby. He grew up in New York City, and at the age of 13 he began working with a cameo cutter, because he realized, even then, that he wanted a career as an artist. Saint-Gaudens took night classes at Cooper Institute and the National Academy of Design. Later, in 1867, he traveled to Paris, then Rome to study sculpting.[29]

The sculptor's first important commission upon returning to the United States occurred in 1881—a statue of Admiral David Farragut to be placed in Central Park. The success of the early work spawned a series of commissions for the young artist. In short order, he sculpted both a standing and sitting Abraham Lincoln in Chicago; a memorial to Deacon Samuel Chapin in Springfield, Massachusetts; a monument at the grave of Mrs. Henry Adams in Rock Creek Cemetery in Washington, D.C.; and a bronze weather vane atop Madison Square Garden.[30]

In 1897 Saint-Gaudens unveiled a Civil War memorial on the edge of Boston Commons which immortalizes Colonel Robert Shaw and his men, the Union's Fifty-Fourth Massachusetts Regiment, who were all black volunteers, some of whom had been slaves. The powerful work shows the men marching, perhaps south, to their final battle at Fort Wagner in South Carolina. In 1863 the regiment attempted to take the fort, despite the overwhelming odds against them, an almost suicidal mission. They all died in the battle and were buried in a mass grave. The poet Robert Lowell said Saint-Gaudens's sculpture "sticks like a fishbone in the city's throat."[31] The commission marked the first time an American sculptor had been asked to represent blacks as heroes. The memorial was also the first American sculpture to commemorate a group, rather than an individual.

For all the power and poignancy of the Massachusetts piece, Saint-Gaudens outdid himself in 1903 with the unveiling of a gold-leaf statue of General William Tecumseh Sherman and Nike, the goddess of victory. On the southeast edge of Central Park, near Fifth Avenue and Fifty-ninth Street, Sherman rides a great war horse, with Nike by his side, her right arm outstretched leading the general forward. The statue is so powerful with its glimmering cover, that when the original gold wore off the monument, New York real estate tycoon Donald Trump paid for it to be re-gilded.[32]

Tragedy struck Saint-Gaudens in 1900 when he was diagnosed with cancer, and underwent two operations. Somehow, he managed to keep up his frenetic pace. A fire in his studio in 1904 destroyed a year's worth of work and many of his cherished treasures, but Saint-Gaudens remained optimistic and upbeat, even though he was known as an extreme perfectionist.[33] In 1907 he designed a twenty-dollar gold eagle, which has been called the most beautiful coin ever minted. He tinkered with the design of the coin, making 70 different versions before deciding on the best one.[34]

Until his dying day, on August 3, 1907, Saint-Gaudens worked on his projects and encouraged other young sculptors. America's foremost critic in the 1900s, Royal Cortissoz, said Saint-Gaudens "was not only our greatest sculptor, but the first to break with the old epoch of insipid ideas and hide-bound academic notions of style, giving the art a new lease of life and fixing a new standard."[35]

Frederick Remington

Another form of sculpture in the 1900s was less formal and perhaps more popular with the general public: Native American and frontier works. Frederic Remington (1861–1909), also a painter and illustrator, created powerful works of cowboys and horses that rival Bellows's boxing paintings for their raw energy and vitality.

From an early age, Remington loved the outdoors. He studied art at Yale, but left for the West where he visited Indian camps, cavalry posts, and cowboy ranches. Remington repackaged the West with heavy doses of nostalgia. He even fabricated a story about fighting in the Indian wars with the American cavalry. He settled down in New York but made frequent trips west in search of material. In his lifetime he produced more than 2,700 paintings.

Remington gained his initial reputation as a magazine illustrator, but he wanted to be taken seriously as an artist. By the early 1900s, his paintings and sculptures came to symbolize the West for many observers. His status as an artist grew steadily throughout the decade. His friendship with Theodore Roosevelt bolstered his sales and his image as a hard strewn Westerner. Remington's sculpture *The Bronco Buster* (1890) shows a remarkable eye for detail, while taking nothing away from the power of the muscled bronze horse. Over the course of the 1900s, Remington produced his sculptures *The Cheyenne* (1901), *Comin' Through the Rye* (1902–1904), and *The Cowboy* (1908). Remington died at the age of 48 of appendicitis.[36]

Gutzon Borglum

Gutzon Borglum (1871–1941) also created bronzes of bucking broncos and wild horses. His *Mares of Diomedes* (1904) portrays a series of horses in full gallop and jumping in stride. The piece was the first sculpture produced by an American artist to be purchased by the Metropolitan Museum of Art. Borglum is even better known as the sculptor of Mount Rushmore in South Dakota. His portraits of four of the nation's great presidents (George Washington, Thomas Jefferson, Abraham Lincoln, and Theodore Roosevelt) constitute one of the largest sculpting projects ever undertaken. The great monument was commissioned by the state of South Dakota in 1927 and finished in 1941, although Borglum died just before it was finished, and his son completed the project.

Artists in the early twentieth century, regardless of specialty, worked diligently to gain the acceptance of the European art establishment, and quickly prove that American artists were equal—if not superior—to their Old World colleagues. The 1900s served as an important stepping stone for artists in the United States. Like the young upstart nation itself, artists had a chip on their shoulders and were bound and determined to prove that an independent art scene could thrive here. Many artists, whether coming to the conclusion themselves or as part of a larger group, decided that there would be depictions of American life and that they were every bit as important as those coming from the Continent. Even if they had to fight against all norms in the art world, there would be interpretations that attempted to capture the American spirit.

The artists of the 1900s bridged the gap between the aging group that lived through the Civil War era and the modernists coming to age around the 1913 Armory Show, which ushered in the modern era. But, in fact, that was just one role they played. They were much more important for their contributions to the history of American art, which superceded their collective standing as a link between the two eras. Keep in mind, this was the age of Bellows, of Henri, of Stieglitz—these were true masters, innovators, radicals, and rebels.

Of these artists, the inclusion of Bellows, in particular, might shock modern observers. He has been singled out as possessing a conservative touch that gained quick acceptance among the art circles of his day. However, examining *Both Members of This Club* or *Stag at Sharkey's* reveals the true energy and grace of Bellows' art. Arguably being as dominant as any of the modernist paintings displayed at the Armory exhibition, these works stand among the triumphs of the twentieth century.

Cost of Products in the 1900s

Women's shoes: $1.50

Women's skirt: $4

Women's corset: $.40

Women's shirt waist hats: $1.75–$3.95

Hatpins: $.05

Women's silk-lined raincoat: $12.50

"The St. Louis," a ¾-length women's coat designed for the World's Fair: $22

Girl's tailored suit: $7.50

Men's shirt: $.50

Men's hat: $2

Men's summer suit: $15

Boy's three-piece suit (age 10–16): $5–$10.50

Brass bed: $16.25–$20

Reversible Brussels carpet: $12.50

Grandfather clock: $31.50

Rocking chair: $2.95

Wooden ice box: $8.92

Borax, ½ lb. package: $.04

Dr. Worden's Female Pills: $.33

Hair-waving iron: $.11

Restaurant sandwich: $.07

Slice of pie: $.03–$.05

Glass of milk: $.03–$.05
Coffee (per lb.): $.15
Eggs (per dozen): $.12
Sugar (100 lb.): $5.80
Beef (per lb.): $.10
Bacon (per lb.): $.12
Model B Cadillac: $900
Roundtrip ticket to Coney Island on an iron steamboat: $.30
Yearly subscription to the *New York Times*: $8.50

Notes

INTRODUCTION

1. Richard Hofstadter, *The Age of Reform: From Bryan to F.D.R.* (New York: Vintage, 1955), 174–177.

2. George E. Mowry, *The Era of Theodore Roosevelt and the Birth of Modern America, 1900–1912* (New York: Harper and Row, 1962), 92–94.

CHAPTER 1

1. E. Benjamin Andrews, *History of the United States: From the Earliest Discovery of America to the End of 1902*, vol. 5 (New York: Charles Scribner's Sons, 1903), 359–364; Sean Dennis Cashman, *America in the Age of the Titans: The Progressive Era and World War I* (New York: New York University Press, 1988), 8.

2. Mark Sullivan, *Our Times: The United States, 1900–1925*, vol. 1 (New York: Charles Scribner's Sons, 1927), 561.

3. Quoted in Edward Wagenknecht, *American Profile: 1900–1909* (Amherst: University of Massachusetts Press, 1982), 347.

4. Max J. Skidmore, "Theodore Roosevelt on Race and Gender," *Journal of American Culture* 21 (summer 1998): 35–46.

5. John Whiteclay Chambers II, *The Tyranny of Change: America in the Progressive Era, 1890–1920*, 2d ed. (New Brunswick, NJ: Rutgers University Press, 2000), 138.

6. Theodore Roosevelt, "Fourth Annual Message to Congress," in *The Essential Theodore Roosevelt*, ed. John Gabriel Hunt (New York: Gramercy Books, 1994), 155.

7. Robert H. Wiebe, *The Search for Order, 1877–1920* (New York: Hill and Wang, 1967), 166.

8. Harold U. Faulkner, *The Quest for Social Justice, 1898–1914* (Chicago: Quadrangle, 1971), 82–86.

9. Wiebe, *The Search for Order*, 168–170.

10. Roosevelt, "Fourth Annual Message," 161.

11. Howard Zinn, *A People's History of the United States, 1492–Present* (New York: Harper Perennial, 1995), 346.

12. Quoted in Chambers, *The Tyranny of Change*, 184; Zinn, *A People's History of the United States*, 341–346.

13. Chambers, *The Tyranny of Change*, 170.

14. Ibid., 48.

15. William Appleman Williams, *The Tragedy of American Diplomacy* (New York: W.W. Norton, 1972), 59.

16. Cashman, *America in the Age of the Titans*, 440.

17. Quoted in ibid., 441.

18. Roosevelt, "Fourth Annual Message," 175–176.

19. Glenn Porter, *The Rise of Big Business, 1860–1920*, 2d ed. (Arlington Heights, IL: Harlan Davidson, 1992), 92.

20. Mansel G. Blackford and K. Austin Kerr, *Business Enterprise in American History*, 2d ed. (Boston: Houghton Mifflin, 1990), 174–179.

21. Ibid., 178–180.

22. Quoted in H.W. Brands, *Masters of Enterprise: Giants of American Business from John Jacob Astor and J.P. Morgan to Bill Gates and Oprah Winfrey* (New York: Free Press, 1999), 87.

23. Ibid., 88–90.

24. Quoted in ibid., 93.

25. Quoted in Ron Chernow, *Titan: The Life of John D. Rockefeller, Sr.* (New York: Random House, 1998), 595.

26. Brands, *Masters of Enterprise*, 66–68.

27. Ibid., 72.

28. Quoted in Daniel Gross, *Forbes' Greatest Business Stories of All Time* (New York: John Wiley, 1996), 71.

29. Ibid., 59–63.

30. Ibid., 67.

31. Quoted in ibid., 69.

32. Ibid., 72.

33. Melvyn Dubofsky, *The State and Labor in Modern America* (Chapel Hill: University of North Carolina Press, 1994), 38.

34. Ibid., 38–39.

35. Cashman, *America in the Age of the Titans*, 198–202.

36. Margaret F. Byington, *Homestead: The Households of a Mill Town* (Pittsburgh: University of Pittsburgh Press, 1974), 161–163.

37. Ibid.

38. David Montgomery, *The Fall of the House of Labor: The Workplace, the State, and American Labor Activism, 1865–1925* (New York: Cambridge University Press, 1987), 310–315.

39. Quoted in Zinn, *A People's History of the United States*, 323.

40. Ibid., 324.

41. Quoted in ibid., 308–309.

42. Cashman, *America in the Age of the Titans*, 170–172.

43. "Risking Death for a Living," *New York Times*, 5 June 1904, 12.

44. Ibid.

45. Thomas J. Schlereth, *Victorian America: Transformations in Everyday Life, 1876–1915* (New York: HarperCollins, 1991), 288–289.

46. Sullivan, *Our Times*, 380.

47. Ray Ginger, *Age of Excess: The United States from 1877 to 1914*, 2nd ed. (Prospect Heights, IL: Waveland Press, 1989), 314–315.

48. Richard Schwartz, *Berkeley 1900: Daily Life at the Turn of the Century* (Berkeley, CA: RSB Books, 2000), 87–88.

49. Judy Crichton, *America 1900: The Sweeping Story of a Pivotal Year in the Life of the Nation* (New York: Henry Holt, 1998), 211–215.

50. Ibid., 215.

51. Nancy Bernhard, *American Decades, 1900–1909*, ed. Vincent Tompkins (Detroit: Gale Research, 1996), 349.

52. George Lane Jr., "The Day Arcadia Burned," History, Desoto Co FLGenWeb Project, http://www.rootsweb.com/~fldesoto/arcadia.htm (28 November 2001).

53. Quoted in ibid.

54. Spessard Stone, "Arcadia, Florida Early History, Part I," taken from *Tampa Morning Tribune*, 10 January 1909. Available online at http://freepages.geneology.rootsweb.com/~crackerbarrel/arcadia1.html (28 November 2001).

55. Ibid.

56. Wagenknecht, *American Profile*, 123–124.

57. Quoted in ibid., 128.

58. Cashman, *America in the Age of the Titans*, 72.

CHAPTER 2

1. Theodore Roosevelt, *An Autobiography* (New York: Macmillan, 1913), 364.

2. Faulkner, *The Quest for Social Justice*, 177–178; David I. Macleod, *The Age of the Child: Children in America, 1898–1920* (New York: Twayne, 1998), 38–39.

3. Roosevelt quoted in Faulkner, *The Quest for Social Justice*, 10–11.

4. Macleod, *The Age of the Child*, 12–13.

5. Elliott West, *Growing Up in Twentieth-Century America: A History and Reference Guide* (Westport, CT: Greenwood Press, 1996), 20–21.

6. Ibid., 1–3.

7. Faulkner, *The Quest for Social Justice*, 178.

8. Ibid., 178–179.

9. West, *Growing Up in Twentieth-Century America*, 11–13.

10. Ibid., 15–16.

11. Schwartz, *Berkeley 1900*, 71.

12. Macleod, *The Age of the Child*, 76.

13. Ibid.

14. Ibid., 77.

15. Schwartz, *Berkeley 1900*, 71.

16. Faulkner, *The Quest for Social Justice*, 192–193.

17. Macleod, *The Age of the Child*, 83–85.

18. Ibid., 88–89.

19. Folkstom Wallace, "Student Life at Stanford University," *Overland Monthly* 45 (January 1905): 35.

20. Quoted in Robert C. Alberts, *Pitt: The Story of the University of Pittsburgh, 1787–1987* (Pittsburgh: University of Pittsburgh Press, 1986), 56.

21. Quoted in Ibid., 63.

22. Ibid., 66–69.

23. John Spargo, "John Spargo on Child Labor (1906)," in *The Progressive Movement, 1900–1915*, ed. Richard Hofstadter (New York: Simon and Schuster, 1963), 42–43.

24. Dorothy Schneider and Carl J. Schneider, *American Women in the Progressive Era, 1900–1920* (New York: Facts on File, 1993), 58–59.

25. Faulkner, *The Quest for Social Justice*, 186–188; Schwartz, *Berkeley 1900*, 81.

26. Faulkner, *The Quest for Social Justice*, 186–188.

27. West, *Growing Up in Twentieth-Century America*, 37.

28. Ibid., 36.

29. Macleod, *The Age of the Child*, 69–70.

30. Ibid., 101–102.

31. Quoted in West, *Growing Up in Twentieth-Century America*, 34.

32. Macleod, *The Age of the Child*, 101–103.

33. Byington, *Homestead*, 118.

34. Ibid., 125–126.

35. Ibid., 134–136.

36. Ibid., 147.

37. West, *Growing Up in Twentieth-Century America*, 11.

38. Quoted in ibid., 24.

39. Ibid., 24–25.

CHAPTER 3

1. Juliann Sivulka, *Soap, Sex, and Cigarettes: A Cultural History of American Advertising* (Belmont, CA: Wadsworth, 1998), 94.

2. Bob Batchelor, *Yesterday, Today, Tomorrow: Kimberly-Clark 125 Years* (Dallas: Kimberly-Clark Corporation, 1997), 68–73.

3. Sivulka, *Soap, Sex, and Cigarettes*, 96–97.

4. Susan Strasser, *Satisfaction Guaranteed: The Making of the American Mass Market* (New York: Pantheon, 1989), 93–97.

5. Ibid., 97–102.

6. Ibid., 102–106.

7. Sivulka, *Soap, Sex, and Cigarettes*, 96–97.

8. Strasser, *Satisfaction Guaranteed*, 204–206.

9. Ibid., 210.

10. Ibid., 210–211.

11. Sivulka, *Soap, Sex, and Cigarettes*, 95.

12. Strasser, *Satisfaction Guaranteed*, 212–213.

13. Ibid.

14. Ibid., 213–214.

15. Strasser, *Satisfaction Guaranteed*, 128–129; Wagenknecht, *American Profile*, 141–142.

16. Wagenknecht, *American Profile*, 144.

17. Stephen Fox, *The Mirror Makers: A History of American Advertising and Its Creators* (New York: William Morrow, 1984), 40.

18. Quoted in Fox, *The Mirror Makers*, 41.

19. Jackson Lears, *Fables of Abundance: A Cultural History of Advertising in America* (New York: BasicBooks, 1994), 198–204.

20. Fox, *The Mirror Makers*, 46.

21. Sivulka, *Soap, Sex, and Cigarettes*, 100–101.

22. Ibid., 99–100.

23. Wagenknecht, *American Profile*, 150–152.

24. William Wrigley Jr., "The Story of the Wrigley Company," http://www.Wrigley.com/gum/storcomp.htm (27 November 2001).

25. Ibid.

26. Quoted in Fox, *The Mirror Makers*, 57.

27. Ibid., 61.

28. Quoted in Fox, *The Mirror Makers*, 61.

29. Ibid., 62–63.

30. Sivulka, *Soap, Sex, and Cigarettes*, 117–119; Lears, *Fables of Abundance*, 156.

31. Wagenknecht, *American Profile*, 137–138.

32. Ibid., 140.

33. Ibid., 140–141.

34. Sivulka, *Soap, Sex, and Cigarettes*, 119–120.

CHAPTER 4

1. Robin Langley Sommer, *American Architecture: An Illustrated History* (New York: Crescent Books, 1996), 70; Robert Hughes, *American Visions: The Epic History of Art in America* (New York: Knopf, 1997), 276.

2. Hughes, *American Visions*, 277–278.

3. Sommer, *American Architecture*, 70.

4. Wagenknecht, *American Profile*, 99–100.

5. Sommer, *American Architecture*, 71.

6. Ibid., 73–75.

7. Ibid., 75.

8. Spiro Kostof, *America by Design* (New York: Oxford University Press, 1987), 38–39.

9. Ibid., 45; David E. Shi, *Facing Facts: Realism in American Thought and Culture, 1850–1920* (New York: Oxford University Press, 1995), 173–174.

10. Daniel M. Mendelowitz, *A History of American Art* (New York: Holt, Rinehart and Winston, 1960), 405–407.

11. Shi, *Facing Facts*, 174–178.

12. Kathy Peiss, *Cheap Amusements: Working Women and Leisure in Turn-of-the-Century New York* (Philadelphia: Temple University Press, 1986), 34–35.

13. Ezra Bowne, ed., *This Fabulous Century, 1900–1910* (Alexandria, VA: Time-Life Books, 1969), 169.

14. Quoted in Hughes, *American Visions*, 395–396.

15. Ibid., 396; Sommer, *American Architecture*, 90–92.

16. Brendan Gill, *Many Masks: A Life of Frank Lloyd Wright* (New York: G.P. Putnam's Sons, 1987) 193–195.

17. Meryle Secrest, *Frank Lloyd Wright* (New York: Knopf, 1992), 169.

18. Ibid.

19. Quoted in Gill, *Many Masks*, 164–173.

20. Ibid., 347.

21. Ibid., 354; Hughes, *American Visions*, 398–399.

22. Robert A.M. Stern, *Pride of Place: Building the American Dream* (Boston: Houghton Mifflin, 1986), 253–254.

23. Robert Twombly, *Louis Sullivan: His Life and Work* (New York: Viking, 1986), 290–292, Quote 329–330.

24. Quoted in Twombly, *Louis Sullivan*, 330.

25. Ibid., 379–382.

26. Quoted in Twombly, *Louis Sullivan*, 390.

27. Stern, *Pride of Place*, 255.

28. Ibid.

CHAPTER 5

1. Bowne, *This Fabulous Century*, 158–161.

2. Quoted in Sullivan, *Our Times*, 388.

3. Quoted in O.E. Schoeffler and William Gale, *Esquire's Encyclopedia of 20th Century Men's Fashions* (New York: McGraw-Hill, 1973), 74.

4. Ibid.

5. Chambers, *Tyranny of Change*, 33.

6. Bowne, *This Fabulous Century*, 182–183.

7. Sullivan, *Our Times*, 193–195.

8. Quoted in Sullivan, New York *World* quote, 195.

9. Bowne, *This Fabulous Century*, 180.

10. Kathy Peiss, *Working Women*, 34, 62.

11. Ibid., 63.

12. Ibid.

13. Ibid., 64–65.

14. Caroline Rennolds Milbank, *New York Fashion: The Evolution of American Style* (New York: Harry N. Abrams, 1989), 48.

15. Quoted in Byington, *Homestead*, 108.

16. Ibid., 83–84.

17. Ibid., 86.

18. Ibid., 100–106.

19. Schoeffler and Gale, *20th Century Men's Fashions*, 124.

20. Estelle Ansley Worrell, *American Costume, 1840 to 1920* (Harrisburg, PA: Stackpole Books, 1979), 145.

21. Richard Maltby, ed., *Popular Culture in the Twentieth Century* (London: Grange Books, 1988), 28.

22. Kathy Peiss, *Hope in a Jar: The Making of America's Beauty Culture* (New York: Henry Holt, 1998), 50–51.

23. Ibid., 55.

24. Ibid., 94–95.

25. Schoeffler and Gale, *20th Century Men's Fashions*, 2–3.

26. Ibid., 4.

27. Ibid., 4–5.

28. Quoted in Sullivan, *Our Times*, 393; 395–401.

29. Sullivan, *Our Times*, 397–399.

30. Worrell, *American Costume*, 146–149.

31. Quoted in Schoeffler and Gale, *20th Century Men's Fashions*, 478.

CHAPTER 6

1. Cashman, *America in the Age of the Titans*, 10–12.

2. Paul Johnson, *A History of the American People* (New York: HarperCollins, 1997), 594–595.

3. Cashman, *America in the Age of the Titans*, 40–42.

4. Byington, *Homestead*, 65.

5. Ibid., 63.

6. Ibid., 108.

7. Ibid., 64.

8. Ibid., 65.

9. Hamilton Hold, ed., *The Life Stories of Undistinguished Americans, as Told by Themselves* (New York: Routledge, 1990), 25–28.

10. Ibid., 28.

11. Harvey A. Levenstein, *Revolution at the Table: The Transformation of the American Diet* (New York: Oxford University Press, 1988), 98–103.

12. Ibid., 104.

13. Ibid., 105–108.

14. Ibid., 30–31.

15. Chambers, *Tyranny of Change*, 38.

16. Quoted in Hofstadter, *The Age of Reform*, 109.

17. Quoted in ibid., 125.

18. Ibid.

19. Ibid., 125–130.

20. William E. Mason, "Food Adulterations," *The North American Review* 170 (1900): 548–549.

21. Ibid., 549–553.

22. Ibid., 553.

23. Cashman, *American in the Age of the Titans*, 82.

24. Ibid., 83.

25. Quoted in H.W. Brands, *T.R.: The Last Romantic* (New York: BasicBooks, 1997), 549.

26. Quoted in Cashman, *American in the Age of the Titans*, 87.

27. Brands, *T.R.: The Last Romantic*, 550–551; Cashman, *American in the Age of the Titans*, 88–89.

28. Ibid.

29. Levenstein, *Revolution at the Table*, 33; Wagenknecht, *American Profile*, 144–145.

30. Wagenknecht, *American Profile*, 144–146.

31. Ibid., 146–147.

32. Levenstein, *Revolution at the Table*, 34.

33. Margaret Visser, *Much Depends on Dinner: The Extraordinary History and Mythology, Allure and Obsessions, Perils and Taboos, of an Ordinary Meal* (New York: Grove Press, 1986), 41–44.

34. Wagenknecht, *American Profile*, 148–149.

35. Kraft Foods, *Kraft Foods History 1900–1910*, available online at http://www.kraftfoods.com/jell-o/history/1900.html (13 February 2001).

36. MSNBC, *The American Century in Food: With 1900s Comes Culinary Change*, available online at http://www.msnbc.com/news/320398.asp?cp1=1 (13 February 2001).

37. Wagenknecht, *American Profile*, 152–153.

38. Ibid., 153–154.

CHAPTER 7

1. Theodore Roosevelt, "The Life of Strenuous Endeavor," in *Theodore Roosevelt*, ed. Dewey W. Grantham (Upper Saddle River, NJ: Prentice-Hall, 1971), 38.

2. Theodore Roosevelt, *An Autobiography* (New York: Macmillan, 1913), 52.

3. Benjamin G. Rader, *American Sports: From the Age of Folk Games to the Age of Televised Sports*, 2d ed. (Upper Saddle River, NJ: Prentice-Hall, 1990), 119.

4. Ibid., 120.

5. Peiss, *Cheap Amusements*, 115.

6. Byington, *Homestead*, 114.

7. G. Edward White, *Creating the National Pastime: Baseball Transforms Itself, 1903–1953* (Princeton: Princeton University Press, 1996), 48.

8. Quoted in Charles C. Alexander, *Our Game: An American Baseball History* (New York: Henry Holt, 1991), 78.

9. Ibid., 78–79.

10. For a detailed study of early baseball contracts and the subsequent ramifications, please see Chapter 2 of White, *Creating the National Pastime*, 48–83.

11. Alexander, *Our Game*, 95–97; Rader, *American Sports*, 159–161.

12. Ibid; quoted in Alexander, *Our Game*, 97.

13. Rader, *American Sports*, 159–160.

14. Brian J. Neilson, "Baseball," in *The Theater of Sport*, ed. Karl B. Raitz (Baltimore: Johns Hopkins University Press, 1995), 37.

15. Alexander, *Our Game*, 85–86.

16. Ibid., 89; Rader, *American Sports*, 153.

17. Allen Guttmann, *The Olympics: A History of the Modern Games* (Urbana: University of Illinois Press, 1992), 1–10.

18. Ibid., 10–15.

19. Ibid., 18.

20. Ibid., 22–23.

21. Ibid., 24–25; Jane Leder, *Grace & Glory: A Century of Women in the Olympics* (Chicago: Triumph Books, 1996), 13.

22. Guttmann, *The Olympics*, 25–27; Mark Dyreson, *Making the American Team: Sport, Culture, and the Olympic Experience* (Urbana: University of Illinois Press, 1998), 86–88.

23. Guttmann, *The Olympics*, 28–31.

24. Allison Danzig, *Oh, How They Played the Game: The Early Days of Football and the Heroes Who Made It Great* (New York: Macmillan, 1971), 149.

25. John Durant and Otto Bettmann, *Pictorial History of American Sports: From Colonial Times to the Present* (New York: A.S. Barnes, 1952), 110–111; H.W. Brands, *T.R.: The Last Romantic* (New York: BasicBooks, 1997), 553–554.

26. George Gipe, *The Great American Sports Book* (Garden City, NY: Doubleday, 1978), 177.

27. Ibid., 171.

28. Ibid., 168.

29. Durant and Bettmann, *Pictorial History of American Sports*, 120–122; Faulkner, *The Quest for Social Justice*, 287.

30. Arthur R. Ashe Jr., *A Hard Road to Glory: A History of the African-American Athlete, 1619–1918* (New York: Amistad, 1988), 30–32.

31. Quoted in ibid., 32.

32. Ibid., 33.

33. Ibid., 34.

34. Ibid., 35.

35. Quoted in ibid., 38.

36. Joseph Dorinson, "Black Heroes in Sport: From Jack Johnson to Muhammad Ali," *Journal of Popular Culture* 31 (winter 1997): 115–135.

37. Faulkner, *The Quest for Social Justice*, 289–290.

38. Thomas J. Schlereth, *Victorian America*, 209.

39. Ibid., 233–234.

40. Ibid., 234.

41. Faulkner, *The Quest for Social Justice*, 306–307.

42. William Martin Aixen, "St. Louis's Exposition Biggest Show on Earth," *New York Times*, 20 June 1904, sec. A.

43. Dyreson, *Making the American Team*, 81–83.

44. Ibid., 88–89.

45. Quoted in ibid., 89.

46. Ibid., 88–90.

CHAPTER 8

1. George Santanyana, "The Gentile Tradition in American Philosophy," *Selected Critical Writings of George Santanyana*, vol. 2 (Cambridge: Cambridge University Press, 1968), 85–107.

2. Quoted in Bowne, *This Fabulous Century*, 12.

3. Peter Conn, *Literature in America: An Illustrated History* (New York: Cambridge University Press, 1989), 297–301.

4. Richard Hofstadter, ed., *The Progressive Movement, 1900–1915* (New York: Simon and Schuster, 1963), 5.

5. Wagenknecht, *American Profile*, 209.

6. Jay Martin, *Harvests of Change: American Literature, 1865–1914* (Upper Saddle River, NJ: Prentice-Hall, 1967), 12.

7. Shi, *Facing Facts*, 106.

8. Ibid., 104–107.

9. Ibid., 121.

10. J. Leonard Bates, *The United States, 1898–1928: Progressivism and A Society in Transition* (New York: McGraw-Hill, 1976), 9–10.

11. Vernon Louis Parrington, *Main Currents in American Thought: An Interpretation of American Thought from the Beginnings to 1920* (New York: Harcourt, Brace, 1930), 241.

12. Warner Berthoff, *The Ferment of Realism, American Literature, 1884–1919* (New York: Free Press, 1965), 65.

13. Quoted in ibid., 61.

14. Henry James, *The American Scene* (London: Chapman and Hall, 1907), 131, 231.

15. Quoted in Shi, *Facing Facts*, 225.

16. Quoted in ibid., 232.

17. Quoted in George Snell, *The Shapers of American Fiction, 1798–1947* (New York: E.P. Dutton, 1947), 227–228.

18. Howells quoted in Shi, *Facing Facts*, 238.

19. London quoted in Kevin Star, "Introduction," in Frank Norris, *The Octopus: A Story of California* (New York: Penguin, 1986), xxx.

20. Quoted in Shi, *Facing Facts*, 238.

21. For an extended discussion of neurasthenia, see Tom Lutz, *American Nervousness, 1903: An Anecdotal History* (Ithaca, NY: Cornell University Press, 1991), 38–62.

22. Theodore Dreiser, *Sister Carrie* (New York: Signet Classics, 1900), 26.

23. Quoted in Fred Lewis Pattee, *A History of American Literature Since 1870* (New York: Century, 1915), 402.

24. Quoted in ibid., 392.

25. Faulkner, *The Quest for Social Justice*, 260.

26. Richard Ohmann, *Selling Culture: Magazines, Markets, and Class at the Turn of the Century* (New York: Verso, 1996), 220.

27. Cashman, *America in the Age of the Titans*, 81–82.

28. Wagenknecht, *American Profile*, 219–221.

29. Martin, *Harvests of Change*, 246.

30. Arthur Weinberg and Lila Weinberg, eds., *The Muckrakers: The Era in Journalism that Moved America to Reform—The Most Significant Magazine Articles of 1902–1912* (New York: Simon and Schuster, 1961), 206.

31. Upton Sinclair, *The Jungle* (New York: Bantam, 1906), 60–61.

32. Chambers, *The Tyranny of Change*, 9.

33. Faulkner, *The Quest for Social Justice*, 11.

34. Katherine Joslin, *Edith Wharton: Women Writers* (New York: St. Martin's, 1991), 52–53.

35. Margaret B. McDowell, *Edith Wharton*, rev. ed. (Boston: Twayne, 1991), 8.

36. Joslin, *Edith Wharton*, 130.

37. Quoted in ibid., 130–131.

38. McDowell, *Edith Wharton*, 74.

39. Ibid., 131.

40. Quoted in Peter Conn, *The Divided Mind: Ideology and Imagination in America, 1898–1917* (New York: Cambridge University Press, 1983), 120.

41. W.E.B. Du Bois, "Resolution at Harper's Ferry, 1906," in *Black Writers of America: A Comprehensive Anthology*, eds., Richard Barksdale and Keneth Kinnamon (New York: Macmillan, 1972), 377.

42. Paul Dunbar, "The Party" and "Sympathy," in *Black Writers of America*, eds., Barksdale and Kinnamon, 355, 358.

43. Conn, *Literature in America*, 329.

CHAPTER 9

1. H. Wiley Hitchcock, *Music in the United States: A Historical Introduction* (Upper Saddle River, NJ: Prentice-Hall, 1974), 144.

2. Edith Borroff, *Music Melting Round: A History of Music in the United States* (New York: Ardsley House, 1995), 122.

3. Wagenknecht, *American Profile*, 301.

4. Ibid., 305.

5. Hitchcock, *Music in the United States*, 141.

6. Nicholas E. Tawa, *Mainstream Music of Early Twentieth Century America: The Composers, Their Times, and Their Works* (Westport, CT: Greenwood Publishing, 1992), 120.

7. Ibid., 123.

8. Quoted in ibid., 106.

9. Ibid., 106–108.

10. Wagenknecht, *American Profile*, 113.

11. David Ewen, *All the Years of American Popular Music* (Upper Saddle River, NJ: Prentice-Hall, 1977), 153.

12. Ibid.

13. Wagenknecht, *American Profile*, 121.

14. Ewen, *All the Years*, 154.

15. Ibid., 155.

16. Quoted in Hitchcock, *Music in the United States*, 121.

17. Susan Curtis, *Dancing to a Black Man's Tune: A Life of Scott Joplin* (Columbia: University of Missouri Press, 1994), 35.

18. Ibid., 38.

19. Ibid., 70.

20. Ibid., 129–145.

21. Ibid., 189.

22. Grace Lichtenstein and Laura Dankner, *Musical Gumbo: The Music of New Orleans* (New York: W.W. Norton, 1993), 26–27.

23. Ibid., 28.

24. Ibid., 28–29.

CHAPTER 10

1. Schlereth, *Victorian America*, 204–205.

2. Ibid., 205.

3. Byington, *Homestead*, 111.

4. Hollis Alpert, *Broadway!: 125 Years of Musical Theater* (New York: Arcade, 1991), 41.

5. Ibid., 43.

6. Ibid., 44–45.

7. Richard Mansfield, "Man and the Actor," in *119 Years of the Atlantic*, ed. Louise Desaulniers (New York: Atlantic Monthly Company, 1977), 224–228.

8. Faulkner, *The Quest for Social Justice*, 300.

9. Alpert, *Broadway*, 45–48.

10. Faulkner, *The Quest for Social Justice*, 302–303.

11. Alpert, *Broadway*, 48–54.

12. Schwartz, *Berkeley 1900*, 275.

13. Quoted in Faulkner, *The Quest for Social Justice*, 299.

14. Wagenknecht, *American Profile*, 265.

15. Ibid., 266.

16. Gerard Greaves, "The Bullet That the World's Greatest Magician Was Meant to Catch Tore into His Body," *Daily Express*, 6 May 2000, available online at http://www.lineone.net/express/00/05/06/features/f0200magic-d.html (1 June 2001).

17. Wagenknecht, *American Profile*, 268.

18. Schlereth, *Victorian America*, 196.

19. Wagenknecht, *American Profile*, 256.

20. Schlereth, *Victorian America*, 202–203.

21. Ibid., 204.

22. Ibid., 200.

23. Faulkner, *The Quest for Social Justice*, 296.

24. Peiss, *Cheap Amusements*, 88.

25. Quoted in ibid., 88.

26. Ibid.

27. Fredrika Blair, *Isadora: Portrait of the Artist as a Woman* (New York: McGraw-Hill, 1986), 16–18.

28. Ibid., 30.

29. Ibid., 400–401.

CHAPTER 11

1. Schlereth, *Victorian America*, 214.

2. Lutz, *American Nervousness*, 1–30.

3. Quoted in Schlereth, *Victorian America*, 216.

4. Ibid., 216–217.

5. Quoted in Lutz, *American Nervousness*, 90.

6. Quoted in Theodore Roosevelt, "Speech at Yellowstone National Park," in *The Essential Theodore Roosevelt*, ed. Hunt, 120–121.

7. Lutz, *American Nervousness*, 90–92.

8. Brown, *This Fabulous Century*, 216–219.

9. Ibid., 220.

10. Dunne quoted in Wagenknecht, *American Profile*, 135.

11. Frederick Lewis Allen, *The Big Change: America Transforms Itself, 1900–1950* (New York: Harper and Row, 1952), 34–37.

12. Faulkner, *The Quest for Social Justice*, 141.

13. Ibid., 142.

14. Ibid., 143–144.

15. Sullivan, *Our Times*, 488–490.

16. Quoted in ibid., 499–500.

17. Cashman, *America in the Age of the Titans*, 267–268.

18. Ibid., 268–269.

19. For several examples of classic automobile posters targeting affluent consumers, please see Brown, *This Fabulous Century*, 237–240.

20. Bob Batchelor, "The Rubber City," *Inside Business*, October 1998, 22.

21. Quoted in Faulkner, *The Quest for Social Justice*, 135.

22. Ibid., 136.

23. Walter Lord, *The Good Years: From 1900 to the First World War* (New York: Harper and Brothers, 1960), 91–94.

24. Ibid., 94–98.

25. Chambers, *The Tyranny of Change*, 124–125.

26. Lord, *The Good Years*, 99–100.

27. Chambers, *The Tyranny of Change*, 124–125.

28. Schlereth, *Victorian America*, 26.

29. Wiebe, *The Search for Order*, 244.

30. Cashman, *America in the Age of the Titans*, 442–444.

31. Schlereth, *Victorian America*, 26–27.

32. Cashman, *America in the Age of the Titans*, 444–446.

CHAPTER 12

1. Hughes, *American Visions*, 216.

2. Marshall B. Davidson, *The American Heritage History of the Artists' America* (New York: American Heritage, 1973), 170–180; Hughes, *American Visions*, 220–223.

3. Davidson, *History of the Artists' America*, 251.

4. Ibid.

5. Hughes, *American Visions*, 237–239.

6. Ibid., 239.

7. Ibid., 242.

8. Daniel M. Mendelowitz, *A History of American Art* (New York: Holt, Rinehart and Winston, 1960), 428–429.

9. Quoted in Davidson, *History of the Artists' America*, 191.

10. Hughes, *American Visions*, 261–264.

11. Ibid., 265–266.

12. Davidson, *History of the Artists' America*, 252–253.

13. Hughes, *American Visions*, 353–357.

14. Ibid., 323.

15. Ibid., 325.

16. Shi, *Facing Facts*, 252–259.

17. Donald Braider, *George Bellows and the Ashcan School of Painting* (Garden City, NY: Doubleday, 1971), 24.

18. Ibid., 26–29.

19. Hughes, *American Visions*, 330.

20. Ibid., 330–332.

21. Joyce Carol Oates, *George Bellows: American Artist* (Hopewell, NJ: Ecco Press, 1995), 18–20.

22. Braider, *George Bellows*, 39–43.

23. Oates, *George Bellows*, 3–5.

24. Hughes, *American Visions*, 350.

25. Ibid., 352.

26. Davidson, *History of the Artists' America*, 280.

27. Crichton, *America 1900*, 92–93.

28. Ibid., 94.

29. Wagenknecht, *American Profile*, 293–294.

30. Ibid., 294.

31. Quoted in Hughes, *American Visions*, 209.

32. Ibid., 207–209.

33. Wagenknecht, *American Profile*, 294–301.

34. Hughes, *American Visions*, 210.

35. Quoted in Wagenknecht, *American Profile*, 297.

36. Mendelowitz, *A History of American Art*, 481.

Further Reading

Alexander, Charles C. *Our Game: An American Baseball History*. New York: Henry Holt, 1991.

Blackford, Mansel G., and K. Austin Kerr. *Business Enterprise in American History*. 2d ed. Boston: Houghton Mifflin, 1990.

Brands, H.W. *T.R.: The Last Romantic*. New York: BasicBooks, 1997.

Byington, Margaret F. *Homestead: The Households of a Mill Town*. Pittsburgh: University of Pittsburgh Press, 1974.

Cashman, Sean Dennis. *America in the Age of the Titans: The Progressive Era and World War I*. New York: New York University Press, 1988.

Chambers, John Whiteclay II. *The Tyranny of Change: America in the Progressive Era, 1890–1920*. 2d ed. New Brunswick, NJ: Rutgers University Press, 2000.

Chernow, Ron. *Titan: The Life of John D. Rockefeller, Sr.* New York: Random House, 1998.

Conn, Peter. *The Divided Mind: Ideology and Imagination in America, 1898–1917*. New York: Cambridge University Press, 1983.

Crichton, Judy. *America 1900: The Sweeping Story of a Pivotal Year in the Life of the Nation*. New York: Henry Holt, 1998.

Curtis, Susan. *Dancing to a Black Man's Tune: A Life of Scott Joplin*. Columbia: University of Missouri Press, 1994.

Dubofsky, Melvyn. *The State and Labor in Modern America*. Chapel Hill: University of North Carolina Press, 1994.

Dyerson, Mark. *Making the American Team: Sport, Culture, and the Olympic Experience*. Urbana: University of Illinois Press, 1998.

Ewen, David. *All the Years of American Popular Music*. Upper Saddle River, NJ: Prentice-Hall, 1977.

Faulkner, Harold U. *The Quest for Social Justice, 1898–1914*. Chicago: Quadrangle, 1971.

Fox, Stephen. *The Mirror Makers: A History of American Advertising and Its Creators*. New York: William Morrow, 1984.

Gill, Brendan. *Many Masks: A Life of Frank Lloyd Wright*. New York: G.P. Putnam's Sons, 1987.

Heinrich, Thomas R. *Ships for the Seven Seas: Philadelphia Shipbuilding in the Age of Industrial Capitalism*. Baltimore: Johns Hopkins University Press, 1997.

Hofstadter, Richard. *The Age of Reform: From Bryan to F.D.R.* New York: Vintage, 1955.

Hold, Hamilton, ed. *The Life Stories of Undistinguished Americans, as Told by Themselves*. New York: Routledge, 1990.

Hughes, Robert. *American Visions: The Epic History of Art in America*. New York: Knopf, 1997.

Lears, T.J. Jackson. *No Place of Grace: Antimodernism and the Transformation of American Culture, 1880–1920*. Chicago: University of Chicago Press, 1981.

Livesay, Harold C. *Andrew Carnegie and the Rise of Big Business*. Boston: Little, Brown, 1975.

Lutz, Tom. *American Nervousness, 1903: An Anecdotal History*. Ithaca, NY: Cornell University Press, 1991.

Macleod, David I. *The Age of the Child: Children in America, 1898–1920*. New York: Twayne, 1998.

Montgomery, David. *The Fall of the House of Labor: The Workplace, the State, and American Labor Activism, 1865–1925*. New York: Cambridge University Press, 1987.

Mowry, George E. *The Era of Theodore Roosevelt and the Birth of Modern America, 1900–1912*. New York: Harper and Row, 1962.

Peiss, Kathy. *Cheap Amusements: Working Women and Leisure in Turn-of-the-Century New York*. Philadelphia: Temple University Press, 1986.

Porter, Glenn. *The Rise of Big Business, 1860–1920*. 2d ed. Arlington Heights, IL: Harlan Davidson, 1992.

Roosevelt, Theodore. *The Essential Theodore Roosevelt*. Edited by John Gabriel Hunt. New York: Gramercy Books, 1994.

Schlereth, Thomas J. *Victorian America: Transformations in Everyday Life, 1876–1915*. New York: HarperCollins, 1991.

Schneider, Dorothy, and Carl J. Schneider. *American Women in the Progressive Era, 1900–1920*. New York: Facts on File, 1993.

Schwartz, Richard. *Berkeley 1900: Daily Life at the Turn of the Century*. Berkeley, CA: RSB Books, 2000.

Shi, David E. *Facing Facts: Realism in American Thought and Culture, 1850–1920*. New York: Oxford University Press, 1995.

Wagenknecht, Edward. *American Profile: 1900–1909*. Amherst: University of Massachusetts Press, 1982.

West, Elliott. *Growing Up in Twentieth-Century America: A History and Reference Guide*. Westport, CT: Greenwood Press, 1996.

Wiebe, Robert H. *The Search for Order, 1877–1920*. New York: Hill and Wang, 1967.

Zinn, Howard. *A People's History of the United States, 1492–Present*. New York: Harper Perennial, 1995.

Index

About the Author

BOB BATCHELOR is an award-winning business writer and historian. Trained at the University of Pittsburgh and Kent State University, he currently lives with his wife, Katherine, in San Rafael, CA.